Dr. JAC™

Phonics Friendly Books

TEACHING PHONICS THROUGH CHILDREN'S LITERATURE

Joyce Armstrong Carroll

Absey and Company
Spring, TX

"That is question now;
And then comes answer like an Absey book.
King John, i, 9
Shakespeare

Acknowledgements
Judy Wallis, Kelley Smith, and Nancy Stone

Absey & Co.
5706 Root Road, Suite 5
Spring, Texas 77389
281-257-2340

Published by Absey & Co., Spring, Texas
Manufactured in the United States of America

ISBN 1-888842-11-3

ISBN 1-888842-11-3

Table of Contents

continued

⊷⊐ INTRODUCTION ⊏⊷

Sitting here at my computer, the content of *Phonics Friendly Books* in the hands of editors, I am about to write its introduction. Unwilling to enter into the debate that seems to endlessly rotate around the question of how someone learns to read--explicit decoding, phonics, basic-skills instruction versus whole-language, naturalistic, emergent literacy, literature-based instruction--I find myself moving momentarily away from the pile of research next to my desk and deeper into my own reading experiences.

For me, reading came easy; I read even before Dick, Jane, Sally, Spot, and Puff cavorted across the pages of my pre-primers, primers, and what we called *reader books*. But reading did not come easy for some of my friends or some of my students. The mysterious act of decoding words and comprehending their meaning shadowed them, and others like them, throughout life, popping up like a specter while taking a test, filling out forms, following a road map, even when figuring the correct dosage of medicine. For these people, reading was tedious, difficult, sometimes demeaning, and always a Herculean task. Their eyes did not race across a line causing images to dance in their heads; they could not predict what might happen next because they were too busy struggling to understand what was happening at the moment. Blind-sided by the text's literal meaning, inferring or interpreting became impossible for them, and the notion of reading for pleasure was never their option.

Even after almost four decades in teaching, I still remember Chester, a classmate in the primary grades, stumbling his way through the simple sentences, "Come, Dick. Come and see." He could not get the the words *come* and *see* straight. He said *see* when it was *come* every time. No amount of repetition seemed to help. I wondered about that even then. Yet, just last month I watched another Chester in another classroom stumbling his way through another equally simple line of type.

They rarely catch up.

Case in point: About a year ago, I needed an audiotape of a story segment. "Perfect," I said to my husband. "Our friends are coming over. I need two male voices and two female voices. This will only take a couple of minutes." When they arrived, I presented my tiny project, gave them their parts, and turned on the tape. It never occurred to me there would be a problem until this very successful electrical contractor, faltered over common, one-syllable words. I watched in horror as the color rose in his cheeks, as he coughed and cleared his throat. Recognizing these distractions, since students use them all the time, I half expected him to ask to use the pencil sharpener or the restroom. Still he tried to accommodate me as he must have tried to accommodate his teachers, but he literally could not read. Where did we lose this bright man? I asked myself.

What makes learning to read so easy for some and so difficult for others? Perhaps some highly sophisticated tomography machine will enable us to examine the brains of readers and pinpoint the "learning to read" place. Perhaps some brilliant scholar will happen along and unravel this highly complex ability that continually demands connections that are motor, perceptual, cognitive, and experiential. Then teaching reading will become uniform and perfect, enabling all children to learn with great joy, excitement, and success.

Perhaps this very dream drove teachers throughout our American educational history to find the reading equivalent of the fountain of youth. They searched for a spring from which all children could drink so that the United States would be guaranteed an informed citizenry.

For nearly two hundred years we have, as a nation, troubled ourselves over reading. Pioneers used the act of reading as a vehicle to instill values in their young. The concept of childhood, as we know it, did not exist. Children were considered incomplete adults and as such were expected to read books for ethical instruction, for moral growth. Teachers used sounds and sight words, alphabet books, books with lessons such as the fables of Aesop, and the Bible--a trend that continued into the nineteenth century.

On the one hand, early textbooks that favored phonics often contained entire pages filled with totally unrelated words. For example, one page I examined contained only three-letter words complete with an array of diacritical marks that went beyond the diaeresis, macron, and breve to marks for the subtonics and atonics, and cedillas to mark certain C sounds. Just looking at these pages was overwhelming. Reading indeed must have been a chore!

On the other hand, textbooks that favored the whole word method, such as Thomas Gallaudet's 1835 *Mother's Primer*, were criticized because while the students could pronounce the words, which they did repeatedly, orally, and in unison, they often did not understand the meaning of the words they were saying.

The famous *McGuffey Eclectic Readers*, introduced in 1836 and popular for fifty years, also advanced moral values. Reading was conducted aloud, in unison or in turn, with students working their way through the five-book series of graduated difficulty.

Although the *Baldwin Readers*, published in 1897, were the first to use color pictures, it was not until the early twentieth century that a substantial shift occurred in the content of books used to teach reading.

Enter William S. Gray, a reading specialist, and Zerna Sharp, a reading consultant. Together in the 1930s they created Dick and Jane textbooks based on the "show don't tell" principle. A popular replacement for the monotonous approaches of the preceding centuries, Dick and Jane textbooks primarily used a controlled vocabulary and stilted story lines geared to middle America. Sight word reading, called "look-say," was the predominant approach with phonics taught incidentally. These books welcomed readers into the life of Dick, Jane, Sally, Mother, Father, Spot, Puff, and Tim for thirty years.

Gone were the repetitive memory drills of sounds and words in isolation with students sitting in rows, the teacher, ruler in hand, pointing as students chorused their responses.

ā says /ā/
ā, as in āge
ă says /ă/
ă , as in ăt
ä says /ä/
ä, as in ärt
a̧ says /a̧/
a̧, as in a̧ll
å says /å/
å, as in båre

$\overset{.}{a}$ *says* /$\overset{.}{a}$/
$\overset{.}{a}$, *as in* $\overset{.}{a}sk$

Gone were sentences that made little sense and often called into question phonic and spelling regularity such as this line found in an old textbook,

O, no! Oh fy!

Since these two sentences convey little meaning, consider the confusion of spelling and sound that the interjections *O* and *Oh* must have created for young readers and writers.

Gone were incoherent paragraphs that held little interest for the reader:

The dog has a bed of tow. Ann has a cat. Her cat can mew.
My son has a hog. Has he a toy hoe? Yes; and he can use it, too.

So where does reading instruction stand today? Currently, reading textbooks are literature-based anthologies. They contain unabridged authentic children's stories. Most are broad and eclectic, drawing from a variety of reading theories which provide many options for implementation by teachers.

What is the future of reading instruction? Empirical research suggests that textbooks will employ a balanced approach, a combination of all the *best* in the field of teaching reading coupled with well-trained teachers who know how students learn and who recognize and meet the individual differences, processes, and learning styles of their students. Dorothy Strickland, Professor of Reading at Rutgers University, says it simply yet eloquently as she describes Dorothy Fowler's first-grade classroom in the introduction to her book *Teaching Phonics Today*, "Teachers like Dorothy artfully balance the development of skills and strategies within the framework of a rich language and literature program. They know that all aspects of a child's literacy development are interdependent." She goes on, "For it is good teaching that helps make phonics work for children as they learn to read and write."

The truth remains, reading demands an overlapping and intertwining of the senses--the readers look, as Frank Smith tells us, but the brain sees. And what is seen or understood happens because it is heard--as if the reader momentarily trades eyes for ears--even when the reading is silent. (Interestingly, silent reading did not emerge until the Middle Ages when spaces were made between written words. These spaces enabled readers to distinguish words without sounding them aloud.) David Abram in *The Spell of the Sensuous* contends that people "learn their native language not mentally but bodily" (75). He points to the crying, laughing, squealing, babbling, mimicking of children. As they echo the sounds in their experience, they appropriate new words and phrases first through their tonality and texture; second, through their meaning.

Looking out the window I see three neighborhood children playing between our houses. They range in age from two to eleven. The two older girls stray from the house, down the block a bit. The two-year-old brother follows them. When next I look up, Mom stands, arms akimbo. I cannot hear her words, but there is no mistaking the downcast eyes and shuffling feet of the girls. They have been reprimanded. Mom disappears into the house. Then, all of a sudden, the little guy places his hands on his hips in imitation of Mom. I see his lips moving. I know I am privy to a reenactment of the greater drama. My bet is that he tries on the words *and* the tone. My bet is he tries to capture the texture of Mom's speech. He knows it sounds different than when she plays with him in the pool, tucks him in at night, or reads a story. Fertile ground here for the relationship of sound and meaning, for the reverberations, resonance, and registers of the sounds of English.

Phonics Friendly Books: Teaching Phonics Through Children's Literature attempts to help the art and science of good teaching as described by Dr. Strickland by providing the skills and presenting suggested strategies all within the framework of sixty focal children's books rich in language and literature. As Strickland says, "Teachers using trade books as core materials are more likely to capitalize on the opportunities for phonics instruction presented in the literature rather than rely on rigidly applied hierarchy of skills" (30).

As with other Dr. JAC™ books, the format of *Phonics Friendly* fits the needs of the busy teacher. The **TITLE** and **author** of the focal book, the PHONICS CONCEPT or CONCEPTS, (and when appropriate a *generalization* or *generalizations*), the LANGUAGE ARTS CONCEPT or CONCEPTS, a suggested **artifact**, and the **summary** are laid out briefly at the onset of the *lesson*. These are followed by the *lesson*, which, while uniquely embedded within a READING/WRITING CONNECTION, incorporates the concepts, and invites students to engage in some *writing experience*. The writing attempts of young students encourages them to both explore the alphabet and realize its importance. EXTENSIONS enable reteaching, additional work on the concepts, or more challenging work. The RELATED BOOKS offer a broad spectrum of further reading and writing, often across disciplines. Each Dr. JAC concludes with a PUBLISHING suggestion.

The *focal books* are classics in children's literature such as *The Three Billy Goats Gruff*, versions of classics such as *Wake Up, Sleeping Beauty!*, books that reflect divergent cultures such as *Shake Shake Shake*, or contemporary books that relate to phonics, the alphabet, or ones that highlight letters, sounds, or words in ways that students find interesting, motivating, and easy to learn and remember such as in *The War Between the Vowels and the Consonants*.

Lessons in *Phonics Friendly* may be used in the sequence presented, or the sequence that meets the needs of the students and fits the determination of the teacher. **Concepts** may be taught then retaught in a variety of ways by using the extensions and the related books, or they may be reinforced by reading the focal book several times. Often many phonics concepts are offered in the same Dr. JAC. These may be taught together in an integrated way or one concept at a time, returning to the focal book again and again as necessary and thus making explicit the implicit lesson that good literature deserves to be read and reread. Subsequent readings yield more depth of understanding and often illuminate elements missed on the first read. Sometimes the same phonics concept is repeated in another Dr. JAC using a different book with a different approach. For example, C (K sound) may be found in Dr. JAC 3, 9, and 33. (See the "Phonics Concept Index" for other cross references.)

I chose the word *generalization* over the word *rule* to suggest that these statements about how letters sound, while sometimes helpful and handy as tools for the memory, are not really *rules* because they often are not valid or have many exceptions. (See Clymer.) I believe students are best served by learning **generalizations** that are valid *most* of the time; and, even then, they should not be taught as absolutes. I use the word *student* over the word *children*, even though these lessons are obviously geared to the elementary level, to place the lesson in an academic setting. While most lessons in this book are most appropriate for **primary students, intermediate students** would also benefit from then. Experiencing them helps students see a multitude of applications for phonics, helps patch any holes that may have occurred in previous reading instruction, and aids in their spelling skills.

Assessment in *Phonics Friendly* is intrinsic to each lesson since each lesson may be instructional or evaluative simply by changing its focus. In this way the assessment is both on-going and authentic. I encourage teachers, because of the plethora of standardized diagnostic test batteries with tests and subtests, commercial instruments that measure various aspects of metalinguistic competence, screening devices, informal checks, and end-of-year analyses, to exercise professional and prudent judgment in selecting and administering tests. Consideration should be given to school district recommendations, and all assessment tools should meet the needs of individual students.

Phonics Friendly also contains a *Phonics Map* and a *Phonics Concept Index*. The former enables readers to follow the commonly used terms in this arena of language. The latter serves as a handy cross reference. The *Bibliography* contains full information for all the books referenced, *Books and Articles for Teachers* provides theory and research references, and *Resources for Teachers* supplies addresses and phone or FAX numbers for materials. Also, a *Glossary of Language Arts Concepts* presents an easy refresher of the standard literary terms used in the book.

In closing this introduction, permit me one additional word: this book has been created as a **blueprint** to aid teachers in **balancing phonic skills** with **language development** within the context of reading. As Marilyn Jager Adams' synthesis of Jeanne Chall's research maintains, "As a complement to connected and meaningful reading--systematic phonic instruction is a valuable component of beginning reading instruction" (39). I invite teachers to use the lessons again and again for each is rich with ideas and possibility. And I remind teachers of the enormous potential of each student in their care. We need to be reminded and rereminded of what Stickland and Cullinan state in the "Afterword" to Adams' book:

> Current naturalistic research strongly suggests that phonics is best learned in the context of reading and writing. If learning is to occur, we must give children good stories that intrigue and engage them; we must give them poetry that sings with the beauty of language; we must enchant them with language play; and we must give them opportunities to write. In short, we must surround them with literature that helps them understand their world and their ability to create meaning. We must read to children from the very beginning and read to them every day. We won't need to remind them when it's time for stories; they won't let us forget it! That's the magic of stories. In countless demonstrations of story reading and experimentation with writing, children develop the knowledge of the way print works. (428)

Written in 1990, their words find support in recent neuroscientific research which informs us of the wondrous, complex structure of the human brain. As teachers, we best promote the dendritic growth within that brain through an **interactive/active learning environment** that encourages the students' construction of knowledge. By leading them to conceptual understandings through concrete contexts that hold meaning for them; and by treating them with dignity, we acknowledge them as the *phenomenal learners* they are.

Dr. JAC

Dr. JAC™

Phonics Map

AN EASY GUIDE THROUGH PHONICS

Phonograms (sometimes called rimes or word families) are a succession of letters that occurs with the same phonetic value in several words. For example: the at in *bat, sat, mat, cat, rat*.

Word families sometimes called "psychological units of syllables," "chunks," or "orthographic patterns" by linguists, are comprised of *onsets* and *rimes* (Moustafa). Other linguists define a word family as a basic phonogram to which an initial consonant, blend, or digraph may be added to make it a word. *Onsets* refers to all the letters before the vowel, and *rimes* refers to the vowel and what follows

Word families are made up of any consonants which may come before the vowel sound, an obligatory vowel sound, and any consonants which may come after it (Fry, Kress, & Fountoukidis). Fry lists the most common phonograms as: *ay, ill, ip, at, am, ag, ack, ank, ick, ell, ot, ing, ap, unk, ail, ain, eed, y, out, ug, op, in, an, est, ink, ow, ew, ore, ed, ab, ob, ock, ake, ine, ight, im, uck, um* (621).

Phrased another way, onsets are all the letters before the vowel, and rimes consist of the vowel and what follows. Students find this an easy way to divide words for word attack and reading. For example, the word *small* is more easily divided into *sm -all* than into *sma-ll* or *s-m-a-l-l*. This also helps students sound out other words with the same rime: *call, ball, stall* and so forth.

Still other linguists call word families phonograms. These usually consist of words that have the same vowel and ending letters and that rhyme (Cunningham). Therefore, *sheep/cheap* could be considered as an onset/rime because SH and CH are the onsets while EEP and EAP have the same vowel sound. Considered another way, EEP and EAP are different phonograms or word families because while they carry the same long E sound and final consonant P, they have different letters.

Phonograms or rimes have been used since Colonial times to teach reading and are especially effective with young readers, at-risk readers, and ESL readers. An excellent source for phonograms is *The Reading Teacher's Book of Lists*.

---

ne way.

l to know the difference between vowels and conso-
n students according to their abilities, interests, and
helps them remember the letter and sound; for oth-

then releasing it as in P, B, T, D, K, G;
F, V, TH *thing*, DH as in *that*, S , Z, SH, ZH;
ie breath is momentarily closed off at the beginning
d the C sound in *chill*;

, N, NG;

e most musical of the consonants as in W, Y, and H.
d as in *wind*;
ng I sound;
it.

Systems of Language

Orthography is the writing and spelling systems of a language.

Phonology is the study of the history and theory of the system of sounds an oral language uses.

Vowels

A **vowel** is a sound that allows the air to flow through the mouth without any obstruction.

Vowel sounds are often determined by word structures that are visually apparent. The following generalizations will alert you to these visual cues:

Vowel Generalization One: When there is one vowel in a word and the word ends in a consonant, the vowel is usually short. (*get, bag, rid, at, is*)

Vowel Generalization Two: When the only vowel in a word is at the end, that vowel is usually long. (*go, he, me*)

Vowel Generalization Three: When a word has two vowels, one of which is a final E separated from the first vowel by one consonant, the first vowel is usually long and the E is usually silent. (*ride, rope, make, use, rose*)

Vowel Generalization Four: When there are two consecutive vowels in a word, the first is usually long and the second is usually silent, unless they are vowel diphthongs such as OI, OY, OW, OU, or variant vowel digraphs such as AU, EA. (*rain, eat, boat, meet*)

Consonant Categories

A **consonant** is a sound in which the air flow is obstructed

(Note: The following information is for the teacher. Student nants, letters and sounds. But additional labels may be share learning styles. For some students, knowing the label, "frica ers it is a deterrent. Always, it is the teacher's call.)

Consonants
- stops or plosives—closing off the breath momentaril
- fricatives—creating audible friction in the mouth as
- affricatives—a combination of a stop and fricative si but there is some friction before the vowel starts as i
- gutturals—vibrating sound in the throat as in G, GI
- nasals—diverting some air into the nasal passages as
- liquids—interrupting the air flow as in R, L;

Semi-vowels
- sometimes called glides, are so called because they
- W literally makes the sound of the double U, an OC
- Y sometimes takes the long E sound and sometimes
- H is an almost voiceless version of the vowel that f

Pull Sheet Open Here

$\mathcal{S}$uggested $\mathcal{G}$uidelines $\mathcal{S}$

- Teaching phonics is not synonymous with t
- Reading and spelling require much more th
- Phonics is a means to an end, not the end it
- Phonics is one of several enablers or cueing
- Phonics is one of several strategies for spell
- Memorizing phonics rules does not ensure
- Learners need to see the relevance of phonic
- Teaching students to use phonics is differen
- The best context for learning and applying

(Strickland, *Te*

Sounds of English

Diphthongs combine two vowel phonemes within one syllable. For example, OI is a diphthong in the word oil. A diphthong is a vowel sound.

A **blend** is a one-syllable combination of two or three consecutive consonants, each with a distinct sound. For example in the word splash, SPL is a three-letter blend. A blend is a consonant sound.

A **digraph** is composed of two letters that make one sound. There are normal digraphs, such as the EE in *meet*, and consonant digraphs, such as the CH in *chin*.. A digraph is a vowel or consonant sound.

Reading Terms

...**oding** sometimes means using phonics to pronounce a word. For example, a reader may ...de the word cat by separating each phoneme C A T. Strickland, however, defines decod-...as the entire set of strategies readers use to "unlock the code" (15).

...**ding comprehension** refers to the understanding of a word in context. For example, ...r decoding *cat*, the reader knows that those three letters and the sound *kat* refers to the ...ily's furry pet in the sentence, story, or picture.

Units of Language

Phoneme is the smallest unit of sound in the language. For example, the B in *bat*; the C in *cat*. It is generally acknowledged that English has approximately forty phonemes.

Morpheme is the smallest unit of meaning in the language. For example, *go* is one morpheme; *don't* contains two morphemes.

Grapheme is a letter, a unit of written language. For example, there are two graphemes in the written word *at* ; there are three in the written word *fat* and in the written word *chat*. The word chat has three graphemes because CH in the spoken word represents one phoneme.

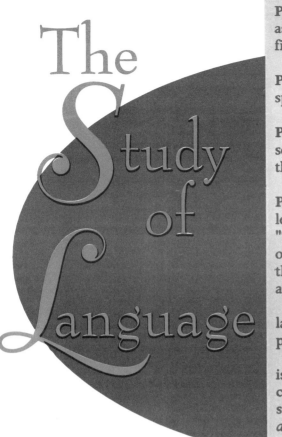

The Study of Language

Phonetics is the study of the characteristics of speech sounds, such as how the human ear hears a sound or how a sound may be classified.

Phonological awareness refers to the knowledge of sounds in the spoken language.

Phonemic awareness refers to the knowledge of the separable sounds of spoken language by learning to identify and manipulate the sounds (phonemes) within spoken words.

Phonics is the knowledge of how sounds are represented by letters letter combinations in written language to help people read and speak "Teaching phonics refers to a system of teaching reading that builds on the alphabetic principle, a system of which a central component the teaching of correspondences between letters or groups of letters and their pronunciations" (Adams, *Beginning to Read*, 50).

    • **synthetic phonics**--sounds are identified with letters in isolation and then put together as a whole as in *c• a• t* taken as three parts before being considered as the whole word *cat*.

    • **analytic phonics**--sounds are associated with letters not isolation but in context. Learners begin by identifying the phonic concept in the words under study, usually in a meaningful context such as the T sound in the sentence *Two teeny tiny turtles turn around in the tank.*

The Three Cueing Systems in Reading

Graphophonics describes the relationship between the sounds of the language and written letters or spelling patterns. For example, readers using **graphophonic cues** tap their knowledge of letters, letter blends, and corresponding sounds.

Semantics describes the understanding of the meaning of a word. For example, readers using semantic cues tap the context of a word.

    • **background knowledge**--refers to the experiences a reader brings to the text. For example, readers using background knowledge tap what they know about the world. A reader may not know the word *mittens* even after sounding out and pronouncing the word because he or she lives in a warm climate and never wears mittens.

Syntax refers to the understanding of word order, the function of words, and the grammar and structure of language. For example, readers using syntactic cues tap grammar to figure out the meaning.

    • **structural analysis**--involves the use of the structural elements in a word to identify it. For example, readers using structural analysis cues tap endings, prefixes, suffixes, roots to understand the word.

for Learning Phonics

hing reading.

phonics.

f.

stems that help us read.

plication of those rules.

or themselves in their own reading and writing

om teaching them about phonics.

onics is actual reading and writing.

hing Phonics Today, 25)

Dr. JAC

Phonics Friendly Books

Dr. JAC 1

Vowels & Consonants

THE WAR BETWEEN THE VOWELS AND THE CONSONANTS

Farrar Straus Giroux

Priscilla Turner

PHONICS CONCEPTS:
• Letters are divided into two categories: vowels and consonants (linguists add another category called semivowels);
• Identification of vowels and consonants;
• Vowels make their sounds by letting the air flow through the mouth unobstructedly;
• Consonants make their sounds by obstructing the air flow through the mouth in various ways.

LANGUAGE ARTS CONCEPTS:
• Letters make words;
• Every word must contain at least one vowel;
• Words make sentences;
• Sentences make paragraphs.

Artifacts: Alphabet cereal letters
Summary: Personified vowels and consonants, once enemies, discover the power of working together.

READING/WRITING CONNECTION

1. Previous to this lesson, go through the alphabet cereal letters to make certain there are vowels and consonants and the letters to spell the word STOP.
2. Show the dust jacket. Ask students if they can name the letters on it.
3. Turn the pages of the book. Ask students to name the letters they recognize. For oral language experience, encourage students to talk about what the personified letters are doing on the different pages (playing football, piloting airplanes, singing, boxing).
4. Read the book. Exaggerate the names of the letters and their sounds as you read. Point to each letter when appropriate.
5. Invite the students to echo the names of the letters they hear and identify them as you point to them.
6. Students pick letters from the alphabet cereal box. Each student calls out his or her letter. Help students who have difficulty. Make this a fun, not a threatening, experience.
7. Students holding vowels line up on one side of a long strip of butcher paper on

which scrawling, scribbles have been drawn with wide colored markers to look like those in the book. Students holding consonants line up on the other side of the butcher paper.

8. The teacher calls out each of the letters S - T - O - P in turn. The students holding these letters march forward. They stand together and say aloud the word they spell. This reinforces the idea that individual letters spell words.

9. Invite students to call out other words they know. Write these words one-by-one on another strip of butcher paper. Students holding these letters march forward and say the word. Repeat the procedure with different words.

10. Teach that letters are divided into vowels and consonants. Explain that every word must contain at least one vowel.

EXTENSIONS

1. Continue the above activity in the same manner except do it with sentences.
   - Challenge students to put words together to make sense—to make a sentence.
   - Write the sentences offered by the students on colorful sentence strips.
   - Read them aloud.
   - Students read them again as the teacher points to each word.
   - This activity may be repeated many times.

2. Use the reference in the book to paragraphs as an opportunity to show students what a paragraph looks like. Show them how it is "dented in." Together write a paragraph about the story or about something related to school. The purpose here is not to teach paragraphing but to sow the seeds for longer writing.

3. Use the reference in the book to pages.
   - Look at pages in different books from around the room.
   - Talk about the writing on those pages.

RELATED BOOK

The Alphabet Tree by Leo Lionni tells the story of isolated letters finding strength when the "word bug" helps them become words. Then, at the urging of the caterpillar, these words discover the power of meaning something when they combine to form sentences.

1. To continue the story line in this book, distribute colorful paper.
2. Each student draws and cuts out a colorful paper leaf.
3. Divide students into small groups. Each student in the group decides upon a word and writes that word on the paper leaf.
4. Advanced students may work as a group so that their words could be combined into sentences. For example, a group of three students might write, "We love school."

PUBLISHING

Students glue their cereal letters onto colorful paper. They use the remaining part of the paper to write the letter, to write their letter into words, into their names, or even into sentences, depending upon their level and abilities. Display the long strips of butcher paper used earlier and affix the students' work on it to reinforce the connection of moving from scribbles to knowing letters. Title the display WE KNOW OUR LETTERS!

OLD MACDONALD HAD A FARM

Orchard Books or any version of this all-time favorite

Nancy Hellen

PHONICS CONCEPT:
• Learning the Vowels A, E, I, O, U

LANGUAGE ARTS CONCEPT:
• Reinforce that every word contains at least one vowel.

Artifacts: Flat plastic disposable gloves (available in the paint departments of discount stores)

Summary: Stylized simplicity characterizes this version of the traditional children's song. The farm animals are described verse by verse on board pages with die cuts. The book also contains the music to accompany the lyrics, which is printed on its end pages.

READING/WRITING CONNECTION

1. Show the cover of the book.
2. Students identify MacDonald as the farmer and each of the animals pictured.
3. Talk about these animals, what they produce, how they help us.
4. Ask students to tell what they know about farms.
5. Introduce the song by singing it, but instead of singing the classic repeated phrase of

          E - I - E - I - O,
          sing the vowels
          A - E - I - O - U.

6. Make VOWEL GLOVES. Using one of the plastic gloves as a model, write A on the tip of the pinky finger, E on the tip of the ring finger, I on the tip of the middle finger, O on the tip of the index finger, an U on the tip of the thumb. (Use Sharpies ™ for best results.)
7. As you sing, wiggle the finger with the corresponding vowel.
8. Distribute the gloves to the students. Model how to write the vowels on the fingertips.
9. Students write the vowels on the tips of the plastic gloves' fingers and put them on.
10. Students sing the book and reinforce the concept of vowels with finger play. They wiggle the finger that corresponds to the vowel they are singing.

EXTENSIONS

1. Reread the book. On this subsequent reading, encourage students to look at the pictured object. For example, when they see the bags of flour, they predict what animal those bags will become when the page is turned, a cow.

2. Create a story mural.
   • Tape a long piece of butcher paper on the wall.
   • Divide the paper into six sections.
   • After starting with the farmer, students name each animal in the order in which it appears in the book. (If you use a version with more animals, divide the paper accordingly.)
   • In the first section, write the word *farmer*.
   • In the subsequent sections, write the names of the animals.
   • Divide students into six groups and assign a section to each group.
   • Working in six small groups, each group draws the farmer or the appropriate animal in their section. They may elaborate their section with background.
   • When all the inhabitants of the farm are in place on the mural, sing the song again. Students may point to the words that correspond to the song.
   • As students sing A, E, I, O, U write the vowels, or choose students to write the vowels, beneath the character on the mural.
3. Reteach that every word contains at least one vowel.
   • Students identify the vowels in the words in each section of their mural.
   • Students wear their vowel gloves and wiggle the appropriate finger.

RELATED BOOKS

Old MacDonald Had a Farm illustrated by Carol Jones presents a more detailed look at this cumulative story classic. It depicts seven animals which the reader predicts by looking through a peep hole. The illustrations invite rich oral language experiences.
1. Remind students of A, E, I, O, U before reading or singing this book.
2. Show them the page with the peep hole. Explain that what appears in that peep hole is a hint about the next animal on the farm.
3. Point to each word as you read the first page and make the prediction together. Individual students can make the predictions for the pages that follow.
4. After reading the book, go through it again by singing it.

A board version of *Old MacDonald* by Rosemary Wells (from the *Bunny Reads Back* series) captures the delight of this classic for young readers.
1. Read the book as you point to the words.
2. Cover the e-i-e-i-o with Post-it ™ Correction & Cover-up Tape and write the vowels on the correction tape.
3. Students sing the vowels.

Old MacDonald Had an Apartment House by Judi Barrett with illustrations by Ron Barrett was first published in 1969 and has been reissued. This classic lives as a celebration of cities, veggies, and old-fashioned ingenuity. In this book, MacDonald is an apartment house super who turns his building into a four-story farm.
1. Students may add the jingle of vowels after appropriate pages in the book.
2. Teacher writes on sentence strips several simple sentences related to the book. Students take turns pointing out the vowels in the sentences.
   • A cow moved in.
   • Fruit trees took their place.
   • Carrots didn't smudge doorknobs.
   • Cucumbers didn't leave muddy footprints.

• Potatoes didn't bang on the radiators for more stem.

PUBLISHING

1. Give each student two pages stapled so that the pages open horizontally and will look like the pages in the book.
2. The top page has the sentence
        Old MacDonald had a farm.
   Under the sentence, provide a line for students to write the five vowels. (Some students may be ready to write the entire sentence and the vowels.)
3. Under the writing, have a two or three inch peep hole cut out.
4. Under the peep hole, write
        And on that farm he had a ...
5. Students draw an animal on the second page under the peep hole so that just a part of it shows through the peep hole.
6. One by one the students take the Author's Chair while the other students sing the song and predict each others' animals.
7. Display the students' books around a large round paper (to approximate the peep hole in the book) on which is written OLD MACDONALD HAD A FARM OF VOWELS!

I SPY IN THE GARDEN

and its companion book

I SPY ON THE FARM

Puffin

Richard Powell

PHONICS CONCEPTS:
- The consonants called STOPS or PLOSIVES;
- B Sound as in *Butterfly, Bee;*
- C (K Sound) as in *Cat, Cow, Caterpillar;*
- D Sound as in *Dog, Duck;*
- G (hard) as in *Garden, Goat, Goldfish;*
- K Sound as in *Kitten;*
- P Sound as in *Pig;*
- T Sound as in *liTtle;*
- *Generalization:*
  WHEN TWO OF THE SAME CONSONANTS ARE SIDE BY SIDE, ONLY ONE IS HEARD.

LANGUAGE ARTS CONCEPT:
- By looking closely at the letter, picture, and part of the hidden picture, students begin to develop the skill of close reading for meaning.

Artifacts: Miniature plastic magnifying glasses (available from Oriental Trading Co.)
Summary: Both of these lift-the-flap books begin each double-page spread with the same sentence stem: "I spy with my little eye something beginning with...." The reader then examines the clues and predicts the animal or object hidden behind fences and flowers, in bushes, or under leaves. The major clue is the beginning letter which identifies the animal or object. The second clue is the portion of the hidden animal or object. Predictions may be validated by lifting the flap.

READING/WRITING CONNECTION

1. Keep the books, a large magnifying glass, and the artifacts hidden from the students. Begin by playing the game "I Spy" with the students gathered around. Talk about what "spy" means. For example, you might say, "I spy with my little eye someone wearing something brown." Then the students guess. The person guessing correctly gets to be the "spy." If the students do not guess, add another feature such as, "I spy with my little eye someone wearing something brown with a bow in her hair."
2. After everyone has had a turn, take out the large magnifying glass. Talk about what

magnifying glasses do and who uses them. Tell the students that when they read they often have to look closely to understand what the words say.

3. Tell students there are seven letters that are fun to look closely at and even more fun to say. These letters are the consonants that stop the air coming out of the mouth for a moment, let the air build up behind the lips, teeth, or tongue, and then let it out with a tiny explosion. Because these consonants stop the air, they are sometimes called STOPS. Because they end in a tiny explosion, they are sometimes called PLOSIVES (as in explosives).

4. Write these letters on the board or chart paper. Say each letter as you write it. Students hold their hands a bit away from but in front of their mouths as they echo each letter. They will feel a tiny burst of air as they say:

    B, C, (K sound), D, G, K, P, T.

5. Take out one of the books. Read the "I Spy" sentence stub, pointing to the words.

6. Ask for a volunteer to read. That student comes up, faces the group, takes the book, reads, identifies the clue letter, and makes a prediction about the hidden object or animal. If correct, that student chooses the next student. (Since every page contains the same sentence stub and since you have already played the game, every student can read, although some may need gentle nudging.)

7. Continue this procedure throughout the book. (Note: there are a few pages in these books with objects or animals that begin with letters other than PLOSIVES. You may skip these to avoid confusion, place them in another category, or take your turn reading.)

8. Follow the same procedure as above with the companion book.

9. Distribute the miniature magnifying glasses. Students look closely at the seven consonants you have written on the board or chart.

10. Place these seven letters, magnetic or foam, in a writing center for students to explore. Give students paper to practice writing them. Advanced students may use these letters in words or sentences.

EXTENSIONS

1. Students name the seven consonants that stop the air and then release it in a tiny burst or explosion.
    • Write these on the board or chart as students name the consonants.
    • Ask students why they are called (stops or plosives).

2. Students brainstorm objects or animals that start with these letters. Write down their offerings.

3. Ask students if they remember the "I Spy" sentence stub. Write it on the board or chart paper.

4. Students make an "I Spy" book.
    • Distribute colorful paper.
    • Students fold the paper in half, short end to short end.
    • Students draw a picture of an animal or object on the right side.
    • Encourage them to think of something that begins with a STOP or PLOSIVE.
    • Challenge them to think of other objects or animals than those they read about in the books or brainstormed on the board.
    • On the left side of paper, students write (or copy from the board–depending upon their level) the "I Spy" sentence stub.
    • Then they write first letter of the animal or object they drew under the stub.

5. Students share their books as part of an oral language experience.
   - Students cluster around the Author's Chair.
   - In turn, each student reads his or her "I Spy."
   - Other students predict the animal or object based on the first letter.

RELATED BOOKS

Although *Big Dog and Little Dog Going for a Walk* by Dav Pilkey is a simple board book for children ages one to three, it does reinforce all the PLOSIVES except the hard C sound.

1. Review the seven STOPS or PLOSIVES.
2. Tell students that sometimes the sounds can be heard in the middle or at the end of a word as well as at the beginning of a word. They must listen carefully, e.g. *walK* or *liKe* as well *Big* or *Dog*.
3. Read a sentence (the sentences are short).
4. Students again hold their hands a bit away from but in front of their mouths as they repeat the sentences.
5. Students identify the words with the STOP or PLOSIVE sounds by remembering the letters or by the feel of the tiny explosion. Write these words on large index cards.
6. Students in groups of two may use the index cards to practice reading the words.

In her delightful book, *Kisses*, Alice McLerran describes all kinds of kisses from daddy and mummy's kisses to puppy licks.

1. Since this book repeats the word *kiss* so often, it reinforces the letter K and its sound. By repeatedly showing students the letter K and pronouncing its sound, they will be able to distinguish the letter K from the letter C when it makes the K consonant sound, sometimes called the hard C.
2. Give students candy kisses and ask them to write about kisses.

PUBLISHING

Under a banner which reads WE ARE EXPLODING WITH SOUNDS! display the seven STOPS or PLOSIVES, the students' "I Spy" books, and the words on the index cards.

Dr. JAC 4
qu

THE QUILT STORY

G. P Putnam's Sons

Tony Johnston

PHONICS CONCEPTS:
- QU: the KW Sound as in *QUilt;*
- *Generalization:*
  THE LETTER Q IS NEVER USED WITHOUT THE LETTER U.
- *Generalization:*
  THE QU USUALLY MAKES THE KW SOUND BUT SOMETIMES MAKES ONLY THE K SOUND AS IN *PICTURESQUE* OR *UNIQUE.*

LANGUAGE ARTS CONCEPT:
- Sequencing

Artifacts: 5" X 5" squares of patterned fabric and 5" X 5" squares of colorful paper
Summary: A pioneer mother makes a quilt for her daughter Abigail. Years later another mother mends it for her little girl. Tomie dePaola's illustrations enhance the story.

READING/WRITING CONNECTION

1. Make a 2' Q and a 2' U out of cardboard. Cover with pieces of fabric so the letters look like quilts. Use plastic re-usable adhesive to attach these letters to the chalkboard.
2. Pointing to each letter, identify it. Students echo. Ask students what the covering on the letters looks like. (If available, bring a quilt to class to show students, to nudge them into identification.)
3. When they see the connection of QU to a quilt, point to the letters and say the KW sound. Invite the students to echo. This association of fabric and object to letters and sounds helps solidify it in the memory.
4. Write the letters ILT after the QU; say the word *quilt*; invite students to echo.
5. Ask students to think of other words beginning with QU. As they offer words, write them next to the enlarged QU. Some words might be: *quart, question, quick, quit, queen, quiet, quack, quake.* If students are slow to respond, provide hints: "Think of a word that starts with qu and goes with king." "Think of a word that we use when we get too noisy. Remember the word begins with QU."
6. Read the story. Every time you are about to read the word quilt, point to the enlarged letters and invite the students to chorus the word with you.
7. After the story, distribute the fabric squares and paper to each student. Write the word *square* on the board or chart and underline QU.
8. Each student glues the fabric square onto the paper square.
9. At this time, point out that the letter U always follows the letter Q. Distribute additional paper and encourage students to write on the paper. Depending upon level,

this writing may range from copying the two letters, writing sentences about a quilt, paraphrasing the book, or composing an entirely new story.

10. Students share what they have written by sitting in the Author's Chair with classmates clustered around.

EXTENSIONS

1. Follow the same procedure with the enlarged QU and the medial KW sound. Some words might be: *square, equal, squirrel, liquid, squash, squeak, squirm.* On board or chart, write the letters before and after the enlarged QU to make the word. This method is especially helpful for visual learners. Again, point out to students that the letter U always follows the letter Q.
2. Using the tune to the folk song "Oh, A-Hunting We Will Go," students sing, "Oh, A-Quilting We Will Go..." emphasizing the "KW" of QU:

   "Oh, a-quilting we will go, a-quilting we will go!
   Quick, quiet, sew ee oh
   A-quilting we will go!

RELATED BOOKS

Five Little Ducks illustrated by Jose Aruego and Ariane Dewey is one of the *Raffi Songs to Read* series. Through this delightful blending of sequence, rhyme, and rhythm, students sing the song of mother duck who repeatedly calls for her ducks, "Quack, quack, quack, quack!"
1. Students sing the song "Five Little Ducks" to the music provided in the book.
2. When they get to the "Quack, quack, quack, quack!" section, students put their hands together palm-to-palm and clap them together to the words.

Quick as a Cricket by Audrey Wood reinforces the Q as the KW sound in the title. This is book enables students to role play each of the adjectives: *quick, slow, happy, sad,* and so forth.

The Quilt by Ann Jonas tells the story of a little girl who finds memories in her new quilt.
1. Read the story.
2. Students join in calling for "Sally."

Eight Hands Round: A Patchwork Alphabet by Ann Whitford Paul is a terrific book to reinforce the letters of the alphabet.
1. Show students how patchwork pieces can be sewn together into quilts just like letters can be "sewn together" to make words, sentences, paragraphs, and stories.
2. Read the Q page and point out how that pattern looks like a queen's crown.

PUBLISHING

Students display their quilt squares in a sequence to form a large quilt. After all the quilt squares are hung, students count the number of fabric squares aloud and then count the number of paper squares. Call the display A QUILTING WE WILL GO!

AMAZING ANTHONY ANT

Random House

Lorna and Graham Philpot

PHONICS CONCEPTS:
- A Vowel Sound: Schwa as in *Amazing;*
- A Vowel Sound: Long A as in *amAzing;*
- A Vowel Sound: Short A as in *Anthony* and *Ant;*

LANGUAGE ARTS CONCEPTS:
- Emphasizing the concept of word;
- Distinguishing fiction;
- Distinguishing non-fiction;

Artifacts: Miniature plastic ants (available from Oriental Trading Co.)

Summary: This book marries mathematics to music by showing ants marching and singing "The Anthony Ant Song" to the tune of "When Johnny Comes Marching Home" as they follow a maze and count off by twos, threes, and so forth to tens. Added incentives offer four choices for the last line of the stanza under four flaps plus the challenge to find Anthony Ant.

READING/WRITING CONNECTION

1. Show students the book's cover. Call students' attention to the ants marching around its edge. Point to the directions: "Lift the Flaps" and talk about what that means. Then show the flaps and how they work. Follow this same procedure for the other directions on the cover: "Find Anthony Ant," "Follow the Maze," and "Sing the Song."

2. After students are thoroughly familiar with the book's format, show the title and the first stanza which has been written on a page of chart paper large enough for all students to see.

3. Tell students they can learn the sounds the letter A makes in this book.

4. Put the words *amazing, Anthony, ant* in a pocket chart with the words separated on sentence strips to emphasize the concept of word. Highlight with 2" highlighter tape the first A in the word *amazing* using NoteTape (available from Lee Products or Calloway House). Tell students this A sound has a funny name called *schwa.* Pronounce the sound and pronounce the word. Exaggerate the sounds. Invite students to echo.

5. Next, highlight the second A in *amazing.* Tell students this sound says its own name and is called a long A. Pronounce the sound and pronounce the word. Exaggerate the sounds. Invite students to echo.

6. Finally, highlight the A in the name *Anthony* and in the word *ant.* Tell students this sound is called the short A because the sound is barely pronounced, barely heard.

Pronounce the sound and pronounce the word. Invite students to echo.

7. Then highlight each word. This reinforces whole to part to whole.
8. Read the book by singing it. Students follow your finger around maze and individual students choose the flaps. Reread the book with the students joining in the singing. This may be done four times or more in order to discover what is under each flap.
9. Distribute the artifacts and plain white paper. Each student draws a maze on his or her paper (or they could work in small groups) and glues the ant somewhere in the maze.
10. Depending on the level, students write "Amazing Anthony Ant" on the paper or even some or all of the "Anthony Ant Song." Advanced students may follow the model of the book and label the areas or streets on their maze.

EXTENSIONS

1. Students line up by twos and march around the room, cafeteria, or outside, singing the "Anthony Ant Song." They increase their numbers each time they make a full turn.
2. Students identify other creatures in the book.
   • Write these names on chart paper.
   • If there is an A in the creature's name, together try to determine what sound it makes. For example, the A in the word snake says its own name, so it is a long A.
   • Find and identify the vowel or vowels in the creature's names.

RELATED BOOKS

One Hundred Hungry Ants by Elinor J. Pinczes tells the story of ants heading to a picnic, but they take so much time forming lines divisible by 100 that they lose out on the food.
1. Students form the lines as the ants do in the book by using plastic ants, counters, or beads.
2. The rhyme in this book may also be used to reinforce the long O sound as in *so*, *slow*, and *row*.

Bernard Most's *There's an Ant in Anthony* is a wonderful book to show students how small words can hide in bigger words.
1. Students, like Anthony, try to find the word ant in words they find around the room or in their books, as in *praying mantis, pant*, and so forth.
2. Students may find a small word in their names, in the name of the school, town, or something else familiar to them and then try to find that word in other words.

The Fascinating World of Ants by Maria Ángels Julivert is a non-fiction book which explores facts about ants from their various species to their anatomy, from their colonies to their enemies.

Ants by Ruth Berman, another non-fiction book, covers much the same material as Julivert's book, but in a simpler language with large print.
1. Use one or both of these non-fiction books and the focal fiction book to explain the

difference between fiction and non-fiction.

2. Students may talk about how these two books differ from the counting books or other fiction books about ants.

3. Students may become A detectives looking for words that contain the letter A. When found, they may try to sound out the word using what they know about the A sound.

PUBLISHING

Divide the class into three groups. Each group receives a sheet of chart paper. On one is written SCHWA with an example such as the word *alone*; another says LONG A with an example such as *may*; the third shows the SHORT A with the example such as *at*. Students find words with their sound for the letter A to write on their charts. Display these on a wall under the headline WE KNOW THE ANTICS OF A!

GOOD-NIGHT, OWL!

Aladdin

Pat Hutchins

PHONICS CONCEPTS:
- OW Vowel Sound: OU Diphthong as in *OWl*;
- Locating the sound in the beginning, medial, and final position of a word

LANGUAGE ARTS CONCEPT:
- Onomatopoeia

Artifacts: Large plastic "eyes," (available in craft stores) and 6" brown or white paper bags (available in discount stores)

Summary: Owl is unable to sleep all through the day because other birds, the bees, and the squirrel keep him awake. That night, owl turns the tables.

READING/WRITING CONNECTION

1. If possible, focus the students with an owl puppet. (Folkmanis has a beautiful snowy owl with a head that turns.) Invite students to talk about owls, what they look like, their color, their habits.

2. Show the book's cover. Point out the OW sound at the beginning of the word owl. Say the sound. Students echo.

3. Separate the sound OW in the word *owl* from the onomatopoeic sounds owls make such as *whoo* and *screech*.

   • Tell students that sometimes words sound like what they mean, for example *splash*. Sometimes owls say *whoo*, and we write it w•h•o•o. Show this on board or chart.

   • Sometimes owls say screech, and we write it s•c•r•e•e•c•h. Show this on board or chart. *Whoo* and *screech* are words that sound like what they mean. Depending upon their level, tell students we call these words onomatopoeia.

   • Note: be careful when asking students, "What sound does owl make?" They are more likely to say "whoo" than they are to identify the OW sound. If you want the OW sound in *owl*, it is better to write *owl* on board or chart, underline or highlight the OW, and focus students with, "What sound does the OW make in the word *owl*?"

4. Call the students' attention to the owl's eyes. Ask students why the owl might have one eye open and one eye closed. Talk about the book's title.

5. Open to the first double page spread. Talk about the meaning of the word tried. Ask students if they ever "tried to sleep." What might keep them from sleeping. Receive all answers.

6. Since owls sleep during the day, ask students to predict what might keep an owl awake.

7. Distribute one large plastic "eye" and the small paper bag to each student.

8. Students glue the one open "eye" to the top flap of the bag and make a curved line somewhat like a U for the closed eye. Their owls will resemble the owl on the cover of the book. They may cut off about one inch of the bag's bottom to use for the pointed ears and beak.

9. Then students repeatedly write the word *owl* in brown or black crayon all over the bag. As they write the word, they say the word to themselves. When completed, the repeated word looks like feathers. This is a good way for students to practice the OW sound.

10. When the students have finished making their owls, they place one hand inside, curl their fingers around the inside flap, make the head move up and down, and practice owl sounds, the OW sound as well as *whoo* and *screech*.

EXTENSIONS

1. Divide the class into ten small groups: bees, squirrels, crows, woodpeckers, starlings, jays, cuckoos, robins, sparrows, and doves.
   • Each group practices their appropriate sound: the bees *buzz*, the squirrels *crunch*, the crows *caw*, the woodpeckers *rat-a-tat*, the starlings *twit-twit*, the jays *ark*, the cuckoos *cuckoo*, the robins *pip*, the sparrows *cheep*, and the doves *coo*.
   • Reread the book.
   • When you get to a specific group, that group provides the necessary sound. In this way, the groundwork is laid for future work on onomatopoeic words and poetry.

2. Write OW on a chart or board (or use a pocket chart). Add letters before and after the OW to show the sound in different positions. For example: *OWl, cOW, prOWl*. Students suggest letters or words. Students replicate this activity at their places with letters from their mini-folders, their magnetic letters and boards, tactile letters, or foam letters.

RELATED BOOKS

The Owl and the Pussycat by Edward Lear with illustrations by Jan Brett places these classic characters in the Caribbean. As usual, after a courtship voyage of a year and a day, Owl and Pussy finally buy a ring from Piggy and get married. Brett's detailed illustrations perfectly match Lear's charming poem.

1. It is important to read this classic to young students. Encourage oral language experience by asking them to point out the things they notice in the illustrations.

2. Before rereading, divide the class into two parts: one part makes the owl's sound when his name is read; the other side makes the purring sound of a cat when her part is read.

Owl Moon by Jane Yolen tells the story of how a young girl and her father go owling for the Great Horned Owl.

1. Turn the lights down as you read the book.

2. Students softly join in making the "Whoo-whoo-who-who-who-whooooooo" sound.

Owl Babies by Martin Waddell is the story of three owl babies whose mother has gone in the night, and they try to stay calm.

1. Members of class chorus the recurring line "all owls think a lot" during the reading.
2. Students talk about things they do to stay calm when their mothers are away.

The Owl Scatterer by Howard Norman takes the reader to Canada where lazy old Jake lives. When the town is overrun with owls, however, it is Jake who knows how to scatter them.

1. Students enjoy making the owl sounds in this book.
2. This book offers an opportunity for problem solving. Students suggest ways to scatter the owls.
3. Students role play Jake when he scatters the owls.

Two non-fiction books on owls lend themselves to the activities listed below.

•*The Fascinating World of Birds of Prey* by Maria Ángels Julivert is an especially good non-fiction book on nocturnal hunters. It has a a wonderful picture of a mother barn owl holding a mouse as she is about to feed her young. It shows the tawny owl in camouflage, another owl turning its head, and pictures of many species of owl.

•*Amazing Birds* by Alexandra Parsons contains a clear picture of an eagle owl with particular emphasis on its "ears," actually tufts of feathers, and on its huge claws or talons.

1. Show students the pictures and share the details about owls.
2. Divide students into groups. Give each group a bag of feathers.
3. Students categorize the feathers by size, color, or type.

PUBLISHING

Place a large strip of brown butcher paper vertically up a wall to look like the owl's tree in the book. Cut smaller strips and attach them horizontally to look like branches. Hang the students' bag owls from the branches. Across the top of the tree, on green paper leaves, proclaim WE KNOW OUR OWL SOUNDS!

SHAKE SHAKE SHAKE

Red Wagon

Andrea and Brian Pinkney

PHONICS CONCEPT:
• Consonant Digraph SH as in *SHake*, *SHoe*, or *SHapes*

LANGUAGE ARTS CONCEPT:
• Apostrophe

Artifacts: Miniature baby rattles (available in party stores)

Summary: This easy-to-read sturdy board book is based upon two little children experiencing a "shekere" (pronounced shay-kur-ray), which is an African percussion instrument.

READING/WRITING CONNECTION

1. Before beginning this lesson, make a 2' SHOE WORD BANK out of butcher paper cut into the shape of a shoe.
2. Begin by playing "Simon Says Shake Your..." (head, left hand, right arm, legs, body, foot, finger, and so forth) with the students.
3. Bring a dry gourd that rattles to class; shake it for the students; let them take turns shaking it.
4. Show the book to the students. Point to each word in the title as you read it. Repeat so students may also read the title.
5. Invite students to stand around you as you read the book. Help students see the connection between the gourd in the classroom and the shekere in the book.
6. Every time you read the word shake, tell students to shake themselves.
7. Point out the SH sound. Tell students that these two letters, S and H come together to make one sound. Invite students to put their fingers to their lips and whisper the SH sound. Then give them the rattles, invite them to rattle and say the SH sound out loud.
8. Divide the shoe word bank in half. Write "QUIET SH WORDS" on one side and "LOUD SH WORDS" on the other side.
9. Students brainstorm words with SH sounds, tell what side the word belongs, and give their reasons. (This is a fine high level thinking skill activity although some hints may be necessary.) Examples: "Sunshine belongs on the quiet side because it never makes a sound." "Put dishes on the loud side 'cause they break." "Shirt is quiet because it just hangs on you."
10. Reread the book by calling upon individual students to read each of the double spread pages. When the student gets to the repeated word *shake*, all students shake their rattles and chorus the word.

EXTENSIONS

1. Display a number of small gourds each with a 1" hole in the top and bottom, or tell students to bring one to class. Students choose their gourd. Each student writes his or her name, followed by an apostrophe, followed by the word shekere on the gourd. Explain that the apostrophe shows who owns the shekere. Tell them that they will be making a shekere somewhat like the one in the story.
    - Place newspaper somewhere in the room where the air circulates. Explain to students that the gourds must first dry out. Students choose a place to put their gourds making sure no gourd touches another gourd during this drying process or both may rot.
    - Once each morning for approximately two weeks the students tend to their gourds by taking old sheeting and wiping their gourds dry. When they replace their gourds, they put them in new positions, again being careful they do not touch.
    - Students will know the gourds are dry when the seeds inside rattle.
    - When all the gourds rattle, students wash their gourd with warm water and soap.
    - They paint the outside with self-polishing floor wax and let them dry overnight.
    - The next day they can reread the story and shake their shekeres.
2. Together write a song that can be sung while shaking their rattles.

RELATED BOOKS

Shoes, a Reading Rainbow Big Book, by Elizabeth Winthrop is perfect to reinforce the SH digraph. The word shoes is repeated, there is rhyme, and the added interest of different kinds of shoes makes this book a natural for the young student.

1. After the first reading of the book, ask students to name the shoes pictured. For example, *ice skates*, *ballet slippers*, *flippers*, *rollerblades*, and so forth. Students may be challenged to name other types of shoes not pictured in the book. Write these on the Shoe Word Bank for later writing.
2. Give each student a piece of brown cardboard from old boxes. Each student traces his or her foot on the cardboard. Cut it out. Punch six holes at the sole of the outline—two holes on each side and two holes at the heel—one hole on each side.
3. Students write their name with an apostrophe followed by the word shoe on their shoe outline, for example, Maria's shoe, Joe's shoe, and so forth.
4. Each student chooses one piece of yarn from different colors. They use the yarn to lace their shoes.

Shoes, a fascinating non-fiction book by Margery G. Nichelason, traces the development of different kinds of footwear, shoe fashions, and interesting facts and folklore about shoes. Students will especially enjoy the house covered with shoes and the house shaped like a shoe—not Mother Goose but a real house in York, Pennsylvania.

1. Students design a new use for an old shoe.
2. Students plan a display of different kinds of shoes.

So Many Kinds of Shoes! Book-and-Mobile Set by Max Grover is geared to toddlers who love shoes. It complements the work on shoes by showing many kinds of shoes on its end pages and reinforces the SH sound.

1. Students identify the different kinds of shoes pictured in the book.
2. Use the mobile as a model for the shoes students outlined from cardboard.

Sea Shapes by Suse MacDonald introduces the elementary geometry of shapes amid beautiful pictures of the sea's fauna and marine animals. Interesting sea facts are given at the conclusion of the book.

1. Students identify the shape picture, read the word for that shape, and find the shape in the pictures. Advanced students may identify what is pictured in more detail, for example, star, starfish.
2. Students may choose a shape and create their own sea creature. As an added challenge, students may name their creature something beginning with the letters SH.

PUBLISHING

On a section of the floor, display the students' shoes in and around the SHOE WORD BANK. Make little shoe prints upon which you spell out WE ARE SHAKING IN OUR SHOES OVER SH! Tack these over the display as if someone with small feet had walked by and left his or her prints. Arrange the students' shekeres around the shoes.

CHARLIE THE CHICKEN

Red Wagon

Nick Denchfield
and
Ant Parker

PHONICS CONCEPTS:

- CH Consonant Sound: CH Digraph as in *CHarlie* and *CHicken;*
- WH Consonant Sound: WH Digraph (HW blend) as in *WHy* and *WHeat;*
- TH Consonant Sound: TH Digraph voiced as in *THat* (the DH sound, sometimes called the voiced TH to distinguish it from the digraph TH as in *THank* or *THing,* which is sometimes called the voiceless TH sound);
- *Generalization:*
  WHEN THE C AND H ARE NEXT TO EACH OTHER, THEY MAKE ONLY ONE SOUND.
- *Generalization:*
  CH IS USUALLY PRONOUNCED AS IT IS IN *KITCHEN*, *CATCH*, AND *CHAIR*, NOT LIKE SH.

LANGUAGE ARTS CONCEPT:

- Cause and effect

Artifacts: Chenille Fuzzy Chicks (available from Oriental Trading Co.)
Summary: Charlie's tummy, beak, and feet pop-up in this delightful book that holds a big surprise that folds out at the end.

READING/WRITING CONNECTION

1. Before beginning the lesson, make an enlarged version of Charlie on yellow butcher paper. Use Charlie from the cover as a model for the CHICKEN WORD BANK. Display near students.
2. Show the book. Point to the CH in the word *Charlie* and in the word *chicken*. Tell students these two letters make one sound, the CH sound. Make the sound. Invite the students to echo.
3. Explain that there are two other words repeated in the book that also have two letters that make one sound. Write the word *That's* on the board or chart and the word *why*.
4. Say the TH sound and the WH sound. Invite the students to echo.
5. Ask students to say other words that begin with CH. Write the words the students

offer on the CHICKEN WORD BANK.

6. For advanced students or for an added challenge, ask students to come up with tongue twisters using the CH sound, e.g. Charlie Chicken cheerfully chased children to church.
7. Follow the same procedure for the TH and WH sounds, although the tongue twisters may be more difficult for these sounds.
8. Read the book. Since it is an easy book with large letters, point to each word as you read it. Students orally join in on the phrase "Charlie the chicken..." and "That's why...."
9. Read the book several times with students participating.
10. Distribute the artifacts and invite students to talk and write about their experience with chickens, Easter, and other books about chickens.

EXTENSIONS

1. Students create a pop-up book of their own. They make a chicken, which they name, with a beak that opens.
    • Fold a standard-size piece of yellow construction paper in half short end to short end. Cut a two-inch slit in the middle of the paper, perpendicular to the fold.
    • With the paper still folded, take one side of the cut at the fold and crease it into a deep triangle. Follow the same procedure with the other side of the cut. (The paper will look like a V-neck collar.)
    • Bend the triangles back to their original positions.
    • Make a tent with the paper with the center fold as the peak.
    • Gently push the two triangles through. Recrease them on the inside of the paper. (When you close the paper, there is a clean V on the outside. Inside, there is a moving beak, a smaller version of the one in the book.)
    • Students draw a chicken around the beak and title their books.
2. Students, according to their abilities, write the three digraphs, the name of their chicken, or a story about their chicken in their pop-up book. Encourage them to use words that begin with the CH, TH, or WH sound.
3. Go back through the book. Ask students to identify the cause by giving them the effect. For example, "Why did Charlie the chicken get such a big fat tummy?"
4. Then go through the book again. This time give the cause and students identify the effect. For example, "What happened to Charlie the chicken after he ate lots of barley?"

RELATED BOOKS

Chicka Chicka Boom Boom by Bill Martin, Jr. and John Archambault provides a rhythmic way to reinforce the CH sound. This book personifies the letters of the alphabet by having them climb a coconut tree and fall off with a boom!
    • Students clap out the rhythm of the book's title as it is read.
    • This reading/clapping may be repeated several times.

That's Good! That's Bad! by Margery Cuyler reinforces the TH sound. In this book, a little boy experiences a series of adventures that end with a refrain—one or the other sentences of the title.

• As the story is read and the refrain reached, students predict which sentence it will be—good or bad—by chorusing one or the other lines. The reader's intonation can provide the clue.
• Point out to students that the sentences give the effect of each cause.

I Like It When... by Mary Murphy reinforces the WH digraph through a simple story of a little penguin sharing his favorite things with his mother.
• Students together say the repeated sentence stub, which is the effect.
• The reader (who could be a competent student) completes the sentence and provides the cause. This is a good book to show students that the cause is not always given first; sometimes the effect is given first.

PUBLISHING

Arrange the students' pop-up books on a table or shelf in the room. Display a long banner behind the books that says, WE POP OVER CH, TH, WH SOUNDS!

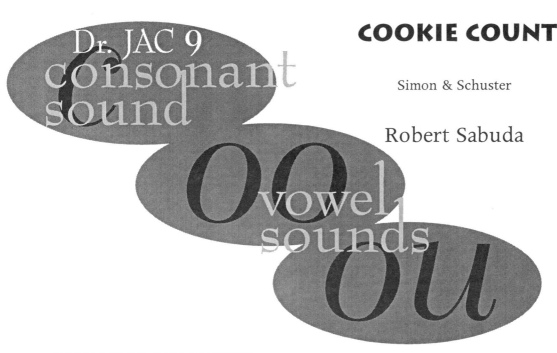

COOKIE COUNT

Simon & Schuster

Robert Sabuda

PHONICS CONCEPTS:

- C Consonant Sound: K Sound, sometimes called the hard C as in *Cookie* and *Count;*
- OO Vowel Sound: 1-Dot U or Short OO as in *cOOkie;*
- OU Vowel Sound: OU Diphthong as in *cOUnt;*
- *Generalization:*
  WHEN THE LETTER C IS FOLLOWED BY O OR A THE SOUND OF K IS LIKELY TO BE HEARD.

LANGUAGE ARTS CONCEPTS:

- Numeration, counting by numbers;
- Changing numbers as symbols (1,2,3) to spelled-out numbers as words (one, two, three)

Artifacts: Chocolate chip cookies

Summary: This mouth-watering book takes the pop-up book to new heights. Each double-page spread is an intricate weaving of paper cookies of all types. It begins with ONE chocolate chip cookie and ends with a gingerbread cookie house with TEN windows. This delightful book enables the teaching of phonics and numeration in a tasty, whimsical way.

READING/WRITING CONNECTION

1. Before the lesson begins cut a two-foot circle out of brown butcher paper. Make darker brown "chips." This is the COOKIE WORD BANK. Also, cut out brown three-inch circles with "chips" to approximate chocolate chip cookies (at least ten per student).
2. Begin by giving each student one chocolate chip cookie. Ask them to identify the kind of cookie they are holding. Everyone takes one big bite. Ask them what letter they are holding (C).
3. Engage students in talk about cookies, their favorites, when they usually eat cookies. Ask if they ever helped make cookies.

4. Write their responses on the COOKIE WORD BANK.

5. Introduce the book by telling students that the author made cookies out of paper much the way a baker makes cookies out of dough.

6. Read through the book so that students catch the number pattern. Invite students to anticipate the next number.

7. Take time for students to talk about each cookie. Use this as an oral activity.

8. Before students take turns reading the book, write C on the COOKIE WORD BANK. Pronounce the sound; students echo. Say the words *cookie* and *count*. Write OO on the COOKIE WORD BANK. Pronounce the sound and say it again in the word *cookie*. Students echo. Write OU. Pronounce the sound and say it again in the word *count*. Point out these three sounds in the book's title. Explain how knowing the sounds can help them read the title. Write the title on the COOKIE WORD BANK.

9. Each student gets the opportunity to read a page and count the pictured cookies. The other students follow along by counting their pre-cut brown circle "cookies" at their places.

10. Distribute a 6" X 4" index card to each student. Students use these to make cookie pop-up book marks.
    • Fold the card in half long side to long side;
    • On the fold, measure two inches in on each side and mark vertically;
    • Measure one inch down from the fold and mark horizontally;
    • Cut on each of the two inch marks and fold on the one inch mark;
    • Push the rectangle through to the inside of the card, inverting the crease, to form the portion that will pop out (When the pop-out is folded in, the back of the card will look like a block letter C.);
    • Inside, on the pop-up, the students paste a drawing of their favorite cookie;
    • Depending upon level, students write C, OO and OU or sentences about their favorite cookie. Advanced students may write the recipe on the back;
    • These may be used as bookmarks in their favorite "tastiest" books.

EXTENSIONS

1. Using alphabet cookie cutters (available from U. S. Toy) and play dough, students make letters.
    • Sure-fire play dough comes from the following recipe in Mary Ann F. Kohl's book *Scribble Cookies* (89).
    Mix and cook on LOW until a ball forms, then knead:

1 Cup flour	1 T. cream of tartar
1 Cup water	add food coloring, tempera powder,
1 Cup salt	Jello™, Kool-Aid™, or leave natural

    Roll out with a rolling pin. (Store in snap-on plastic containers or coffee cans.)
    • Students cut the dough into letters.
    • They use the letters to form words on tiles, heavy-stock paper, or plastic cafeteria trays.

2. Return to the book. Write the number symbol on the board or chart. Write the word next to it. Students practice saying their numbers and reading their numbers.

3. Students sing "C Is for Cookie," which can be found on the tape *Sesame Street Platinum All-Time Favorites*.

RELATED BOOKS

Laura Joffe Numeroff's *If You Give a Mouse a Cookie* is a young boy's theorizing a cycle of requests a mouse might make if you gave it a cookie. The book allows for reinforcement of the C, OO and OU sounds.

1. Show the book. Ask students to point out in the book's title the word cookie. Then ask them to point out the two sounds they are learning in that word.
2. Read the book.
3. Bring box cookie dough into class. Add water and bake in a toaster oven.
4. To approximate the book, give students white paper and crayons. Ask them to draw a picture the mouse would draw. As they are working, share the cookies.

The Doorbell Rang by Pat Hutchins (also available in a Big Book edition) recounts what happens to a plate of cookies Ma made each time the doorbell rings. When the cookies run out, Grandma appears at the door with an enormous tray of more cookies. This book enables the same circular reading as Numeroff's.

1. Students use their pre-cut brown circles that represent cookies for simple mathematical calculations such as adding and subtracting. Following are some samples. These should be geared to the level of the students.
   • Add your cookies to those of your friend. How many do you have together? How many do you have if another friend joins you?
   • If the principal comes in to visit and you share two cookies, how many will you have left?
   • If the school nurse brings a tray of cookies to the classroom and everyone gets another cookie, how many will you have?
2. Students role play the book.

PUBLISHING

Display students' pop-up books around the enlarged COOKIE WORD BANK. Call the display, IF YOU GIVE STUDENTS THE C, OO AND OU SOUNDS, THEY WILL...

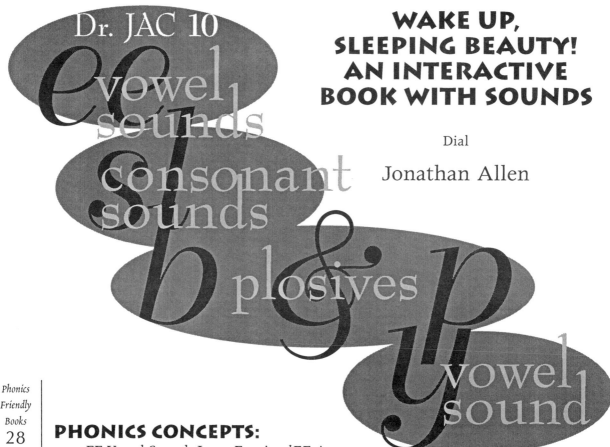

Dr. JAC 10

ee vowel sounds
sl consonant sounds
b & p plosives
y vowel sound

WAKE UP, SLEEPING BEAUTY! AN INTERACTIVE BOOK WITH SOUNDS

Dial

Jonathan Allen

PHONICS CONCEPTS:
- EE Vowel Sound: Long E as in *slEEping;*
- *Generalization:*
    WORDS HAVING EE USUALLY HAVE THE LONG E SOUND;
- SL Consonant Sound: SL Blend as in *SLeeping;*
- B and P Plosives as in *Beauty, sleePing,* and *uP;*
- Y Vowel Sound: Long E as in *BeautY;*
- *Generalization:*
    WHEN Y OR EY IS SEEN IN THE LAST SYLLABLE THAT IS NOT ACCENTED, THE LONG SOUND OF E IS HEARD.

LANGUAGE ARTS CONCEPT:
- Different versions of the same story

Artifacts: Crowns, student-made (For directions, see *Huzzah Means Hooray* by Laurie Carlson.)

Summary: This wonderfully interactive book plays on the idea of waking Sleeping Beauty by using various sounds—whistles, gongs, and so forth. A variation of the classic tale, the high interest of this book invites a way into important phonics concepts.

READING/WRITING CONNECTION

1. Ask students if they know the story of Sleeping Beauty. Listen to their renditions of that classic fairy tale.

2. If they do not know the story, read one from an anthology of fairy tales. A recent publication that presents a relatively concise retelling of the story can be found in *The Candlewick Book of Fairy Tales* by Sarah Hayes.
3. Read the "Wake Up" version all the way through.
4. On the second reading, invite individual students to carefully pull the tabs to initiate the sounds. Talk about how this version is like and unlike the original or other versions.
5. Write EE, SL, P, B, and Y on board or chart. Explain that just as the prince made sounds to wake up the princess, letters make sounds to wake up meaning.
6. Pronounce each of the five sounds. Students echo. Point out these sounds in the title of the book. Read the title. Students echo.
7. Help students realize that by making the sounds, saying the words, and understanding what the words mean, they are reading.
8. Students design crowns on large sheets of goldenrod paper.
9. They copy the letters that make the sounds they have studied around the crown as a decoration, whispering the sounds as they write.
10. They cut out the crowns and affix them together so they can wear them.

EXTENSIONS

1. Hang a long strip of butcher paper horizontally on a wall. Divide it into nine sections.
    • Ask students to name the prince and his assistant. Invite students to tell you what these characters intended to do at the beginning of the story. Write that in the first section.
    • Students tell the first way the prince tried to wake up the princess? Write that in the second section.
    • What was the second way? Write that in the third section.
    • What was the third way? Write that in the fourth section.
    • What was the fourth way? Write that in the fifth section.
    • What was the fifth way? Write that in the sixth section.
    • What happened after the prince gave up? Write that in the seventh section.
    • What happened next? Write that in the eighth section.
    • What happened at the end of the story? Write that in the final section.
2. After that review of the story and the sequencing of events, divide the class into five groups.
    • Give group one plastic whistles.
    • Give group two aluminum pie plates that can be crashed together.
    • Give group three inexpensive toy guitars (or rubber bands on cardboard).
    • Give group four play drums.
    • Give group five plastic clickers.
3. Read the story mural as each group provides the sound for that section. For section seven, students make a "kissing sound"; for the last section they make their sounds together!

RELATED BOOKS

Reading the following books with the students will reinforce the phonics for this unit.

Sleepless Beauty by Frances Minters is a rhythmic, updated version, introduced by a modern-day *choragos* saxophone player, who reappears throughout the book as a type of Greek chorus.* Beauty cleverly outwits the wicked witch and arranges her own happy ending. This book would also work well for older students who are having trouble reading because of its "rock star" interest and upbeat poetry. It reinforces the EE, SL, B, P, and Y sounds.

Eeney, Meeney, Miney, Mo by B. G. Hennessy also reinforces the EE, long E sound as the initial sound of the first character's name and the medial sound in the second character's name. Also, the EY sound in the last syllable of the third character's name reinforces the generalization: When Y or EY is seen in the last syllable that is not accented, the long sound of E is heard.

Think of an Eel by Karen Wallace is an unusual picture book that repeats the word *eel* throughout this beautiful non-fiction book and thereby reinforces the EE sound. Students sing out *eel* as the teacher reads the book.

Ira Sleeps Over by Bernard Waber reinforces the SL consonant blend, the P plosive, and the EE sound.

PUBLISHING

Display the students' crowns in and around the mural. Above it display a banner that proclaims: WE THINK SOUNDS ARE ENCHANTING!

* In Greek tragedies, the fifteen member chorus and its leader (the choragos) usually introduced the play to the accompaniment of a flute. Throughout the play, they remained in the orchestra performing not only its odes but sometimes exchanging dialogue with the characters.

I WENT WALKING

Gulliver

Sue Williams

PHONICS CONCEPT:

- I Vowel Sound: Long I as in I, *kInd*, *Idea*, and *mIce*

LANGUAGE ARTS CONCEPTS:

- Patterning;
- Questions and answers;
- Question marks and periods;
- Color words;
- Capital I;

Artifacts: Tiny plastic animals or animal stickers (available from Oriental Trading Co. or U. S. Toy)

Summary: While walking, a young boy sees and identifies a menagerie of colorful animals. The repetition of the title sentence invites a reinforcement of the long I sound and introduces the pattern. The second pattern is the question, "What did you see?" and invites prediction. The third pattern is a double-spread page which gives the answer.

READING/WRITING CONNECTION

1. Begin this lesson by bringing a small bag or basket to the reading area in which you have placed crayons to match the colors given in the book: black, brown, red, green, pink, and yellow.
2. Hold up each crayon in turn and ask the students to identify its color.
3. As the students identify the colors, write the colors on the board or chart. Tell students they will see these colors again in the book you are about to read and they will be able to read the names of the colors.
4. Point to the first word in the book's title as you say *I*. Tell students that the long I says its name when it stands alone and even sometimes when it is tucked inside a word. It is capitalized when it stands alone. Repeat the word. Students echo.
5. Read the book, exaggerating a bit the rising inflection of voice for the question.
6. Since the book's pattern is repetitive, *I* appears in the initial sentence and again in the answer to the question. Encourage students to read *I*, remember the pattern, identify the animal, and name its color. When they do, they are reading the book.
7. Upon second reading, call upon individual students to read the statement and question. Point out that the statement ends with a period and the question with a question mark. Remind students that their voice should go up at the end of a question. Help students who still have not caught on to the pattern. The reader then plays teacher and calls on another student to predict the answer. The student who

answered gets a turn to read and so on.

8. Distribute a sticker, picture, or tiny plastic replica of an animal and a large sheet of white paper to each student. Tell students they are about to write an *I Went Walking* book. Caution them to keep their animal a secret.

9. Students fold the paper into four equal parts. (Modify for very young students.)
   • In quadrant one, they write "I went walking" and draw themselves.
   • In quadrant two, they write the question and draw a picture that hints at their plastic animal or the one on their sticker.
   • In quadrant three, they draw a related picture.
   • In quadrant four, they identify the animal and its color.

10. Students sit in a circle. Begin with one student who reads up to quadrant three (or the question and hint for very young students). Other students predict the animal. Go around the circle until every student reads his or her book.

EXTENSIONS

1. Students practice singing the following song adapted to the tune of the traditional song "I've Been Working on the Railroad."

I've been working on my long I sounds
All the livelong day.
I've been working on my long I sounds
To learn them all the way.
Don't you hear the teacher saying
"The long I says its name"?
Don't you hear the students saying,
"The long I says its name"?

Long I starts *idea*,
Long I starts *icicle*,
Long I always says its name, its name.

Long I is in *kind*,
Long I is in *mice*,
Long I always says its name.

Spider's always use the long I,
Lions always use it too- o-o-o
Triangles love the long I,
And so do I– I do.

Fee-fi, fiddle-i-o
Fee-fi, fiddle-i-o, i-o-o,
Fee-fi, fiddle-i-o,
The long I always says its name.

2. Students may sing the song with actions. Advanced students, working individually or in groups, may find other words that start with long I, other words that have long I in them, or other words that use the long I .

3. Write the words found by students on chart paper and add the song's verses.

RELATED BOOKS

I Took My Frog to the Library by Eric A. Kimmel tells about a young girl who brings her strange pets to the library. The delightful ending not only reinforces the long I, but also the concept of modeling and the power of reading.

    1. Read the book and show the pictures. Check if students can identify the long I.

    2. Students write or talk about other pets and what might happen if their pet went to the library.

The Bear's Bicycle by Emilie Warren McLeod remains a great favorite of students. As the young boy takes a bicycle ride, his toy bear, come to life, does the same. The boy is careful and obeys the rules. The bear is foolhardy.

    1. Read the book and show the pictures. Challenge students to identify the long I.

    2. Upon second reading, invite individual students to pair up as readers. One reads the words about the boy's adventure; the other reads the pictures about the bear's adventures.

Teeny Tiny retold by Jill Bennett allows practice of the long I in the medial position. Because the words *teeny tiny* are repeated several times on each page, students are able to hear the long I say its name over and over again in the word *tiny*.

    1. Tell students you will give them a signal. When they see that signal, they are to say "teeny tiny." (An apt signal is to use the thumb and index finger to indicate a small amount.)

    2. Students make a teeny tiny eight-page book and write their version of the tale.

Three Kind Mice by Vivian Sathre tells the story of three generous mice who bake a birthday cake for their mysterious friend. The rhyme enhances the charming story.

    1. Point out the long I vowel sound in the title, in both words *kind* and *mice*.

    2. Students, working in small groups and with strips of cash register tape, generate a list of words with the long I in the IND family: *bind, find, blind*; and in the ICE family: *dice, nice, rice* and so forth.

PUBLISHING

Display all the work students have generated in the hallway or on a classroom wall. Call the display I WENT WALKING AND I SAW THE LONG I!

FIX-IT

Unicorn

David McPhail

PHONICS CONCEPTS:

- I Vowel Sound: Short I as in *fIx, It, Inch*;
- Fricative F Sound as in *Fix*;
- X Consonant Sound: KS Sound as in *fiX*;
- Long I Vowel Sound as in *I*;
- The Plosive T as in *iT*;

LANGUAGE ARTS CONCEPTS:

- Writing a book;
- Cover with title and author's name;
- Dedication page;
- "About the Author" page

Artifacts: Miniature books (student-made)

Summary: In this simple classic, Emma wants to watch television one morning but discovers it is broken. Her mother, her father, and the fix-it man try to get it working. To distract her, Mom reads and rereads a book. Then, even after the television works, Emma has become too involved with her book to care.

READING/WRITING CONNECTION

1. Make a 1' copy of each letter in the book's title using felt material. Attach to board or wall within students' view. With FIX IT as a focus, explain that all the letters in this title have sounds. This is a perfect time for students at their places to use their magnetic or tactile letters to write the words.
2. Point to the fricative F sound. Show students how they put their teeth momentarily on their bottom lips to interfere with the airflow from the lungs in order to make the F sound. (If necessary, review the difference between vowels and consonants in Dr. JAC 1.) Make the sound. Students echo.
3. Tell students that the letter I makes two sounds. The long I sound says its own name. Students echo. Then make the short I sound. Students echo.
4. Introduce the X consonant sound which sounds like KS. Make the sound. Show stu-

dents how to bring their teeth together and hiss like a snake. Students echo.

5. Put all three sounds together to read the first word in the title.

6. Sound the short I sound and the plosive T. Students echo each and then use their knowledge of sounds to read the title.

7. As you read the book, show students the words *fix it* when they appear. Encourage the students to read those words.

8. Show a model of a miniature eight-page book and demonstrate how to make it.
   • Fold a 5 1/2" X 4 1/2" paper in half, short end to short end. Crease.
   • Fold back one side halfway and crease; fold back the other side halfway and crease. (If opened, the paper would show four long rectangles.)
   • Keeping the paper folded, fold it short end to short end and crease. (If opened, the paper would show eight rectangles.)
   • Unfold until the paper is in half. Flip the two bottom rectangles up one way and the other two bottom rectangles up the other way so that the paper makes a small tent.
   • Carefully tear or cut down from the peak of the tent on the center crease to the fold.
   • Place the thumb and index finger of one hand on one side of the tear or cut and the other thumb and index finger on the other side of the tear or cut. Pull down so the paper resembles a star. Recrease the one fold.
   • Simply turn the pages against each other to form the book.

9. Students write FIX IT on the cover and their names as the authors. Inside the cover they dedicate their book to someone. On the back cover they write "About the Author," and they write something about themselves. If available, students may paste small school pictures of themselves on the back cover. On the remaining five pages they write any of the following options depending upon their level:
   • The letters of the alphabet they know;
   • A list of things that can be fixed;
   • A story about a time when they couldn't watch television;
   • Some things about a book they like to have read to them;
   • Something about books they like to read to themselves or to their toys;
   • An original story.

10. Author's Chair Share.

EXTENSIONS

1. Use *Fix-It* as a means of sowing the seeds of inferential thinking.
   • Students look at the picture of Mom trying to fix the television and infer what she tries to do to make it work.
   • Students examine the picture of Emma's father trying to fix it and infer what he tries to do to make it work.
   • Students follow the several pictures of the fix-it man and infer what he tries to do to make the television work.
   • Students inspect the picture of Emma's father finding the problem. They infer by the picture what that problem was. Look back to the title pages to find an early inference of the cause of the problem.

2. Discuss with students the difference between hearing a book read, reading a book themselves, and watching television. Nudge students into realization of the importance of creating images connected to the words in their minds when they read as

opposed to having the images given to you.

RELATED BOOKS

Leo Lionni's classic *Inch by Inch* tells the story of a smart inchworm who outwits a robin ready to gobble him up by measuring the robin's tail. The inchworm continues to measure parts of other creatures until a nightingale wants his song measured. Again the inchworm uses his wits.

1. Students hear the short I vowel sound repeated throughout the book in the word *inch* and should echo the sound during the reading.
2. Tell students another name for the inchworm is the "looper" because this type of caterpillar moves with a looping movement by alternating its front and back legs.
3. As a quick mathematics connection, students measure a 4" X 1" paper inchworm. They cut this strip of paper and name their inchworm.
   - They fold it in half and lay the strip flat in front of them.
   - They place their left index finger on the left edge of the strip and their right index finger on the right edge of the strip.
   - As they sing the following verse, they alternately push the paper with their right index finger and pull it with their left thereby making their paper inchworms move. The object of singing this verse is to emphasize the word *inch* and the short I vowel sound. (Sing to "Merrily We Roll Along.")
     Merrily we inch along, inch along, inch along,
     Merrily we inch along, all day long.

What's Inside? Insects, a non-fiction book conceived, edited, and designed by DK Direct Limited, describes the behavior, anatomy, and interior workings of eight insects, one of which is the caterpillar. Its double-spread page of the caterpillar helps students understand the movement of the inchworm (see *Inch by Inch* above). Its repetition of the word *insects* reinforces the short I vowel sound and the plosive T.

Four Famished Foxes and Fosdyke by Pamela Duncan Edwards challenges the reader at the outset to find objects in the story that begin with the letter F, a great activity to study the fricative F sound. Additionally, since this alliterative book deals with four foxes, the KS sound of X is repeated in delightfully reinforcing ways students are sure to remember.

Fox on the Job by James Marshall tells about how Fox tries to earn the money for a new bicycle by working several different jobs.
1. The word fox appears approximately fifty times in this book, allowing ample practice with the X consonant sound.
2. Point to *fox* each time and ask individual students to read the word.

PUBLISHING

Students choose one of the felt letters that spell FIX IT and affix or pin their miniature books. As they choose the letter, they identify the letter and say its sound. On a sentence strip write in large print WE CAN and place in in front of the felt letters. After the felt letters, place another sentence strip that states, WE CAN READ! The entire display then proclaims: WE CAN FIX IT! WE CAN READ!

BAT JAMBOREE

Morrow Junior

Kathi Appelt

PHONICS CONCEPTS:
- Affricative J: Consonant Sound as in *Jamboree;*
- *Generalization:*
    ENGLISH WORDS DO NOT END IN J; THEREFORE, WHEN THIS SOUND IS HEARD AT THE END OF A WORD, IT IS DGE AFTER SHORT VOWEL SOUNDS AND GE OR NGE AFTER LONG VOWEL SOUNDS.
- The EE Vowel Sound: Long E as in *jamborEE*

LANGUAGE ARTS CONCEPTS:
- Constructing larger words by putting small words together
- Idioms

Artifacts: Bat erasers or bat rings (available from Oriental Trading Co. and U. S. Toy)
Summary: In this humorous counting book, fifty-five bats entertain a crowd of animals in an abandoned outdoor movie theater. They begin with a single singing bat act and continue in sequence through to ten "acro-bats." As a finale, they create a pyramid in reverse numerical order with a twist of an idiom as the last sentence.

READING/WRITING CONNECTION

1. In order to help students understand the word *jamboree*, explain that words are like families; they are related. They are like a child who looks a little like her mother or has a nose like her father or the eyes of a grandparent. The word *jamboree* is like that child.
2. Write the word *jabber* on the board or chart. Ask all the students to say their names out loud several times at once. When they do, tell them that they were jabbering. Write the word *shivaree* on the board or chart. Give the students an assortment of pans, horns, and other noisemakers. At a signal, they all make their noise. Tell them that is a shivaree.
3. Put the two words together on the board or chart to make the word *jamboree*. Say the word with verve. Ask students if they can figure out what the word means by putting the words and their meanings together. Receive all offerings. If the correct definition is not forthcoming, nudge students into realizing the word is a noisy gathering, usually for entertainment and fun.

4. Show the book. With the meaning of *jamboree* under their belts, invite students to speculate about what the bats might do in the book.

5. Introduce the J sound by explaining that the letter J sounds like two sounds quickly rubbing together. Say the sound. Students echo. Say the word *jamboree*, accenting the J sound and the EE sound. Students echo.

6. Read the book all the way through. Talk about the idiom "...until the fat lady sings." Show the twist of that idiom at the end of the book.

7. Give students their bat artifacts and big pieces of colorful paper.

8. Ask students to brainstorm other jamborees the bats may attend: letter jamborees, food jamborees, jelly jamborees, sport jamborees, and so forth.

9. Write these suggestions on board or chart. Students choose one of these jamborees and write their version of Bat Jamboree.

10. Share in small jamborees!

EXTENSIONS

1. Students play around matching rhyming words with JAM and BOREE to create other kinds of noisy celebrations. For young students, supply a list of rhyming words (see Babs Bell Hajdusiewicz or Sue Young in bibliography).

2. To help students, tell them there is an actual celebration in East Texas, where they grow lots of sweet potatoes, called a Yamboree! People get together to enjoy entertainment, see the Yam Queen crowned, watch a parade, and eat lots of food.

3. Encourage students to have fun with the word play. Some "celebrations" students have created doing this activity have been: CLAM BOR SEA (a clam bake); GREAT GRAM BAKERY (the day Great Grandmother makes cookies); HAM FACTORY (a comedy show). Younger students have offered: SAM BUMBLE BEE (a bunch of bees with one named Sam) ; a WHAM KNEE (hitting your knee but not crying); SLAM A FLEA (when your dog picks out a flea with his teeth); and the self explanatory offering of A LAMB NAMED LEE.

RELATED BOOKS

Just Like Daddy by Frank Asch builds on the affricative J sound by repeating the phrase "just like Daddy." A baby bear models his daddy's activities all day with a surprise ending.

1. After introducing the book, say the title and invite the students to echo. Practice several times.

2. Give students a signal. When they see the signal, they are to chorus the phrase "just like daddy," except for the final twist.

The Pop-Up, Pull-Tab, Playtime House That Jack Built by Nadine Bernard Westcott follows the pattern of the classic Mother Goose nursery rhyme but updates it with whimsical illustrations, pop-ups, and pull-tabs.

1. Invite students to join in with the words and phrases they know as you read this book.

2. On second reading, ask individual students to read the page, and work the tabs. Again, invite the students to join in with the words and phrases they know. Emphasize the J sound.

The Judge by Harve Zemach (a Caldecott Honor Book) is the story of a Judge who disbelieves the descriptions of the monster offered by prisoners and sentences each to jail only to discover too late that they were telling the truth.

1. Point out the initial J sound. Say it; students echo.
2. Call students' attention to the fact that the U does not say its own name, so it is short. Teach the initial J sound and the phonogram DGE after the short U vowel sound.

Pages of Music by Tony Johnston with illustrations by Tomie dePaola is the story of a composer who shares his pages of music with the inhabitants of Sardinia who once shared their pages of music with him.

1. Here the letter A in the word *pages* says its own name, so it is a long A vowel sound.
2. Show students how the GE sounds like J those letters follow a long vowel sound.
3. Brainstorm other words that do the same thing: *cage, village, huge, age*, and so forth.

The Strange Blue Creature by Paul Borovsky threatens to gobble up all the crayons until a princess shows him how to use them and he becomes a great artist.

1. The word *strange* in this book enables students to see how the NGE sounds like J after long vowel sounds.
2. Brainstorm other words that do the same thing: change, danger, range, and so forth.

In *Jamberry* by Bruce Degen, a young boy meets a bear and together they have fun with words and berries.

1. After reading the book, provide students with a list of words that begin with the J sound: *jump, January, jaw, June, joy, jade, jail, Japan, jelly, jet, jig, jigsaw, jog*, and so forth (See Sue Young's book).
2. Students, working in small groups, create a rhyming adventure in the manner of the book and write it on big sheets of paper.

PUBLISHING

Create a collage of all the students' work on the J sound. Call the display WE ARE ENJOYING THE J SOUND!

THE CUT-UPS

Puffin

James Marshall

PHONICS CONCEPTS:
- U Vowel Sound: Short U as in *cUt* and *Ups;*
- U Vowel Sound: 1-Dot U as in *fUll* and *bUshes;*
- UR Vowel Sound: R Sound as in *tURn* and *SpURgle;*
- *Generalization:*
    WHEN A VOWEL IS FOLLOWED BY R, THE R INFLUENCES THE VOWEL SOUND.

LANGUAGE ARTS CONCEPTS:
- Connotation;
- Denotation;
- Figuring out the meaning of a word or phrase in context

Artifacts: Wikki Stix (available from Resources for Reading)

Summary: Spud Jenkins and Joe Turner are cut-ups. They play practical jokes on everyone in their family and in the neighborhood until they meet Mary Frances Hooley. This is a pure James Marshall classic.

READING/WRITING CONNECTION

1. Distribute a wikki stix to each student and a large index card or stock weight paper. Ask students to shape the wikki stix into the letter U and stick it on the card.
2. After they are finished, ask students to identify the letter. When they say U, affirm their responses by telling them that they just made the long U sound. Then tell them U makes other sounds. Tell them they will meet these other U sounds in the book *The Cut-Ups.*
3. Write the words *cut* and *up* on the board or chart paper.
4. Students take their scissors and cut up their wikki stix letters.
5. Explain to students that cutting up their letters is one meaning for *cut up*, but in the book they are about to hear, *cut-up* carries another meaning.
6. Tell students that the short U sound is made by pushing up a grunt with the tongue, cheeks, and lips left slack. What comes up is an UH sound. Challenge students to listen carefully as you read the story to figure out the other meaning of *cut up.*
7. Read the book through once. At the conclusion, ask students to define *cut-up.*
8. Talk about how a word sometimes means something different depending upon how it is used in a story. Give a few examples: bark (dog's) (tree's covering); pop (a sound)

(another name for Dad); tire (to become sleepy) (rubber around a wheel).

9. To reinforce the concept of meaning in context, ask students to line up. As they stand in line, encourage them to talk about the word *up* in the phrase *line up* and the word *up* in other contexts such as: she *upped* and left; the kite flew *up*; the boy took the *up* escalator; she went *up* into the attic; *up* and down; to be on the *up-and-up*; and so forth. Older students may be able to identify the part of speech up takes in each case. (verb, adverb, adjective, adverbs, preposition, noun)

10. Give students paper. They write or draw the sequel to the adventures of Spud, Joe, Mary Frances, and Mr. Spurgle. Share in Author's Chair.

EXTENSIONS

1. Divide a board or chart into three sections. Label one Short U. Label the second column 1-Dot U. Label the third the UR vowel sound. Reread the book. Beginning with the title, place the words with the various U sounds under the proper heading. Be sure to pronounce each word and invite the students to echo.

Short U	1-Dot U	UR vowel sound
cut-ups	full	Turner
Spud		murder
grown-ups	bushes	turn
run		Spurgle

Students copy this list. As they write each word, encourage them to sub-vocalize it.

2. Since Mr. Spurgle never forgets a face, students pretend they are Spud, Joe, or Mary Frances and change their faces through face painting. (See Jacqueline Russon's book *Face Painting*.) Students choose from bears, clowns, bunnies, robots, cats, and others offered in the book. One caveat: To make this maximally productive, students are to explain why they made their choice.

RELATED BOOKS

Ugh, a cave-boy twist on the Cinderella story, by Arthur Yorinks is a perfect companion book for the short U vowel sound.

1. As an introduction to the book, tell students that the short U sound is sometimes called the "shudder vowel" because we often make that sound when we are scared or disgusted. Model a shudder. Ask the students to shudder while saying the sound.

2. Show the book and explain that this is a Cinderella-type story. Ask students about Cinderella's life before the ball. When they say it was miserable, move into that connection to the cave boy's name. Connect it with the shudder vowel.

3. Read the book, giving students a signal every time you are about to read Ugh's name.

Uglypuss by Caroline Gregoire is a wonderful dog story. Marty wants a dog, but when he finally gets one, he is so ugly that Marty ignores him. Uglypuss remains loyal and turns hero.

1. Point out the initial short U sound in the word *ugly* and the 1-Dot U in word *puss*. Talk about how these sounds suggest something not nice. Ask students to predict the story based on the title and picture on the cover.

2. Students draw their version of Uglypuss in pencil, using the drawings on the end

pages as models.

3. Students share their drawings and talk about the story.

A less recent book but one excellent for the short U sound is *The Enchanted Umbrella* by Odette Meyers. In this story Patou is rewarded for his generous spirit and greed is punished. There is a short history of the umbrella at the conclusion of the book.

1. After listening to the story, divide students into groups to design an umbrella.
2. They may write another ending to this story, or they may write a sequel.

PUBLISHING

Out of butcher paper make a rocket ship in the manner of the one pictured in the book. Print on the side WE ARE NO CUT UPS WHEN IT COMES TO THE U SOUND! Display on the wall with the students' sequels to the adventures of Spud, Joe, Mary Frances, and Mr. Spurgle affixed to the ship.

I KNOW AN OLD LADY WHO SWALLOWED A PIE

Dutton

Alison Jackson

PHONICS CONCEPTS:
- KN Consonant Sound: N as in *KNow;*
- *Generalization:*
    WHEN A WORD BEGINS WITH KN, THE K IS SILENT.
- SW Consonant Sound: SW Blend as in *SWallowed*

LANGUAGE ARTS CONCEPT:
- Humor in literature

Artifacts: Small pie tarts (available in bulk in wholesale grocery stores) or pieces of pie
Summary: In this humorous version of the cumulative American folk song "There Was an Old Lady Who Swallowed a Fly," an old lady comes to visit on Thanksgiving Day with a pie and an appetite. She stuffs herself with all the traditional foods including the whole turkey, the pot, and an entire cake to the horror of her hosts and the delight of the children. She is so full at the book's end, she becomes a helium-type floating balloon in a Thanksgiving Day Parade.

READING/WRITING CONNECTION

1. Ask students if they know the American folk song "There Was an Old Lady Who Swallowed a Fly." Sing the song or read a version of the book.
2. Connect the traditional version to this updated, holiday version.
3. Point out the word *know* in the title. Place a small piece of Post-it Correction & Cover-up Tape™ over the K. Ask students about the meaning of the word *silent*. Explain that this letter is called silent because in this word it makes no sound.
4. Tell students there is a generalization that says when a word begins with KN, the K is silent. Write *knee, knit, knock, knuckle, knife* on the board or chart to reinforce the rule. Say each word; cover the K and say the word again. Students repeat. (You may also cover the silent W in know and repeat the process depending upon the level of the students. Caution: For some students covering both silent letters may be confusing, especially since the silent W is not consistent.)
5. Point out the SW blend in the word *swallow*. Talk about what the word means. Ask students to swallow. Talk about why people swallow, its purpose. Challenge students to think of other words that begin with SW. Some possible responses might

be: *swim, sweater, sweep, sweet, swollen, swing,* and so forth.

6. Read the book stopping often to show students the illustrations and to talk about them. Nudge students into noticing the cat, the expressions on the faces of the characters, and how the woman increases in size as she indulges her enormous appetite. Invite students to join in as they remember lines or rhymes. Talk about what in the story makes them laugh and why.

7. Distribute the tiny pies or pieces of pie. As students are eating, remind them of the SW sound in what they are doing– SWallowing.

8. Give students paper and markers. They brainstorm in small groups the names of other foods typically eaten at Thanksgiving, for example, cranberry sauce, string beans, sweet potatoes, ham, and so forth.

9. When students finish eating, challenge them to choose one or more of the foods from their brainstorming and extend the book. (Check *The Scholastic Rhyming Dictionary* for rhyming words .) For example:

> I know an old lady who swallowed a string bean.
> I mean, it was quite a scene,
> She swallowed the bean to go with the...

or

> I know an old lady who swallowed the sauce.
> I mean, she thought she was the boss.
> She swallowed the sauce to go with the ....

10. Make this a fun activity with open sharing even if the rhymes are silly. Students may compose orally or in writing.

EXTENSIONS

1. To connect foods, Thanksgiving, and the book, students make a sugar-free turkey. Previous to class, prepare the fruits and vegetables for this activity. Place the fixings for the turkey in individual plastic baggies (one for each student):
   - a pear for the body of the turkey;
   - the tip off a small yellow squash for the turkey's head;
   - several slices of squash for feathers ;
   - the small end of a carrot for the neck;
   - two slices of carrot for the feet;
   - two whole cloves for eyes;
   - toothpicks to join parts together and for the legs and to use as balance.
   - Students make their turkeys. Display.

2. Students write about how they celebrate Thanksgiving, something funny that happened at Thanksgiving Day dinner, or about a favorite relative that visits on Thanksgiving.

RELATED BOOKS

There Was an Old Lady Who Swallowed a Fly with illustrations by Pam Adams comes close to the original version. Pages contain cut-out circles that when flipped encircle the question "why?"

1. Students, working in small groups, make their own book using different animals. They use the book as a model.

2. Listen to "Peter, Paul & Mommy, Too" a recording by Peter, Paul and Mary. Students then use the music and sing their version of the book to the tune on the recording.

Donna D. Cooner puts a Texas twist on the folk song in her book *I Know an Old Texan Who Swallowed a Fly*. An added attraction to this book is its glossary. Here the reader can find interesting information about all the animals, birds, insects, and reptiles mentioned in the book. There is also a bibliography for young naturalists.
1. After reading the book, students do further research on the critters referenced.
2. Students may compose a book based on their own home state and animals associated with the state, for example, "I Know an Old Floridian Who Swallowed an Alligator."

There Was an OId Lady Who Swallowed a Fly by Simms Taback is a Caldecott Honor Book that uses an ever-expanding die-cut hole tø add a fresh and funny twist to this old favorite.
1. An interesting coda presents a brief history of this favorite American folk poem. Students may add their version by suggesting other animals the old lady could swallow.
2. Discuss the moral at the story's end.
3. Since Taback gives credit to Peter Newell as the creator of *The Hole Book,* students would find it interesting to see that antique book. Reproductions (No. 30241) are available from Merrimack Publishing Corporation, 85 Fifth Avenue, New York, NY 10003.

There Was an Old Lady Who Swallowed a Fly! (available from Constructive Playthings) comes as a poly/cotton book bag format with soft sculpture characters that can be placed into the Old Lady's tummy.
1. Students love reading the story over and over again because of the interactive nature of this book.
2. Students create their own characters out of felt that can be taped with reusable adhesive onto the Old Lady's tummy.

PUBLISHING

On a wall or bulletin board, create a huge woman with a smiling face out of butcher paper. In the center of her tummy place a huge circle in a different colored paper. Students place their creations in her tummy. Label the display: WE KNOW SILENT LETTERS AND WE SWALLOW BLENDS.

YO! YES?

Orchard

Chris Raschka

PHONICS CONCEPT:
• Y Consonant Sound as in *Yo* and *Yes*

LANGUAGE ARTS CONCEPTS:
• Intonation as a way of making meaning;
• Punctuation marks: exclamation mark, question mark, comma, period, apostrophe

Artifacts: Mini yo-yos (available from U. S. Toy); also, students may be encouraged to bring their own regular yo-yos. Just be sure to have one for each student.

Summary: Two lonely boys, representing two different races, meet on the street and become friends.

READING/WRITING CONNECTION

1. Show the dust jacket of the book. Point to the two characters cavorting under the title. Ask students to tell you what they notice about the two characters.
   • Describe what they look like;
   • Talk about the clothes they are wearing;
   • Estimate how old they might be;
   • Tell what they seem to be doing.

2. Explain that these are the main characters in this book. Tell students that even though this book does not have many words, they will be able to figure out what is happening by the word or words on the page, by the punctuation marks, and by looking carefully at the pictures.

3. Point to the two words in the title. Ask students what the word *Yo* means, when it is usually used. Check if this word is in their vocabulary, if the students use the word in its contemporary sense. Model in front of the students by looking the word up in the dictionary. Read them the dictionary definition. Be sure they understand the meaning of "call attention to."

4. Talk about the exclamation mark, the excitement mark after the word. Invite students to speculate about why that mark would be there. Follow the same procedure with the word *Yes* and its question mark. Point out the other punctuation marks as they appear in the reading.

5. Use the copyright and dedication pages to help students realize that some books "begin before they begin," that the author sometimes sets the scene, or gives hints before the first page. Encourage students to describe what is happening on these two pages. Help them look closely at the body language, the position of the characters, and how they look different than they did on the cover.

6. Begin the book by reading the words on the double-page spread. Students repeat

the words. They discuss how the characters must feel and make inferences and predictions about the characters. Follow this procedure throughout the book.

7. When the reading is completed, return to the words in the title. Point to the letter Y and make its sound. Remind students of the difference between consonants and vowels. Ask them to make the sound. Tell them to think about whether or not the breath comes out freely. Help them notice that the breath is somewhat impeded by the tongue, and therefore in both the words *Yo* and *Yes,* the Y is a consonant.

8. Look at all the other Ys in the book and listen for the sounds.
    • In *hey*, the Y is silent and the last sound is a long A sound.
    • In *you*, the Y is the consonant sound.
    • In *why*, the Y vowel sound, the long I sound.
    • In *yow*, the Y is the consonant sound.

9. Distribute the yo-yos. Point out that the letter Y takes the consonant sound with both Y letters. Remind students of the generalization. Allow students to play with the yo-yos. After a suitable time, students return to their places. Talk about how new friends like those in the book might share yo-yos.

10. Students write about sharing their yo-yos with a friend. For example: they might teach a friend a new yo-yo trick, show a friend their new soccer design yo-yo, tell about their yo-yo collection, ask the friend to teach them a yo-yo trick, and so forth.

EXTENSIONS

1. This book lends itself to role-playing.
    • Divide the students into groups of two.
    • With each group, the students decide if they are going to play the character "Yo" or the character "Yes."
    • The teacher or a designated student reads the book stopping after each double-page spread to give the pairs of students time to reenact the unfolding drama.
    • All students jump and shout "Yow" at the end of the book.

2. Extend the role-playing with the yo-yos. Continuing to work in pairs, the students talk, share, experiment, and teach each other tricks.

RELATED BOOKS

Barbara Dugan's *Loop the Loop* with illustrations by James Stevenson places a yo-yo as the central object between a sensitive but bored child (Anne) and a cantankerous old woman (Mrs. Simpson). Both come to poignant realizations by book's end.

1. Show the cover and talk about the girl and the old woman. Ask students what they think about seeing an old woman playing with a yo-yo. Remind students again of the Y consonant sound.

2. Read the book with verve, making the old woman's voice a bit shaky.

3. Engage the students in discussion about the elderly. Connect being bored as a child with being bored as an older person.

4. Sing bits from the songs Mrs. Simpson sings, "Camptown Ladies." Students join in with the "Doo-dah" refrain. Sing "Hold That Tiger" and encourage students to join in. Sing "My Bonnie Lies over the Ocean" and students join in.

5. Students check libraries as Anne did for books on yo-yo tricks. They practice the different yo-yo games as mentioned in the book: "Walk the Dog," "Around the

World," "Loop the Loop," "Rock the Baby (Cradle)," and others.

Yo, Aesop! Get a Load of These Fables by Paul Rosenthal contains bite-sized stories that are perfect for read-alouds or beginning readers. While the "fox and the grapes" or the "lion and the splinter" may be replaced by the "cockroach and the dog" or the "pigeon and the salami," the age-old lessons endure.
1. Students match the lessons to the original Aesop's Fables.
2. Students write their own version of a fable using *Yo, Aesop!* as a model.

The Klutz Yo-Yo Book by the Editors of Klutz Press has a complete compendium of yo-yo tricks from "Rock the Cradle" to "Shoot the Moon."

The Little Book of Yo-Yos by Professor Yo-Yo is a Trumpet Club Special Edition. This non-assuming book contains chapters on the history of yo, getting started, basic tricks, beyond the basics, and resources. Students may
   • join the American Yo-Yo Association (AYYA); the address is given;
   • read other books on yo-yos;
   • watch a yo-yo video;
   • find other publications on yo-yos;
   • add to their yo-yo collections.

PUBLISHING

Cut two enormous circles out of butcher paper to approximate two yo-yos. On one print a large "Yo!" On the other print an equally large "Yes!" Affix string around one yo-yo and festoon it to the other yo-yo. On the string suspend the students' writing.

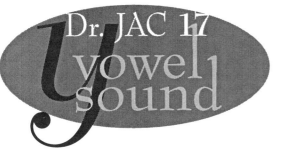

SILLY SALLY

Harcourt Brace Jovanovich

Audrey Wood

PHONICS CONCEPTS:
- Y Vowel Sound: Long E as in *sillY* and *SallY;*
- *Generalization:*
    WHEN Y IS THE FINAL LETTER IN A WORD, IT USUALLY HAS A VOWEL SOUND.

LANGUAGE ARTS CONCEPT:
- Couplets

Artifacts: Six mini-musical instruments: harmonicas; kazoos; fun whistles; two-tone whistles; trumpets; clackers (available from U. S. Toy)

Summary: In this colorful topsy-turvy world, Silly Sally goes to town walking upside-down and backwards. Written in rhyming couplets, this cumulative tale engages young readers in Sally's silly antics.

READING/WRITING CONNECTION

1. Show the book's cover. Tell students that this is a story about a girl named Silly Sally. Ask students what the word *silly* means. Invite them to tell you silly things. Share something silly, such as, "Fish wish they could walk and talk. If the fish got their wish then the sidewalk would squish. Squishy wishy. Wishy squishy."
2. Receive all the silly things the students share. Talk about what makes something silly.
3. Ask students to describe what Silly Sally is doing. Show students how the Y at the end of the word *silly* and the name *Sally* sounds like the long E.
4. Together with the students, examine the two-page spread on the copyright and dedication pages. Using the description of Sally and those pages, invite students to make predictions about the story.
5. Read the book through once. On the second reading, invite students to join in the refrain-like chant about Silly Sally.
6. All the students write their names on small pieces of paper. Draw one name for Sally and one for Neddy (whose name also ends with a Y with a long E sound).
7. Draw names to be in the pig, dog, loon, and sheep groups.
8. Give the student playing Sally a fun whistle and the one playing Neddy a two-tone whistle. The pig group receives the harmonicas; the dog group gets the clackers; the loons take the kazoos; the sheep use the trumpets.
9. Everyone marches around the room, outside, or in the hall backwards playing their instruments.
10. Upon returning to their places, students write about this silly experience. Share.

EXTENSIONS

1. Students make a spiral book that opens from back to front. The spiral represents the road Silly Sally takes to town. Encourage students to put different animals in their books, not the ones in the original book, for example, hen, cat, bird, cow, and so forth.
   - Trace a 5" circle on 8 1/2" X 11" heavy paper;
   - Starting at a point on the edge of the circle, draw a spiral line to its center. Leave about 3/4" between the lines.
   - Cut along that spiral line;
   - Cut off the pointed tip and put the spiral aside for a moment;
   - Fold an 8 1/2" X 14" sheet of heavy yellow paper in half, short end to short end;
   - Unfold it so it looks like an open book;
   - Lay the spiral on the left side of the sheet;
   - Put glue on the underside of the spiral's center;
   - Put glue on the topside of the spiral's end;
   - Close the book and press down holding it until it dries;
   - Open the book to a spiral road for Silly Sally.
2. Students turn their books so they open opposite the way books normally open and write an adventure for Silly Sally.

RELATED BOOKS

The Ladybug and Other Insects, one of the quality books from Scholastic's "First Discovery Book" Series, presents the Y as a long E vowel sound in the medial position. This non-fiction book can be used in conjunction with Eric Carle's fictional *The Grouchy Ladybug*.
1. Give students a quarter of a sheet of transparency film and white paper.
2. Students draw the inside of a ladybug and then they draw it topside using permanent transparency markers. This will resemble the pictures in the book.
3. Then write facts about ladybugs.

Another book for the Y as a long E vowel sound in the medial position is Janet and Allan Ahlberg's *Funnybones*. In this book three skeletons take a walk through a dark town. This book comes with a *Funnybones Picture Card Game* (complete with directions).

For the Y as a long E vowel sound in the final position Ashley Bryan's *ABC of African Poetry*, a magnificent book of sketches and images.
1. After students realize the sound of Y in the word *poetry*, they can listen for other words throughout the book reinforce the Y as a long E vowel sound.
2. Read a poem once. During the second reading, challenge students to listen for the Y as a long E sound.

PUBLISHING

Display the students' silly books under the title WE ARE NOT SILLY ABOUT SOUNDS!

OLD BLACK FLY

Henry Holt

Jim Aylesworth

PHONICS CONCEPTS:
- Y Vowel Sound: Long I as in *flY;*
- *Generalization I:*
    WHEN Y IS THE FINAL LETTER IN A WORD,
        IT USUALLY HAS A VOWEL SOUND.
- *Generalization II:*
    WHEN Y IS USED AS A VOWEL IN WORDS, IT SOMETIMES HAS THE SOUND OF LONG I.
- OO Vowel Sound: 2-Dot U, or Long OO sound as in *shOO;*
- SH Consonant Sound: Digraph as in *SHoo;*
- FL Consonant Sound: FL blend as in *FLy*

LANGUAGE ARTS CONCEPT:
- Alphabetic order

Phonics Friendly Books
51

Artifacts: Miniature soft plastic one-inch flies with hard plastic wings (available from U. S. Toy)

Summary: This delightful alphabet book follows a mischievous old black fly as it lands on various objects around the house. The beginning rhyme and the repetition of the "Shoo fly!" refrain invites participation.

READING/WRITING CONNECTION

1. Before beginning the lesson, write the opening and closing poems in the book on board or chart.
2. Show students the book's cover. Point to Stephen Gammell's illustration of the fly. Together create a web about flies. Put the word fly in the middle and invite students to contribute what they know about flies. (The webbing activity will remind them of how flies are sometimes caught.)
3. Point to the title and call students' attention to the word *fly.* Ask them how the last letter, the Y sounds. Be sure they realize that the Y sounds like an I saying its own name; Y takes the long I sound.
4. Distribute the fly artifacts.

5. Point to the the opening poem on the board or chart. As you read it, point to the words. Invite the students to chant it with you. When it comes to the line "buzzin' around," students hold their flies between their index fingers and thumbs and move them around making a buzzing sound. Otherwise instruct students to hold their flies in the palms of their hands.

6. Write the "Shoo fly!" refrain on the board. Remind students of the SH sound. Make the long OO sound. Put the sounds together. Say the word "shoo." Students echo. When the refrain comes up in the reading, students gently shoo their flies off their palms. Then they quickly pick them up for the next verse. Continue this procedure throughout the alphabet.

7. Read the closing poem from board or chart. Point to the words. Invite the students to chant it with you. When it comes to the line "buzzin' around," students hold their flies between their index fingers and thumbs and move them around making a buzzing sound.

8. Give each student a brightly colored sheet of paper on which you have manuscripted a letter of the alphabet or affixed an alphabet sticker.

9. Students, according to their level, write or draw a poem that starts with the designated letter and ends with the "Shoo fly!" refrain. Three examples:
    One student drew a fly alighting on a flower and wrote:
    > Fly on flower
    > Shoo fly!

    Another traced his hand and said:
    > Fly land on hand
    > right here (The student pointed to the top of the hand where he made a smudge.)
    > Shoo fly!
    > Shoo fly! (copied from the board)
    > Shoo.

    A third student wrote and illustrated:
    > Mr. fly flutter (ed) ("Like a butterfly," the student said as she drew a fly with big butterfly wings.)
    > to peanut butter. (Here she drew a jar of peanut butter with a big peanut on it.)
    > Shoo fly!
    > Shoo fly!
    > Shoo.

10. Students share their poems in the Author's Chair.

EXTENSIONS

1. Write *fly* on the board or chart. Under it make two columns. Label one FL and the other Y. Ask students if they can think of other words that begin with the letters FL (*flag, flat, flea, flip, float, floss.*) Write their offerings under the FL column. This activity helps students with their blends, which many children find difficult.

2. Ask students if they can think of any words that sound like the word fly and end with Y (*my, buy, shy, cry, sly, try, why, dry*). This helps students realize that words with the same vowel and the same ending letters usually rhyme. This, in turn, helps them as a word attack skill when reading.

3. Since *fly* is the central word, a science extension is fitting. Three good books for a closer look at the fly are *What's Inside? Insects*, a Dorling Kindersley book, *Bugs* by Nancy Winslow Parker and Joan Richards Wright, a Reading Rainbow Book, and

ABC of Crawlers and Flyers by Hope Ryden.

RELATED BOOKS

Sir Small and the Dragonfly by Jane O'Connor, a Step into Reading Book, tells the story of a dragonfly who carries off the fair maiden. Sir Small mounts his trusty ant and rides to the rescue.
1. Read the book through once for the story.
2. Before the second reading, divide the board or chart into two columns. Label one column Y vowel sound: long E; label the other Y vowel sound: long I . As you read a word that ends with Y (excepting AY at this point) students listen to its sound to determine its column: *dragonfly, tiny, trusty, penny, pretty, lady, try, party, happy.* Talk about the Y rules.

I Spy: An Alphabet in Art devised and selected by Lucy Micklethwait presents objects in classic paintings for each letter of the alphabet.
1. Students repeat the "I Spy" poem, guess the object, and then try to find it in the painting.
2. Students continue the "I Spy" idea by looking at pictures in their books.

Play Rhymes by Marc Brown and *Tyrannosaurus Was a Beast*, a book of dinosaur poems by Jack Prelutsky, both show the Y vowel sound: the long I sound in the medial position as in *rhYmes* and *tYrannosaurus.*

PUBLISHING

Display students' alphabet poems on a wall or bulletin board. Call the display WE AREN'T SHY ABOUT THE LETTER Y!

PHOEBE AND THE SPELLING BEE

Hyperion

Barney Saltzberg

PHONICS CONCEPTS:
- PH Consonant Sound: F as in PHoebe
- *Generalization:*
  WHEN P IS FOLLOWED BY H, IT IS USUALLY PRONOUNCED AS AN F (EXCEPTIONS ARE WORDS SUCH AS UPHILL, UPHEAVAL, UPHOLD, UPHOLSTERY)

LANGUAGE ARTS CONCEPT:
- The spelling skill of looking at parts of words

Artifacts:
- A spelling list of PH words: *phonics, photo, orphan, alphabet, nephew, trophy, sophomore, telephone, gopher, and graph* .
- Spelling bee certificates for every child: Champion Speller, Master Speller, Victor Speller, Best Attempt, Successful Speller, Winner, Flourishing Speller, Blue-ribbon Winner, Triumphant Speller, Prize-winning Speller, Unbeaten Speller, Flying Colors Speller, Victorious Speller, High Achievement in Spelling, Second Best Speller, Third Best Speller, and so forth. (Be sure every child receives a certificate.)

Summary: Phoebe remembers her spelling words by using her imagination. She also learns what happens when she lies to her friend.

READING/WRITING CONNECTION

1. Show the book's front and back covers. Ask students what they know about spelling bees. Nudge them into talking about:
    - the rules of a spelling bee;
    - why do spelling bees have rules;
    - why students stand in a row during a spelling bee;
    - how the winner feels;
    - how those who do not win feel.
2. Ask them how they remember how to spell a word. Tell them Phoebe, a character in the book, uses several ways to remember how to spell a word.
3. Point out the name *Phoebe*. Ask students what sound they hear at the beginning of that name. Explain that when a P is followed by the letter H it is usually pronounced like F. Remind them that the F sound is a fricative, that something interferes with the airflow from the lungs. Have them place their upper teeth on their lower lip in order to make the sound.
4. Distribute spelling lists, pronounce each word and talk about its meaning.
5. To enhance listening skills, challenge students to listen as you read the story for a word on their list that is also on Phoebe's list (*telephone*). Once identified, ask them

if the F sound is at the beginning, in the middle, or at the end of the word.

6. Help students notice that one way Phoebe remembers to spell a word is by looking at its parts. Invite students to look at each word on their spelling lists for its parts. Explain that one part of a word is sometimes a smaller word. Ask them to look for the smaller words around the PH in each word on their spelling lists, such as the *or* and *an* in the word or PH an.

7. Tell students that Phoebe's method for spelling also works for reading, sometimes when coming upon an unknown word, it is helpful to look at its parts.

8. Ask students if they can spell the words on Phoebe's list. Challenge them to try.

9. Conclude by holding a spelling bee of words on their level. Give certificates to the winners (see artifacts above).

EXTENSIONS

1. Students, working in small groups, generate their own list of spelling words. If possible, depending upon their level, challenge them to include some words that have PH in them. Groups try out their words with other groups. Students, like Phoebe, explain how they remember the words.

2. Talk about Phoebe's lie to Katie. Ask the students to speculate about why Phoebe lied about studying. Discuss lying and why it made Phoebe's stomach feel awful.

3. Students play with language. Give them a PH word and ask them to come up with rhyming words, for example:
   - phony–*baloney, knee*, and so forth
   - Phil–*chill, ill, bill*, and so forth
   - Phoebe–*fiddle-de-dee, bee, see, she*, and so forth
   - telephone–*saxophone, groan*, and so forth
   - phone–*Joan, moan, loan*, and so forth

RELATED BOOK

While any alphabet book would serve the purpose of pointing out the PH consonant sound in the medial position in the word *alPHabet, Grandmother's AlPHabet* by Eve Shaw is contemporary, contains rhyme, and interests students because it shows that grandmothers can be anything from A to Z.

1. Write the word *alphabet* on the board or chart. Ask students to say the word and find the PH as F sound. Ask them the PH generalization.

2. Read the book, invite students to participate by repeating the "...and so can I"

3. After the first reading, ask students to pick a letter. Reread the page that corresponds to that letter. Discuss the possible jobs or professions on that page. Be sure to point out the exception to the PH as F sound in the word *upholsterer*.

4. Share the final page that lists over eighty other jobs or professions. Point out those that have the PH consonant sound: F.

5. Students brainstorm other jobs and professions.

PUBLISHING

Create an large sheet of paper to approximate the paper students use. On it write the words on Phoebe's spelling list and those on the students' spelling list. Attach the spelling lists generated by small groups. Call the display KNOWING SOUNDS CAN HELP US SPELL!

ZACH'S ALLIGATOR

Harper Trophy

Shirley Mozelle

PHONICS CONCEPTS:
- S Consonant Sound: Z Sound as in *Zach'S;*
- *Generalization:*
    WHEN S IS AT THE END OF A WORD, THE S MAY REPRESENT THE SOUND USUALLY ASSOCIATED WITH Z.
- Z Consonant Sound as in *Zach*

LANGUAGE ARTS CONCEPT:
- Exposure to a high interest story with a longer plot, more characters, and language play

Artifacts: Cut alligators out of compressed sponges
Summary: Zach receives an alligator key chain with instructions to water it. When he soaks it in water, it grows into a full-sized adventuresome alligator.

READING/WRITING CONNECTION

1. Before the lesson cut out the shape of an alligator on green butcher paper to create an ALLIGATOR WORD BANK.
2. Give each student (or each group) an alligator out of compressed sponge. Ask them to identify the animal and brainstorm all the things they can think of related to an alligator. Write their responses on the ALLIGATOR WORD BANK.
3. Set out small cups of water at strategic places in the room. Students dip their alligators into the water and watch them grow.
4. Ask students what would happen if their alligators continued to grow and came alive. Receive all answers. Explain that is exactly what happens in the book they are about to hear.
5. Show the book's cover and pronounce the title. Point out the letter Z and exaggerate the sound by closing the teeth together and making its sound. Students echo the sound. Encourage them to place their fingertips on their throats to feel the vibrations the sound makes. (This helps the kinetic as well as the verbal and visual learner.)
5. Tell students that sometimes the consonant S makes a Z sound. Point out the Z sound in *Zach'S*. Again ask them to place their fingertips at their throats and say the following familiar words:
    - *music*   *easy*   *busy*   *those*   *because*   *cheese*
    - *please*   *is*   *as*   *was*   *his*   *hers*

6. Spend some extra time on the word *because* so often misspelled, mispronounced, or misread by students. Show how the S sounds like Z and the E is silent.
7. Read the book, stopping each time Zach's name is used so the students can read, too.
8. Distribute sheets of green paper. Each student writes his or her name with the apostrophe S and the word *alligator*, for example, Bob's Alligator.
9. Students write a story about what would happen if their sponge alligator came to life.
10. Share in the Author's Chair.

EXTENSIONS

1. Students make a design using the letter Z for a Z word key chain.
   • Provide a list of words that begin with the Z Consonant Sound: *zebra, zero, zinnia, zombie, zoo, zig-zag, zeppelin, zipper, zone, zucchini*. Ask the students about the meaning of each word. Lead them into understanding the meaning for the words they do not know.
   • Choose one Z word and model by drawing on the board or chart a key ring design, for example, zinnia, draw a simple daisy and put the letter Z in its center.
   • Distribute the round circular key rings (available in bulk from most discount or hardware stores) and heavy stock paper in various colors. Students transfer their designs onto the heavy paper in the correct size to dangle from the key ring.
   • Reinforce with laminate or tape.
   • Students slide their design onto the rings.
2. Students may write about why they chose the word they chose for their key ring.

RELATED BOOKS

Zomo the Rabbit by Gerald McDermott is a trickster tale from West Africa.
1. Point to the Z and pronounce the rabbit's name *Zomo!* with excitement and verve.
2. Tell students that as you read the story you want them to read along with you and say the rabbit's name when you point to it.
3. Proceed through the book with the students reading the name *Zomo!* (This holds students' attention and aids in letter and word identification.)

Maisy's Colors by Lucy Cousins is another of the "Maisy" primary board books. This one deals with Maisy experiencing colors. This book shows the S consonant that makes the Z sound in both the medial and final positions and that should be pointed out.
1. Write the colors stated in the book in matching markers or crayons on chart paper. For instance, the word *pink* in pink crayon or marker; the word *orange* in orange marker or crayon, and so forth.
2. Divide students into small groups and assign them an area of the room. Give the groups white index cards and crayons or markers. Students find the colors in the room that match the colors in *Maisy's Colors* somewhere in their area.
3. Students write the color on a card with the appropriate crayon or marker and place it near or on top of the object.
4. Groups share their findings.

Captain Whiz-Bang by Diane Stanley deals with a champion cat who ages graceful-

ly.
1. Use this book to show the Z consonant sound in the final position.
2. Students make other words that rhyme with *whiz* on magnetic boards, in groups, with tactile letters, or in writing. Possibilities are: *fizz, frizz, his, is, Liz, quiz, 'tis.*

Miss Tizzy by Libba Moore Gray tells a poignant tale about the power of love and modeling when working with children.
1. Show the double Z as making two Z consonant sounds.
2. When reading the book, point to Miss Tizzy's name for the students to read and invite them to join in the refrain, "And the children loved it."

PUBLISHING

Display students' work under a banner that reads WE KNOW OUR SOUNDS FROM A TO Z!

THE MONSTER BOOK OF ABC SOUNDS

Puffin

Alan Snow

PHONICS CONCEPT:
- Each letter of the alphabet carries a distinctly different sound, (A–Aaaaah!) or can be associated with an onomatopoeic word, ("Yuk!")

LANGUAGE ARTS CONCEPTS:
- Alphabetic order
- Title and characters in a book

Artifacts: Gummy candy letters

Summary: Set up as a hide-and-seek game, each page sequentially presents a letter of the alphabet, gives its sound or an onomatopoeic word, and fills the page with objects and creatures, items, actions, details, or embellishments that begin with the focus letter. Items are encased in a border repeating the featured letter and interspersing it with an animal or object that reinforces the concept and puts it in a meaningful context.

READING/WRITING CONNECTION

1. Begin by asking the students about the sounds certain animals make, "What sounds does a cat make?" "What sounds does a dog make?" Receive their answers.
2. Move to the question "What sounds do people make?" After the students offer suggestions, lead them to see that the words people use have sounds and that letters within the words have sounds. Explain that the book you are about to share is all about the sounds letters and words make.
3. Show the book's cover. Point out and talk about the title, characters, details, and border. Tell students that the author follows this same format throughout the book.
4. Ask students if they know the game hide-and-seek. Talk about the game and its purpose–something or someone is hidden and others try to find it. Tell students that they will be playing that game as they read each page because they will be trying to find animals and things that start with the letter featured on that page.
5. Read the book, allowing time for the students to look at the rich array of pictures and time for them to think and talk about what they see.
6. While on each page, say the sound and ask students to repeat it. Discuss how the sound relates to the letter on the page. Allow plenty of time for students to make connections.
7. At the conclusion of the book, distribute egg cartons (or have the students bring their own from home). Give each student an alphabet gummy candy. Tell them to pretend their gummy is one of the monsters in the book.
8. While they munch on their monster, they draw their version of it on the solid inside cover of the egg carton. Depending upon level, they write a short poem or story

there as well or they write on paper and paste it to the inside cover.

9. Then they list items or animals that begin with the letter of their gummy candy letter and find or draw pictures to place in the tiny egg alcoves.

10. When completed, students share in small groups, challenging their peers to seek and find all the items they have hidden in the sections of their egg cartons.

EXTENSIONS

1. Beginning with the letter A, write the letter on the board or chart. Point to the letter and students respond by saying the sound. At first, proceed in alphabetical order. In time, skip around the alphabet.

2. Play the "Sound Game." Divide the students into two groups:

• A student in Group One calls out a letter and then picks a classmate from Group Two to respond with its sound.

• The chosen student gives the letter's sound from the book, calls another letter, and picks a classmate to respond from Group One.

• A designated student or the teacher marks off the correctly sounded letter from the board or chart so students can track the already identified letters.

• If a student misses the sound, the student who originated the letter gets to choose another classmate.

• Continue this procedure until all letters have been called.

RELATED BOOK

Kalli Dakos has written an intellectually challenging yet fun book, *Get Out of the Alphabet, Number 2*, that combines short verbal puzzle poems with letters and numbers. Building upon the timeless school tradition of designating a daffy day when students and teachers dress differently or do crazy things, such as wearing jeans or funny hats, Dakos calls her day "Wacky Wednesday." On that day letters replace numbers on clocks and get mixed up in interesting ways, while numbers are naughty and get out of line. Since the beauty of this book is enhanced by students who know their alphabet and numbers, it enables them to understand what fun and power they can have because of that knowledge.

1. Read one of the poems, preferably on a designated day once a week; (for example, the last activity on Friday or the first on Monday).

2. Give students time to decode the poem and its puzzle and come up with a solution. Once they understand its meaning, discuss.

3. Celebrate figuring out the silly (yet clever) poem by asking all the students to raise their arms high over their heads, then bend them backwards at the elbows to give themselves pats on the back.

4. Students in small groups practice writing a "Wacky Wednesday" puzzle poem. Distribute large sheets of colorful paper for their drawings and words.

PUBLISHING

Inside a white border of colorful letters and pictures place a la   white square that resembles the cover of the focus book. Print on the square WE ARE MONSTER LEARNERS OF ABC SOUNDS! Display the work the students have accomplished within the border.

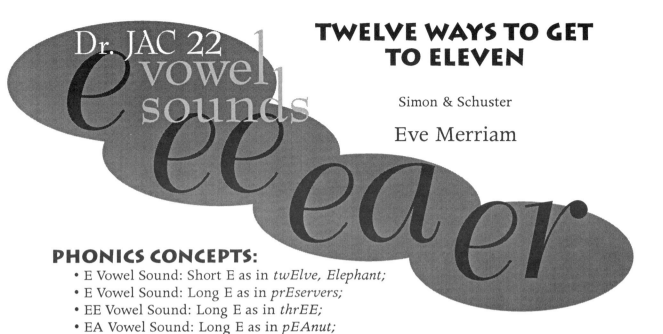

TWELVE WAYS TO GET TO ELEVEN

Simon & Schuster

Eve Merriam

PHONICS CONCEPTS:
- E Vowel Sound: Short E as in *twElve, Elephant;*
- E Vowel Sound: Long E as in *prEservers;*
- EE Vowel Sound: Long E as in *thrEE;*
- EA Vowel Sound: Long E as in *pEAnut;*
- E Vowel Sound: Schwa as in *elevEn, elEphant;*
- E Vowel Sound: Silent as in *onE;*
- ER Vowel Sound: R Sound as in *lettER*

LANGUAGE ARTS CONCEPT:
- Numeration: the skill of reading in words, numbers expressed by numerals.

Artifacts: Assorted stickers of common objects and animals: bears, cars, butterflies, pets, hearts, flowers, barnyard, lizards, frogs, cat, insects, ocean life, stars, smile face, flags, and so forth.

Summary: Merriam opens her book with numbers from one to twelve with eleven missing in the sequence. The answer to the question "Where's Eleven?" becomes the quest that is answered on each double-page spread throughout the book as ordinary objects add up to eleven.

READING/WRITING CONNECTION

1. Show students the book's cover. Count the objects and animals. See how many the students can identify. Read the title and author. In order for students to understand the concept in this book, draw an analogy.
    - Ask all the students to line up in the front of the room.
    - Ask one student to go to the back of the room.
    - Caution the other students to watch exactly how that happens.
    - Challenge another student to go to the back of the room another way.
    - Again caution the other students to watch exactly how that happens and remember how the first student went.
    - Follow this procedure until all students have had a turn. (Students will walk, skip, hop, hold their hands and arms in different ways, weave around desks, even crawl or jump.)
2. After each student has had a turn, draw the analogy: There are many different ways

to go to the back of the room and there are many different ways to make numbers add up to eleven.

3. Open the book to the copyright/dedication pages. Ask students to count the cardinal numbers using their high voices as you point to them. (This is called numeration: the art of reading in words, numbers expressed by numerals.) When you get to the number eleven, ask the students to lower their voices to match where the number appears on the page (bottom).

4. Follow the same procedure as above with the next double-page spread. Students read the numbers that are spelled out.

5. Before you read the book, tell students that this book is a mathematical book, but it also is a book filled with E sounds. The following may be adapted to the students' level. You may introduce all the E sounds at one time, use this for review, or reread this book many times, perhaps adding an additional E sound each time. Be sure to write the phonics concepts on board or chart.

6. Say each of these sounds distinctly. With the silent E words, help students realize that they hear no sound.

7. Read through the book once. Ask students to simply listen to words with E sound.

8. Upon second reading, list the major E words on board or chart, or have the major E words listed and point to each as you read it. Following are the major E words: *pinecones, forest, peanut, shells, banners, pitcher, water, flowers, Eleventh Street, bites, core, stem, seeds, life, preservers, ladder, three, sleeping, nose, teeth, seven, triplets, stroller, piglets, hen, five, eggs, beaks, one.*

9. When the second reading is completed, focus students' attention on the listed words. Go over the E sound in each word. Categorize them into smaller lists. Since students typically write ER words without the E, it is important to stress that E as you add each word to the list.

SHORT E	LONG E	EE/LONG E	EA/LONG E	E/SCHWA	SILENT E	ER/R
forest	preservers	street	peanut	Eleventh	pinecones	banners
shells		seeds	beaks	seven	bites	pitcher
stem		three		eleven	core	water
triplets		sleeping			life	flowers
piglets		teeth			nose	ladder
hen					five	stroller
eggs					one	letter

Note: After completing the categorizing, and depending on the students' level, advanced students may notice some vowel generalizations. For example, they may notice the silent E rule: When there are two vowels, one of which is the final E, the first vowel is long and the E is silent. Or, they may see that in small words (one-syllable words) with a vowel in the middle, the vowel is usually short. Or, when a word has only one vowel letter and ends in a consonant, the vowel is likely to be short. Or, when there are two consecutive vowels, the first vowel is usually long and the second one is silent.

10. Distribute a variety of stickers to each student. Following the book's pattern, students affix different stickers together on colorful paper to make eleven, for example, three stars, plus three flags, plus five butterflies equals eleven. Students may write out what they have done or create a number problem around the number eleven.

EXTENSIONS

1. Distribute eleven counting chips or quiet counters (available from Delta Education) or buttons to each student. As you read through the book, students match the numbers on the pages with their counters. For example, they pick up nine counters to match nine pinecones and two counters to match two acorns. Then together everyone counts to eleven.
2. Distribute paper. Students write the mathematical concept on the paper, (9 + 2 = 11); advanced students write the concept by spelling out the numbers, or they create word problems using eleven as the base.

RELATED BOOKS

Kathi Appelt's *Elephants Aloft* is a concept book built upon prepositions. Two Asian elephants travel to their Auntie Rwanda in Africa.

1. Write the word *elephant* on the board or chart. Point out the two E's. Pronounce the word. Explain that the first E is short and the second is a schwa. Students echo the pronunciation.
2. Give the students cards with each of the prepositions used in the book. When their page is read, they stand and say the preposition. All the students echo the preposition and talk about what is happening in the picture, (the two elephants get in the hot-air balloon basket).

David McKee's *Elmer* is another elephant book. Elmer is not grey like all the other elephants in the jungle; he is a bright patchwork of colors. How Elmer's dilemma is solved proves to be a delightful book with a powerful lesson.

1. Point out the short E vowel sound as well as the ER, R sound in Elmer's name. As you read the book, point to Elmer's name for students to read.
2. Point out the short E vowel sound as well as the schwa in the world elephant. As you read the book, point to the word elephant for students to read or ask students to find the word.

Elmer and Wilbur by David McKee is a companion elephant book. Wilbur is Elmer's cousin and he happens to be a black and white checked elephant. This book reinforces the E sounds by its repetition of Elmer's name and the word elephant. Students write about elephants.

PUBLISHING

Create a huge elephant out of grey paper. Display students work in, on, and around the elephant. Make colorful cards with the E sounds coming out of the elephant's trunk. On the trunk print the following: WE CAN TRUMPET OUR E SOUNDS!

FEATHERS FOR LUNCH

Harcourt Brace Jovanovich

Lois Ehlert

PHONICS CONCEPTS:
- EA Vowel Sound: Short E as in *fEAther;*
- EA Vowel Sound: Long E as in *trEAt, EAt;*
- EA Vowel Diphthong + R: UR Sound as in *EARly;*
- ER Vowel Sound: R Sound as in *feathER;*
- *Generalization:*
    WHEN A VOWEL IS FOLLOWED BY R, THE R INFLUENCES THE VOWEL SOUND.

LANGUAGE ARTS CONCEPTS:
- A glossary;
- Distinguishing fiction and non-fiction;
- Inference

Artifacts: Assorted sizes and colors of feathers (available in craft shops)

Summary: This book combines fiction and non-fiction. The first section recounts cat's search for lunch. The second contains a detailed glossary of the birds cat missed. Punctuating each double-page spread is the bird's sound, the cat's jingle bell, and different colored flowers.

READING/WRITING CONNECTION

1. Begin the book by inviting students to talk about birds and cats. Read the title. Ask students to infer what the title means.
2. Write the word feathers on the board or chart. Underline the EA and pronounce its sound. Students echo. Say the word feather enunciating the EA which makes the short E sound.
3. Take the ER vowel sound which makes the R sound by using the word feather. Read the first double-page spread. Ask students to predict what the cat will do.
4. Read through the book stopping so students notice the details: the position of the cat, the plant or flowers, the bird, the colors, the sounds.
5. When coming upon words *treat, sneaking,* and *eat* ask students to point to the EA in each of these words. Show students that the EA sound in these words is differ-

ent than in the word *feather*. Help them hear that it makes a long E sound. Pronounce and have students echo.

6. When coming to the word feather, ask students to point to the EA, say the sound, and pronounce the word.
7. When coming to the word *early*, pronounce the EA sound, note the R, and help students hear it as different from the EA in *feather* and *eat*. Write the three EA sounds on the board. Pronounce each several times. Students echo.
8. Invite students to infer by the picture what is happening on the last double-page spread of the story. Ask them to infer what is meant by the words accompanying the picture.
9. Show the students the section called "The lunch that got away." Talk about what that means. Give ample time for the students to look at each bird and talk about it.
10. Distribute a brightly-colored feather to each student.
   • Students identify the bird from which it may have come by looking at the birds in the book and in other books. For example: a red feather may come from a cardinal, the breast of a robin, the wing of the red-winged blackbird, or the head of the red-headed woodpecker.
   • They write, according to their level, about their bird, a story about their bird, or they simply copy the EA words from the board or chart.
   • Share.

EXTENSION

After placing a variety of feathers in plastic bags—one bag per group, divide the students into groups of three. Each group designates a job for each person: HANDS, LEGS, MOUTH.
   • LEGS chooses a plastic bag and gets paper and markers for the group.
   • HANDS removes the feathers from the bag. The group, according to their level, does one or more of the following:
      • Categorizes the feathers by color;
      • Arranges the feathers by size: Large, Medium, Small, Tiny
      • Divides the feathers according to the names of the birds: brown for mourning doves, sparrows, wrens, flickers; green for hummingbirds; red for cardinals, robins, red-winged blackbirds, and red-headed woodpeckers, and so forth.
   • HANDS grids the results of the above activities on the paper.
   • MOUTH shares the results.

RELATED BOOKS

A fine non-fiction book that relates to this theme and reinforces the EA vowel sound and the short E sound, is Dean T. Spaulding's *Watching Our Feathered Friends*. What makes this book so fine is not only the fact that it introduces the hobby of bird-watching, birding history, bird-watching, bird feeding, and equipment, but it also includes step-by-step instructions for projects related to birds such as keeping a bird journal.
1. Students keep a bird journal.
2. As a group, students make a bird feeder or a bird house using a large coffee can.
3. Students write:
   National Audubon Society

700 Broadway
New York, NY 10003

Connect this to letter-writing. See Dr. JAC 43 and Dr. JAC 55.

Carmen Agra Deedy's *Agatha's Feather Bed: Not Just Another Wild Goose Story* is a funny book that invites students to consider the source of things.

1. Students look at the objects in the borders, choose one, and research its source.
2. Introduce the concept of idiom. Go back through the book, pulling the idioms, for example, "can spin a yarn." Explain to students that idioms are like cartoons, if you do not understand what is going on, you do not get the joke. See if the students can figure out some of the idioms.

Don't Fidget a Feather! by Erica Silverman is a grand story of one-upsmanship between duck and gander.

1. Since this is essentially a competition between a duck and a goose, it is the perfect book to use with the game "Duck, duck, goose."
   - Students form a circle.
   - One student is designated "It."
   - "It" moves around the circle tapping each student on the head saying, "Duck, duck, goose." Each "goose" leaves the circle until one student remains. That student is "It" for the next round and so forth.
2. Tell students that the sentence "Don't fidget a feather" is an English idiom. Ask students to tell you what it means in their own words (to remain motionless; not to give anything away).
3. On sentence strips write other "feather" idioms. (This could also be done with duck or goose idioms. See Gulland and Hind-Howell's *English Idioms*.)
   - In fine feather (to look or feel good)
   - You could have knocked me down (or over) with a feather. (being surprised)
   - To smooth a person's ruffled feathers (to calm someone down)
   - To make feathers fly (to begin an argument or fight)
   - A feather in your cap (to receive an honor)
   - Birds of a feather flock together. (similar people stay together)
4. "Don't fidget a feather," is a wonderful expression to use when students are on line and need to be still. Challenge them to be like goose and duck and not "fidget a feather." Make it a game. See who can remain the most still and silent the longest.

Mem Fox has written a modern sophisticated fable called *Feathers and Fools* about peacocks and swans who allow their fear of differences to destroy each other. Out of this destruction arises a peacock and swan who do not look at their differences but at their similarities. The moral of the story is clear and worth discussing with students of any age.

PUBLISHING

Display the students' writing and grids on a bulletin board entitled THE EA SOUND IS A FEATHER IN OUR CAPS!

THE THREE BILLY GOATS GRUFF

Harcourt Brace Jovanovich, (or any of the classic versions of this children's favorite).

Janet Stevens
(reteller and illustrator)

PHONICS CONCEPTS:
The gutturals
* G (hard) as in *Goats;*
* GR Consonant Sound: Blend as in *GRuff, GRoaned;*
* CR Consonant Sound: Blend as in *CRoss, CReaked;*
* TR Consonant Sound: Blend as in *TRoll, TRap, TRip, TRamp*

LANGUAGE ARTS CONCEPTS:
* Introduce the folk tale;
* Norwegian folk literature;
* The difference among goats: billy (male), nanny (female), kids (young);
* Introduce degrees of adjectives

*Phonics
Friendly
Books*
67

Artifacts: Troll pencil tops (available from U. S. Toy)

Summary: This is the classic cumulative beast story. Three clever billy goats outwit a mean, ugly troll that lives under a bridge they must cross in order to get to the grassy hillside. Called an almost perfectly constructed short story because no words are wasted, its action is rapid, and its ending is satisfactory.

READING/WRITING CONNECTION

1. Begin by making a GOAT WORD BANK. Then introduce the notion of a guttural sound by asking the students to place their fingers on their throats in order to feel the airflow that is stopped back toward the throat as if bunched-up behind the tongue. Make the hard G sound, the GR sound, the CR sound, and the TR sound. After each sound, students echo. (Since children often have difficulty with blends, saying *twrap* instead of *trap*, for instance, the repetition of words such as *gruff, troll, trip*, and *trap* and other guttural words help develop the muscle control necessary to make the throaty sound and allow for the fine sound differentiations necessary to pronounce these blends.)

2. Ask the students to help as you read the book. Give them one signal for the word gruff and another signal for the words *trip, trap, trip, trap*. Further, ask them to use

their one-inch voices for the youngest billy goat, their regular voices for the second billy goat, and deep voices for the big billy goat. Students also enjoy repeating the couplet which ends the story.

3. Read the book with the students joining in at the appropriate signal. When arriving at the page that asks, "What to do?" stop and challenge the students to do some problem solving.

4. After the reading, distribute the artifacts and talk about trolls as part of Norwegian folk literature. Show students Norway on the map. (A good source for information on trolls complete with other troll stories is *Norwegian Trolls and Other Tales* by Florence Ekstrand.) Also discuss billy goats (male), nanny goats (female), and kids (young goats). Point out that goats have hollow horns and beards.

5. Upon second reading, ask the students to send you a signal every time they hear a word that starts with G, GR, CR, or TR. This is an excellent listening activity since many words beginning with these sounds are used multiple times. When they signal for *Gruff, grass, grew, green, great, troll, trip, trap, tripping, goat, gobble, cross, greedy, creaked, groaned,* write these words on a big piece of butcher paper shaped like a goat. These words will become part of their GOAT WORD BANK.

6. Reread the words. Invite individual students to underline with a colorful marker the blend in the word you call out. Then everyone repeats the word.

7. Add the words *hungry* and *angry* to the list. Challenge students to underline the GR blend in the middle of these words.

8. Brainstorm other animals, birds, or reptiles. Give each of these the last name Gruff, for example, Cow Gruff, Goose Gruff, Sparrow Gruff, and so forth. Write these on the GOAT WORD BANK for further reference. This repetition reinforces the GR sound.

9. Brainstorm other places where the troll might hide (behind trees, in bushes, near a boulder). Write these on the GOAT WORD BANK for further reference. Talk briefly about the other meaning of troll.

10. Invite students to write their own version of a troll story using the story as a model as well as the information they brainstormed. Share in Author's Chair.

EXTENSION

Students make accordion books to help them categorize size and degree:
- Fold a sheet of 8 1/2" x 11" colored paper in half short end to short end.
- Fold one side back halfway.
- Fold the other side back halfway.

The accordion book will thus have a front and back cover and six long, narrow pages counting both the front and back of the paper.

- Students title their books and put their names on the front cover. They title the back cover: "About the Author." There they write something about themselves.

- On each of the three narrow pages, students draw and label pictures of the small (tiny, little), medium (middle, regular), and big (large, huge) billy goats.

- On each of the other three narrow pages, students choose another animal, bird, or reptile and an adjective to express the positive, comparative, and superlative degrees, (short, shorter, shortest or fast, faster, fastest) to identify and illustrate. This is good practice for later work on degrees of adjectives.

RELATED BOOKS

Three Cool Kids by Rebecca Emberley is an urban retelling of the children's classic. In this version Emberley plays with words such as *cool* and *kids* and replaces the horrid troll with a huge, hungry sewer rat. In addition, her turn of the cliché "the grass is always greener on the other side of the street" supplies that satisfactory ending.

1. After reading the story, show students the first double-page picture. Students point to "big," "middle" and "little" since these are not shown in the usual sequence.
2. Students retell the story in its proper sequence.
3. Since Emberley uses cut paper for her medium, students use cut paper scraps which they arrange to depict their version of the three billy goats and the rat.
4. The rat is disturbed by the sounds the goats make on the street. Students have fun pronouncing the sounds such as *kachinga, chinga*, and *kalomp*.
5. Check comprehension by asking the students to identify the character by giving hints, such as the bracelets, sneakers, yellow eyes, and so forth.
6. Talk about the expression "the grass is always greener on the other side of the street." Encourage students to speculate about what that expression might mean. Go back to the book's conclusion to help them understand the meaning.

A Trio of Triceratops by Bernard Most tells how these three dinosaurs undertake different activities such as touching their toes and tasting tangerines.

1. Students may draw comparisons between the three goats and the three triceratops, including that one is a folk tale, and one is not.
2. This book reinforces the TR blend. Students practice saying and reading words in the book with that sound.
3. Point out how the words begin with the same letter or letters. This is the beginning of alliteration.

The Toll-Bridge Troll by Patricia Rae Wolff is an up-to-date version of the classic story. In this story a Troll tries to prevent a young boy named Trigg from crossing the bridge on the way to school only to be outwitted by the boy's riddles.

PUBLISHING

Using *Three Cool Kids* as a model, create three goat silhouettes out of black butcher paper. Hang on a wall in the hall. Affix students work to two of these. Cut out letters to say WE TROLL FOR THE SOUNDS OF WORDS! and paste these on the third goat.

SHEEP IN A JEEP

Houghton Mifflin

Nancy Shaw

PHONICS CONCEPTS:
- Word Families;
- Onsets and Rimes

LANGUAGE ARTS CONCEPT:
- A corpus of work by an author

Artifacts: Woolly sheep cards

Summary: This classic tells the story of sheep who have adventures and misadventures in a jeep.

READING/WRITING CONNECTION

1. Talk about the concept of family, how members of the same family share the same last name. That last name is called the family name.

2. Put your last name on the board or chart and under it write the first names of others in your family. Then read the first and last name, (Smith: Mary, John, Sally, Tom). Then read: Mary Smith, John Smith, Sally Smith, Tom Smith. Tell students Mary and John are the mother and father, and Sally and Tom are the children. They are a family with the same last name.

3. Follow this same procedure with the last names of several students until you are sure the students understand the concept.

4. Draw the parallel to word families. Explain that words sometimes belong to families, too. When they do, we call them word families.

5. Write the word *dip* on the board or chart. Underline the IP. Tell students that the underlined letters are like the last name in a family, for example, Smith. The D is like the first name.

6. Ask students if they can think of other first names that could go with the last name IP to make another member of the word family. Students might suggest: L, S, R, or even SH. Write these under the family name to reinforce the concept.

7. Tell students they are about to hear a book with the following word families, which you previously have written on the board or chart in separate columns:
   EEP (long E), EAP (long E), UD (short U), UG (short U), ELP (short E), OUT (OU), EER (long E), EA (long E).

8. Pronounce each of the families. Students echo.

9. Ask the students to listen for the members of these word families as you read the book. When you come upon a word that belongs to a family, write it under its correct family.

10. Make woolly sheep cards. Show one as a model.

   • Distribute white woolly fabric (available in cloth stores), a square of black felt, and a card of heavy stock to each student;

   • Students cut a small oval face and a slightly bigger body out of the white woolly fabric.

   • They cut two small ears and two stick legs from the black felt;

   • They glue the woolly fabric onto the card. On top of face oval, they glue the black oval. Then they glue the ears and legs in place to make a sheep;

   • On the card, they write the sheep word family, a message, or a story, depending upon their level.

   • Author's Chair Share.

EXTENSION

Students make LIBRARY POCKET WORD FAMILIES.

   • Before beginning this activity, slice the bottom folds off colorful library pockets (available from Top Notch Paper Co.). Print (or use computer labels) a different phonogram sideways on each pocket so that the first letter of the phonogram begins at the mouth of the pocket.

   • Distribute one pocket and a different color sentence strip to each student.

   • Using a pocket with the phonogram AG on it and a sentence strip, demonstrate how students write an onset (digraph, blend, or single consonant) that makes the phonogram (rime) into a word on the sentence strip. Then show students how they can push it through, write another, push, write, and so on. For example, with the phonogram (rime) AG, students may suggest the following onsets: *b, h, t, n, br, sn.* When they push these through the pockets, they spell: *bag, hag, tag, nag, brag, snag,* and so forth.

   • After modeling the lesson, students work on their own pockets and strips. According to their level, students may refer to dictionaries, rhyming dictionaries, their language arts books, or they may work in groups. If students use up one entire side of the sentence strip they may turn it over and write more onsets on the other side.

   • Divide students into circles of three, four, or five, each with different rimes. Each student or group shares.

   • Display.

RELATED BOOKS

1.   Since *Sheep Out to Eat* remains a favorite because students understand why the sheep have difficulty with the food in the teashop, use this for extended work on onsets and rimes.

   • After reading the book, write the phonograms from the book on the board or chart.

   • Students make a story-flap book using the listed phonograms. For example, they may tell a story of the sheep going to eat.

   The first page may read: The sheep want to eat.

   The second page may read: But they don't want to eat _____. The word meat is covered by a flap or Post-it Note ™.

The third page may read: They want a sweet _____. Again, the word treat is covered.

• These stories may be as long or as short as is appropriate for the level. They may contain one phonogram or many.

• Classmates predict the word under the flap during sharing time by considering the phonogram and the context of the story.

2. Share some or all of Shaw's "Sheep" books: *Sheep on a Ship, Sheep in a Shop, Sheep Take a Hike,* and *Sheep Out to Eat.* Tell students that authors often write many books and sometimes these books have the same characters. (Corpus of work)

PUBLISHING

Pin the woolly sheep cards and the students' writing on a bulletin board that has been covered with woolly material. Cut letters out of black felt to spell out WE MADE FRIENDS WITH WORD FAMILIES!

Dr. JAC 26

ROXABOXEN

Lothrop, Lee & Shepard
(The Scholastic book-club edition is available
in both English and Spanish.)

Alice McLerran

PHONICS CONCEPTS:
- O Vowel Sound: Short O as in *ROxabOxen*
- A Vowel Sound: Schwa as in *RoxAboxen*
- R Consonant Sound: Liquid as in *Roxaboxen*
- X Consonant Sound: KS Sound as in *RoXaboXen*

LANGUAGE ARTS CONCEPT:
- Using known words to create new words

Artifacts: Small rocks or stones

Summary: Roxaboxen, created from rocks and boxes, bits of glass and cactus by the author's mother, her mother's siblings, and her mother's friends, lives again through the words of McLerran and the illustrations of Barbara Cooney. This wonderful story captures the imagination of all children who like to pretend and all adults who like to remember.

READING/WRITING CONNECTION

1. Show the book's cover. Ask students to describe what is happening. Explain that the tall girl in blue is Marian who went to a hill in Yuma, Arizona, (you might show students its location on a map) and named it Roxaboxen. Point to its name on the cover.
2. Write *Roxaboxen* on board or chart. Cover all but *Rox*. Pronounce *rox*. Exaggerate the short O sound. Students echo. Ask what *rox* sounds like. Lead them to the word *rocks*. Write on the board or chart.
3. Follow the same procedure as above with *box*. Help students generalize that the X sound may be spelled X or KS.
4. Make the R sound by bunching up the tongue. Students echo. Pronounce it in the word *Roxaboxen*.
5. Make the A vowel sound as a schwa. Students echo. Pronounce it in the word *Roxaboxen*.
6. Put all the sounds together to say *Roxaboxen*. Uncover word as students echo.

7. Read the book. Afterwards explain that Marian made up the name of the town by putting together sounds and smaller words. Talk about why she chose the words *rocks* and *box*. Help students understand the fun of making words. Tell them they can make words, too.

8. Put large cards with OX and KS in a pocket chart or along the chalk ledge. Make other slightly smaller cards with multiples of the letters BL, C, D, F, KN, M, P, R, S, H, M, T, CKS, and O. Create a set of these letters in plastic bags for pairs of students, distribute a bag of letters to each dyad, or students use their sets of letters in their mini-folders, their magnetic letters and boards, or their tactile letters. (This may also be done with individual students or with small groups.)

9. Model the making of words in the pocket chart or on the ledge by beginning with OX, KS. Then add letters, arrange or rearrange them, or combine letters. Have fun making words: *fox, locks, blocks, shocks, pox, clocks*. Praise success and effort. (For advanced students this activity may be done on paper and extended to include compound words such as: mailbox, Reeboks, sandbox, chickenpox.)

10. Distribute the rocks. Depending upon their level, students write a description or a story about their rocks, or they write about the book. Share.

EXTENSIONS

1. Talk about the early 20th century when Roxaboxen was created. Brainstorm stores or shops the children might put in Roxaboxen if they were creating it today, such as a computer store, a mall, a discount center, and so forth.

2. Section off the corners of the room as places for students to create their versions of Roxaboxen. Have available rocks, stones, pebbles; boxes both cardboard and wood, if possible; cardboard of various sizes, shapes, and colors; markers; butcher paper and other kinds of paper, odd objects such as corks, soda pop tops, cans, bottles; round plastic tops of containers; rope and string—and plants! Divide the class into four groups. Each group creates their own Roxaboxen:
   • Stores, houses, other buildings, and a way to designate them;
   • Streets and street names;
   • A name for their town;
   • Its "money";
   • A mayor;
   • Laws and rules.

3. Use the "towns" created by the students for further study:
   • Dramatic play (students pretend play in their towns);
   • Oral language experience;
   • Writing experiences;
   • Cooperative group activities;
   • Extensions across the curriculum:
     • science—the study of rocks, fossils, plants, animals;
     • mathematics—counting, time, parts of wholes;
     • music—singing about places such as "This Land Is Your Land," "The Erie Canal," "She'll Be Coming 'Round the Mountain," "Down by the Bay," "Over in the Meadow," and other folk song favorites;
     • art—drawing or painting in more detail one of the places in their town;
     • social studies—reading more about Yuma, Arizona, during the time of Roxaboxen, how towns form, cities, and so forth.

RELATED BOOK:

The Legacy of Roxaboxen: A Collection of Voices by Alice McLerran is the non-fiction book about Roxaboxen. Very much a family book, its core is a facsimile of "The History of Roxaboxan," written in 1916 by Marian Doan, who became Alice's mother. (The facsimile is removable so that students can handle and read it independently.) Drawing on a host of materials, including the memoirs of her aunt and grandmother as well as a wide variety of photographs, McLerran presents a portrait of the young author in the first part of this century and traces the impact over time of her mother's self-published book.

1. **Fiction/Non-fiction.** For students of all ages, *Roxaboxen* and *The Legacy of Roxaboxen: A Collection of Voices* clearly demonstrate the difference between fiction and non-fiction. Teach these differences by pointing out the genre characteristics in each book.

2. **Phonics.** Review the phonics lessons connected to the title.

3. **Letter Writing.** Each student chooses one of the children pictured as a pretend pen-pal. Brainstorm possible topics or questions: what other games children played early in the century, what their parents did, how they traveled, what school was like. Students may want to tell their pen-pal what it is like today, what they like to do in their spare time, and so forth.

4. **Journal Writing.** Students keep a journal about their favorite play area.

5. **Map Skills.** Students draw a map of the town they created in the room by using the map of Roxaboxen in the book.

6. **Photoarchaeology.** This activity may be more appropriate for older or more advanced students. Distribute old photographs of persons, places, things. Collect these from old books, magazines, or encyclopedias often found in garage sales or flea markets. Challenge students to look for clues in the appearance, clothing, quality of the photo, hair styles, and background to determine the time of the photo much the way an archaeologist studies artifacts from digs.

7. Since Marian Doan wrote her book when she was a child in 1916, encourage students to write their books now. Give students trigger words—words that evoke connections as a way to suggest topics for their books. Possible trigger words may be: *games you play; places you visit; brothers and sisters; kids in the neighborhood; favorite things to do; a fond memory.*

PUBLISHING

CELEBRATE SELF-PUBLISHING! Create a central publishing house, so each student gets published. Display books at the _____ (fill in the name) publishing house.

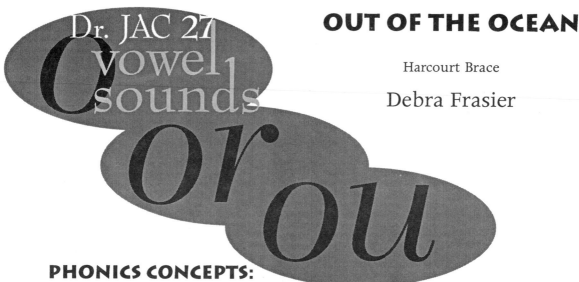

OUT OF THE OCEAN

Harcourt Brace

Debra Frasier

PHONICS CONCEPTS:
• O Vowel Sound: Long O—as in *Ocean;*
• O Vowel Sound: Schwa usually referred to as the unstressed vowel sound as in *Of;*
• OR Vowel Sound: OR Sound as in *seashORe;*
• OU Vowel Sound: OU Diphthong as in *OUt*

LANGUAGE ARTS CONCEPTS:
• The function of a glossary in a book;
• Apostrophe to show ownership

Artifacts: Shells

Summary: This book invites a vicarious walk along the ocean shore where the reader finds all kinds of things. Some small things such as shells fit into the hand; other things such as sun, wind, and ocean waves are too big to carry home. Every object that washes ashore tells a story. This book also features a detailed glossary.

READING/WRITING CONNECTION

1. Write the title of this book on the board or chart. Circle the letter O in different colors. Circle the long O in *ocean* in bright blue; circle the schwa O in *of* in yellow; circle the OU diphthong in *out* in red. Next to the word *ocean* write its synonym *seashore* and circle the OR for the OR sound. Talk about all the sounds the letter O can make. Draw a parallel with all the sounds a person can make.
2. As you read the book, list the things that wash ashore on the board or chart.
3. Talk about each thing after reading the entire book.
4. Show "An Ocean Journal" in the back of the book. Help students understand it as a part of the book and its function. Also share "Illustration Notes" so students will understand the time and work involved in this book.
5. Distribute a shell to each student and two sheets of colorful 8 1/2" x 11" paper for an ocean journal book. Students
    • Fold both sheets short end to short end;
    • Staple along the fold;
    • Write "____(individual name with an apostrophe S to show ownership) Ocean

Journal" on the cover;
- Cut the two inside pages in half so there are four sections between the covers;
- Write "About the Author" on the back cover;

6. In the first section, students write something about their shells. They may identify it, describe it, and tell its story. They may use their imagination about where and how they found their shells.

7. On the other sections (front and back), students record other information they find in books and from talking to others about the ocean. This is a good time to arrange books about the sea, fish, sharks, and environment around the room. Challenge students to find information different from what can be found in the book's glossary.

8. Take students to the library. Show students the section that deals with the ocean. Show students how to find information and pictures about the ocean in reference books. Show students the vast areas of oceans on a map or globe. Identify the oceans of the world: Atlantic, Pacific, Indian and Arctic. Some students may want to record the fact that about 71% of the surface of the earth is covered by water.

9. Students write a brief biography about themselves on the back cover.

10. During National Week of the Ocean, students hold a Read-A-Round. They sit in a circle and share their ocean-related discoveries.

EXTENSIONS

1. Shell Sort
   - Divide the class into groups of four or five and give each group a bag of shells.
   - Students sort the shells into groups of small, medium, large, extra large.
   - Give students large sheets of heavier stock paper and strips of cashier's tape.
   - Students make a grid with the strips. For example, they lay down a strip and place all the small shells in a line on top of the strip, one touching the next but not overlapping it. Then they cut the strip off where the shells end and glue it onto the colorful paper. They do the same for each of the other sizes.
   - After strips are glued and labeled, students may measure the strips and compare their results; for example, which group had the most small shells, the fewest large shells, and so forth.

2. Earth Toss
   - Using an earth balloon ball such as the Balzar Earth Balloon Ball™ (See Resources for Teachers), divide the class into teams.
   - Both teams stand in lines facing each other. One student throws the earth balloon ball to a member of the opposing team. That person catches it and identifies the ocean nearest his or her right thumb.
   - The catcher then throws the ball to someone else on the opposing team and so on. This provides both physical activity and reading skill. Additionally, students are working with map skills. Since 71% of the earth is covered with water, the earth toss reinforces that concept.

RELATED BOOKS

Philip Sauvain's *Oceans* is part of the geography detective series by Carolrhoda Books. This non-fiction book provides interesting information about oceans, the repetition of the long O sound in context, and for advanced or older students there are challenging activities suggested under the heading "Geography Detective."

Keith Faulkner's *A 3-D Look at Oceans* is another fine non-fiction book about oceans. It includes a 3-D Viewer so students can actually see some of the ocean's images dimensionally. This appeals to the visual learner, and the novelty reinforces the O vowel sound concepts.

Always a favorite with students is Scholastic's Magic School Bus Series. *The Magic School Bus on the Ocean Floor* by Joanna Cole recounts still another special field trip. This time Ms. Frizzle's class learns about the ocean and the marine animals and fauna that live there. Using this book with students enables them to learn along with Ms. Frizzle's class. As usual there are many suggestions for writing and reading about the ocean.

PUBLISHING

Celebrate NATIONAL WEEK OF THE OCEAN in April with a display of students' ocean journals, pictures of the ocean, and photographs students may bring in of visits to beaches or the seashore. For more information or to order a celebration kit for teachers, see Resources for Teachers.

WHITE SNOW, BRIGHT SNOW

Mulberry

Alvin Tresselt

PHONICS CONCEPTS:
- OW Vowel Sound: Long O as in *snOW;*
- *Generalization:*
    Sometimes the two letters OW make the long O sound.
- *Generalization:*
    W IS SOMETIMES A VOWEL AND FOLLOWS THE VOWEL DIGRAPH RULE OF TWO VOWELS MAKING ONE SOUND AS IN *crOW.*
- OW Vowel Sound: OU Diphthong as in *OWl*
- *Generalization:*
    W CAN BE CONSIDERED A VOWEL WHEN IT APPEARS IN CONNECTION WITH ANOTHER VOWEL AS IN GR*OW* (LONG O DIGRAPH) OR *NOW* (OW DIPHTHONG).
- *Generalization:*
    A DIPHTHONG REPRESENTS A BLEND OF TWO VOWEL SOUNDS WITHIN ONE SYLLABLE.

LANGUAGE ARTS CONCEPTS:
- Reading and decoding sounds in context
- The same letters may have different sounds.

Artifacts: Styrofoam™ snowballs (available at craft stores or floral suppliers)
Summary: First published in 1947, this classic Caldecott Medal Book and ALA Notable Book captures the wonder and delight children feel during a snowfall.

READING/WRITING CONNECTION

1. Before beginning this book,
    - make a large SNOWFLAKE WORD BANK out of white butcher paper. At the top write in bold: OW–long O sound–SNOW.
    - make a large OWL WORD BANK out of brown butcher paper. Between the ears write in bold: OW–OU sound–OWL.
2. Show the book to the students. Point out the title, especially the word snow. For rich oral language, engage the students in talk about snow: who has seen it, who has not, where and when it falls, what it feels like, what people do in snow, kinds of snow, what can be made out of snow, and so forth.
3. Tell students as you read the book, you will stop when you come to a word that has OW in it. If the OW sounds like the letter O, it is a long O. When they hear that sound, they are to tell you, and you will write that word inside the snowflake.
4. Tell students the OW also has another sound. If the OW sounds like ow as in, "Ow! that hurts," it is a diphthong. That is the OU sounds as if the W (double U; UU) has been squeezed into a U. They hear in the words such as owl, down, and brown. Tell

students when they hear that OU sound, they are to tell you and you will write that word inside the owl. Using these colored graphics help visual and aural learners associate words and sounds with colors and pictures.

5. Read through the book stopping at the following words (even when they are repeated) which go on the snowflake: *snow, snowflakes, low, snowflake, burrows, snowbank, snow houses, snowmen, window, shadows, snowdrifts, snow-light, snowman, snow house, snow fort, snowball, showed, willows, snowman's, slowly, snowdrops;* and the following words which go on the owl: *down, powdery, brown, eyebrows, cows.*

6. After reading the book and recording the words, point to each as you read it. Since many words are repeated in the book, they will be repeated on the lists. This gives students the opportunity to see, hear, and pronounce them many times.

7. Challenge the students to read as many words as they can on the list. Do this together and individually. As the children read, give each reader a snowball artifact even if they read only one word. Do this until every student has read.

8. Distribute white paper doilies. Model for students how to fold the doily in half and then in half again. Cut out pieces from the folded sides in order to make a snowflake.

9. Students make paper doily snowflakes and glue them onto a larger sheet of paper.

10. Students write about snow or copy the words from the SNOWFLAKE WORD BANK, depending upon their level.

EXTENSIONS

Study of Snow. Tell students that in winter when it is very cold, the water in the clouds turns into tiny crystals instead of rain. These crystals sometimes stick to a speck of dust and join together with other crystals to make a snowflake. No two snowflakes are the same.

Snowflakes are really frozen water, but they do not look like ice because the crystals have so many sides the light bounces off and makes them look white.

Why Snowflakes Float. Each student receives two sheets of the same size paper.
- Students crumple one sheet of paper into a ball and hold it in one hand.
- They hold the flat sheet in the other hand.
- They drop both sheets simultaneously.
- They observe that the ball hits the floor first.

Explain that while they are both pulled down by the same gravity, the upward force of air acts differently on the crumpled sheet than on the flat sheet. That is why a raindrop falls fast to earth whereas a snowflake floats.

Study of Winter. Using a globe and a flashlight show students what happens when winter comes.
- Mark the globe where the students live with a non-permanent marker;
- Show how the earth is tilted away from the sun (flashlight) as it goes around the earth;
- Conclusion: the light from the sun does not hit the earth where we live as many hours a day in winter as it does in the summer when the earth is not so tilted.

RELATED BOOKS

To introduce the concept of the OW as the initial sound, use the book *Owen* by Kevin Henkes. Owen's parents try to get him to give up his favorite blanket. Mrs. Tweezers, a neighbor, supplies ideas but nothing works until the final solution which makes everyone happy.

1. Write **Owen** on the board or chart.
2. Ask the students which sound they hear at the beginning as you say the name. When they say O, remind them of that the OW often makes that sound.
3. As you read the story, point to the name on board or chart. Students say the name.

To show students the OW long O sound in the medial position, read Alan Schroeder's delightful Japanese version of the Cinderella folk tale *Lily and the Wooden Bowl*.

1. After pointing out the OW in the middle of bowl, read the book to the students.
2. Talk about how this version is like the Cinderella story and how it is different.

David McPhail's *Snow Lion,* a Children's Choice Award Winner, tells the story of Lion who discovers the wonders of snow.

The *Snowy Day* by Ezra Jack Keats, a Caldecott Award Book, recounts the adventures of a little boy in the city on a very snowy day.

PUBLISHING

Students, holding their snowflakes and their writing, pretend they are snowflakes swirling and dancing in the air to an appropriate piece of classical music. "The Dance of the Sugar-Plum Fairy" or "Waltz of the Flowers" from Tchaikovsky's *Nutcracker Suite* works well. When the music stops, the students fall gently to the floor. In that position, they share their snowflakes and what they have written on them.

OOPS!

Harcourt Brace

Colin McNaughton

PHONICS CONCEPTS:
- OO Vowel Sound: the 2-Dot U or Long OO as in *OOps*
- OO Vowel Sound: the 1-Dot U or Short OO as in c*OO*kie

LANGUAGE ARTS CONCEPTS:
- Literary allusions;
- Story sequels

Artifacts: A strip of faux fur (available in cloth stores) cut to approximate a wolf's tail.
Summary: A slow-witted wolf and a lucky pig are the major characters in this fractured version that combines "Little Red Riding Hood" and "The Three Little Pigs."

READING/WRITING CONNECTION

1. Gather the students around and model several incidents that conclude with the word *Oops!* For example:
   - Pick up chalk or a marker and drop it. Say "Oops!"
   - Sit in the chair, get up, trip a little and say "Oops!"
   - Call on a student by saying the wrong name and say "Oops!"

2. Ask the students if they ever say "Oops!" Encourage students to tell about times when they said "Oops!" Help them generalize that people use the word when they make a mistake, are disappointed, are sorry, or are surprised. Write each of these four reasons on the board or chart for later reference.

3. Write the word on board or chart. Point out that the OO has a long sound. Make the sound; say the sound in fOOd and in *OOps*. Students echo. Write words with the long OO sound: *ooze, tooth, balloon, coo, zoo* on one side of the board. Point out the sound in the initial, medial, and final positions.

4. Compare it to the short OO sound in *cookie*. Say the short sound in c*OO*kie and in l*OO*k. Students echo. Write words with the short OO sound: *look, good, took, wood, wool, cook, book* on the other side of the board.

5. Show students the book. Invite them all to read the title aloud. Talk about the picture on the cover. Ask students which of the reasons for saying Oops! fits the picture. (Either mistake or surprise would fit. Accept both. If the students give other responses, be sure to ask them why. Sometimes their reasons make their less obvious answer work.)

6. Caution students to listen carefully as you read the story because when you come upon the word "Oops!" you will stop to ask which of the four reasons for using the word fit the story.

7. Read through the book, stopping so students can study the pictures, think about

the words, predict, and discuss. Record the reasons students give for each "Oops!" by using slash marks next to the reason written on board or chart.

8. When you get to the last page, open the book so students can see that the front and back covers really depict the end of the story.
9. Distribute the wolf tails and large sheets of paper.
10. Using the covers as the beginning of a new story, students write a sequel.
    • Talk about the sequel to a story.
    • Students glue the faux fur tails on the paper and write their sequels.
    • They may divide the paper into sections or fold it like a book.
    • Issue the challenge to use the word "Oops!" at least once in their stories.
        • Author's Chair Share.

EXTENSION

Since this book contains two literary allusions, one to "Little Red Riding Hood" and one to "The Three Little Pigs," divide the students into two groups.
    • Group One reviews the story of "Little Red Riding Hood" and decides how to present it to the class.
    • Group Two reviews the story of "The Three Little Pigs" and decides how to present it to the class.
Some options are role-playing, writing another version of the story, finding one of the stories and reading it aloud, taking parts, using puppets, sharing, or using drawings to tell the story.

RELATED BOOKS

One of the best books for reinforcing the long OO sound is Bernard Most's *Cock-A-Doodle-Moo!*
    • Point out the long OO sound in the medial position in *doodle* and in the final position in *moo*.
    • Students play rooster and say "cock-a-doodle-doo" every time the rooster does.
    • Designate a student who reads well to read the cow's part, noticing how the cow changes the expression by changing the initial consonants.

For establishing the long OO sound in the medial position, any book with the word *moon* would be effective such as the Caldecott Medal *Owl Moon* by Jane Yolen. Margaret Wise Brown's *Goodnight Moon* enables a comparison of the OO sounds: *Goodnight* contains the short OO vowel sound and *Moon* the long OO vowel sound.

Mrs. Goose's Baby by Charlotte Voake serves two purposes: It provides a version of the ugly duckling theme, and the word *goose*, used repeatedly throughout the book, reinforces the long OO sound.

Steven Kroll's *Loose Tooth*, the story of Fangs and Flapper, twin bats who do everything together, repeats the long OO sound in both words in the title.

Sonny's Beloved Boots by Lisa Stubbs illustrates the long OO sound in the medial position.

PUBLISHING

Design Oops! Day. On that day, students use the word Oops! to signal surprise or disappointment, to say they are sorry, or to admit they made a mistake. Every time someone says the word, they get to write OO on the displayed yellow butcher paper banana peel drawn to look like the one in Oops! At the end of the day, count the OO's and give a rousing Oops! cheer.

A MY NAME IS ALICE

Dial

Steven Kellogg

PHONICS CONCEPTS:
- Letters in names;
- Identifying consonants and vowels in names

LANGUAGE ARTS CONCEPTS:
- Reading names;
- Alphabetical order

Artifacts: Fancy name tags, trimmed with glitter or stars.
Summary: This alphabet book is based on a playground ball game. The idea is to give the letter, follow it with a person's first name, a place that begins with that same letter, and some object. For example: J my name is Joyce. I come from Jersey where I sell jelly beans. This book adds the twist of first a woman's name, followed by her husband's, place, and object. At the bottom of each illustration, the characters are identified also by letter, for example, Alice is an ape; Barbara is a bear and so forth.

READING/WRITING CONNECTION

1. Explain the basis of the book. If possible, bring a tennis ball to class and demonstrate how "A my name is Alice" is played by using your own name. The ball is bounced first to the letter name and then each time a word is said that begins with that letter. For example: J (bounce), my name is Joyce (bounce). I come from Jersey (bounce) where I sell jelly (bounce) beans.
2. Invite students in the class to think about a verse to fit their names.
3. Read through the book to get the alphabetic order.
4. Upon second reading, ask students to suggest a letter. Read the page that corresponds to the letter they suggest.
5. Give students colorful 4″ x 6″ index cards, glitter, stickers, stars for making nametags.
6. Students write their first names in their best writing on the card and decorate their nametags. Encourage them to be individual and creative.
7. While they are working, place the individual letters of the alphabet, which you have printed on the same size index cards, in alphabetical order across one wall of the room.

8. Use these letters as a WORD WALL OF NAMES. Display them low enough to be accessible to students.

9. When the students have completed their nametags, each in alphabetical turn places his or her name under the appropriate letter; for example, Carol under C and Latisha under L and so forth. (Do not worry about the second letter in the name at this point.)

10. Conclude by calling out each letter in alphabetical order. When a letter is called that begins a student's name, that student reads his or her name aloud.

EXTENSIONS

1. This WORD WALL OF NAMES provides a graph of students' names.
   Counting.
   - How many names appear under the letter G? Under K? (and so forth)
   - What letter has the most names under it?
   - Are there two letters in the alphabet with the same number of names under them?
   - Are there three letters with the same number of names under them?
   - Name the letters that have no names under them.

   Mathematics.
   - How many more names appear under the letter N than under the letter P?
   - How many fewer names appear under D than under S?
   - If we added all the names under the vowels, how many would we have?
   - Stand the students in front of the graph according to their names. Give each row a ribbon, tape, or cashier's paper tape. They lay down the tape and stand aside. They have created a human graph. (This is a great activity to introduce graphs.)

   Phonics.
   - Can anyone add all the names under the consonants?
   - If we subtracted the names under the vowels from the names under the consonants, how many would we have?
   - Who can make the sound of the letter above Steven's name?
   - Who can tell me what kind of A sounds we hear in Amanda's name?

   Reading and Predicting.
   - Who can read all the girl's names on our WORD WALL OF NAMES?
   - Who can read all the boy's names?
   - Who can read all the names?
   - If we did this same activity with our last names what might happen?
   - If we invited another class in to do this activity, how would our graph change? How would it stay the same?
   - If we do this graph again next month, would it be the same?

2. Students may add or change the names on the WORD WALL OF NAMES by using the name of the characters in their favorite books, or in stories they read together in class. These names are written on different color index cards and referred to when reviewing the story.

3. Leave the WORD WALL OF NAMES up in the room. When reading, it works even better than the commercial alphabet displayed in rooms because the students own this alphabet and because they associate sounds and letters to their names and the names of classmates.

RELATED BOOKS

While any book that names a character in its title would reinforce this lesson and extend students' awareness of names and their sounds, these four are favorites:

Chrysanthemum by Kevin Henkes tells the story of how Chrysanthemum loved her name until she went to school and the children made fun of it. Fortunately, the music teacher helps her regain her self-esteem.

Knots on a Counting Rope by Bill Martin, Jr. and John Archambault is a powerful story told in tandem by grandfather and boy about how boy got his name.

A Porcupine Named Fluffy by Helen Lester tells about Fluffy's embarrassment about his name until he meets a similarly misnamed rhinoceros, Hippo.

The Legend of the Bluebonnet by Tomie dePaola recounts the Comanche Indian legend of how She-Who-Is-Alone became renamed One-Who-Dearly-Loved-Her-People.

• Students read these books in groups and share their connection to names with the rest of the class.

• Students find other books at home or in the library that deal with a certain character's name.

• Students find books that have the name of the character in the title.

PUBLISHING

Establish PLAY DAY! Have a variety of balls, some different size nets, colored chalk, rope, and string available. Students interview their parents, relatives, friends about games they played when they were kids. Students share these on PLAY DAY! Invite parents and friends to attend, demonstrate, and join in. (Connecting rhyme, chant, and play with sounds, letters, and words remains an intrinsically powerful way for anyone to learn language.)

HANDS

Harcourt Brace

Lois Ehlert

PHONICS CONCEPTS:
- H Consonant Sound: Fricative as in *Hands;*
- A Vowel Sound: Short A as in *hAnds;*
- N Consonant Sound: Nasal as in *haNds;*
- D Consonant Sound: Plosive as in *hanDs;*
- S Consonant Sound: Z Sound: Fricative as in *handS*

LANGUAGE ARTS CONCEPTS:
- Small words embedded in larger words;
- Apostrophe

Artifacts: A HANDbook of Sounds
Summary: This glove-shaped book tells about working and making things with your hands.

READING/WRITING CONNECTION

1. Each student makes an outline of his or her hand on a colorful sheet of paper. On the tips of the fingers, beginning with the pinky finger, they print the letters: H, A, N, D, S.
2. After the students are finished, pronounce the sound of each letter. Students echo. For kinetic learners, connect sounds to movement:
   - For the H sound, students put their hands in front of their mouths to feel their breath;
   - For the short A sound, students give a weak-wrist wave as if saying with the sound and gesture "It's nothing!"
   - For the N sound, students hold their noses to feel the vibration in the nasal passages;
   - For the D sound, students put their hands in front of their mouths to feel the tiny explosion;
   - For the S sound, students put their teeth together to make the Z sound.
3. Invite students to sound out the word *hand* and then the word *hands*. Call their

attention to the clear D sound in *hand* yet the D sound gets absorbed by the Z sound in the plural form *hands*.

4. Read the book. Allow plenty of time for students to examine each page and talk about what they see.

5. Give each student three sheets of 8 1/2" X 11" paper in assorted colors. Students fold each paper in half, trace their hands including one or two inches of wrist, and cut these out. Each student should have six hands.

6. Staple these together at the end of the wrist. On the cover hand, students write their name, apostrophe S, and the words *HANDbook of Sounds*.

7. On the first hand following the cover hand, they print H, on the second hand, A, the third N, the fourth D, the last S.

8. Challenge students to find other words that contain the sound of the letter on each hand and write those words on the proper hand. The H page might contain: *house, happy, overhead.*; the A hand page might hold: *apple, ant, plant, fast.*

9. Students keep their handbooks as an on-going project for several days. Encourage them to gather words at home and outside of class. The idea is to fill each hand, both sides, with words.

10. At the end of the project, students share the letter page they have with the most words. Share. Everyone gives them "a hand" (applause) when they finish reading their page.

EXTENSIONS

1. Show students the small words in the word HANDS: *hand, and, an.*
2. Explain that seeing the small words in big words can help with reading and with spelling. Choose some words from the book and together find the small words in them: marking (*mar, ark, in, king, mark, kin*) and showing (*show, how, ow, wing, in, win, owing*) are good words to use for this modeling.
3. Students enter books they are reading to find big words. They record the big words and as many small words within these words as they can find. This not only reinforces a reading and spelling strategy, but it also expands students' vocabulary.

RELATED BOOKS

That's How It Is When We Draw by Ruth Lercher Bornstein shows a young girl drawing all kinds of wonderful pictures that express her feelings.
1. Discuss the page that begins, "Sometimes I don't know what my hand will draw..."
2. Talk about how sometimes when we are in the act of drawing or writing, another idea pops into our mind that seems to send our hands in another direction. Allow students to talk about that experience.
3. Give students some drawing paper. They may start by drawing their hands as the girl did in the story and see what emerges. Then they may write or talk about what they drew.

Here Are My Hands by Bill Martin, Jr. and John Archambault celebrates the human body by pointing out its various parts.
1. Read through the book.
2. After each part, ask students to come up with another function for that part. For

an extra challenge, see if the students can continue the rhyme or rhythm in the book. For example: hands for drawing and writing—eyes for seeing and sighting, and so forth.

PUBLISHING

Celebrate HANDS with finger or play rhymes which can be found in Marc Brown's *Finger Rhymes* and *Play Rhymes*. Do "Sleepy Fingers," "Whoops! Johnny," "Do Your Ears Hang Low?" and other favorites.

SOME SMUG SLUG

Harper Collins

Pamela Duncan Edwards

PHONICS CONCEPTS:

- S Consonant Sound as in *Some, Summer, Sunday, SenSed;*
- S Consonant Sound: Z Sound as in *shoulderS;*
- SC Consonant Blend as in *SCurrying;*
- SK Consonant Blend as in *SKunk, SKish;*
- SL Consonant Blend as in *SLug, SLope;*
- SM Consonant Blend as in *SMug;*
- SN Consonant Blend as in *SNickered;*
- SP Consonant Blend as in *SPider, suSPicion;*
- ST Consonant Blend as in *SToring, STem;*
- SW Consonant Blend as in *SWallowtail;*
- SCR Consonant 3-Letter Blend as in *SCReamed;*
- SQU Consonant 3-Letter Blend as in *SQUealed;*
- STR Consonant 3-Letter Blend as in *STRand;*
- SHR Consonant 3-Letter Blend as in *SHRug;*
- SH Consonant digraph as is *SHock, SHam, swooSHing, buSH;*
- Initial, Medial, Final

LANGUAGE ARTS CONCEPT:

- Alliteration

Artifacts: Gummy candy worms (called gummy "slugs" in this context)
Summary: This alliterative book, filled with S sounds, tells about a smug slug who ignores the warnings of animals around it and comes to an unexpected end.

READING/WRITING CONNECTION

1. Cut a large 3' X 1' S out of white cardboard so that it approximates the slug on the book's dust jacket. Before beginning this lesson, affix it on the front board or wall.

2. When the students gather around for the story, point to the S. Tell students it sounds like the tail end of a hiss. Say its regular consonant sound. Students echo the sound.

3. Ask students if they can think of insects, reptiles, or animals that start with the S sound. Take them to the library to investigate. (This is great foundation for non-fiction and beginning research.) Write their offerings on the letter.

4. Show students the book's cover.

    • Ask them to identify the creature pictured there. If they do not know what a slug is, tell them it is related to the snail but without the hard shell; they look more like worms.

    • Look at the picture on the back cover of the dust jacket. Talk about how both slugs and snails leave a shiny trail behind them when they travel. Explain that even though slugs live on land, they like moist or wet places.

    • Point to the slug in the picture, ask students to find its head, eyes, mouth, and antennae. Explain that these help the slug sense things. They work like antennae on insects. (For advanced students, who might want to read more about slugs, tell them they are also called gastropod mollusks.)

5. Ask if anyone can read the title. Talk about the meaning of *smug*.

6. Give the author and illustrator's names. Turn to the inside back flap. Tell students you are going to read about the author. Do the same for the illustrator. Since both blurbs are filled with S words, challenge them to think about what letter of the alphabet they will expect in this book.

7. Read the book through, stopping to share the pictures. Talk about the many S words. Tell students when a consonant is repeated, it is called alliteration. Practice with some alliterative tongue twisters.

8. Distribute gummy slugs. Upon second reading, ask students to hold up their slugs every time they hear a word that begins with S. Write these words on the large S.

9. After the second reading, divide the students into fourteen small groups, perhaps pairs. Give each group a long sheet of paper upon which you have written one of the following:

S	SN	SH	SCR
SP	SC		
ST	SK		SQU
SW	SL		STR
	SM		SHR

Instruct students to list all the words they can find on the cardboard S that fits the S pattern written on their sheet. The pattern may appear anywhere in the word. For example: the SH group would have, among other words, *shrieked* and *swooshing* because they both have SH somewhere in the word, but the SW group would also have the word *swooshing*.

10. Students share lists repeating the words so that the sounds are heard several times.

EXTENSIONS

1. Expand students vocabulary by sharing some or all of the names of other gas tropods:

    ABALONE–covered by an ear-shaped shell from which we get mother-of-pearl.
    - Show a picture and talk about how the shell looks like an ear.
    - Try to bring in something mother-of-pearl to show the students.

    CONCH–covered with an overlapping spiral shell. These are often blown as horns and can vary in color from white to red.
    - Show a picture.
    - Simulate the sound of the conch horn by making a deep sound through cupped hands. Students may do the same.
    - Talk about its colors from white to red: pearl, peach, pink, light red.

    SNAIL–covered with a spirally coiled shell.
    - Bring several shells to class for students to see and hold.
    - Ask if students have ever seen a snail in their yard or garden.

    WHELK–covered with a thick-lipped spiral shell with bumps. These are large and can grow up to sixteen inches.
    - Show students sixteen inches on a yard stick.

    LIMBET–covered with a flat conical shell. They like to cling to rocks.
    - Show students a conical shape by rolling a paper into that form.

    PERIWINKLE–covered with a conical spiral shell. They eat algae and seaweed and can be found at the end of water.
    - Bring in dry algae or seaweed from a health food store.
    - Soak in water.

    SEA SLUG–lacks a shell as an adult but is brightly colored. They creep along the bottom of the sea or cling to plants that grow under water. Students might enjoy their other name, "nudibranch."

2. Take students through the challenges offered on the last page of the book.

RELATED BOOK

Toad by Ruth Brown picks up, in a way, where *Some Smug Slug* leaves off. In this book, Toad goes on an adventure and crawls into the jaws of a monster. Unlike the unlucky slug, the monster spits him out.

1. After reading this book, use it to teach descriptive words (adjectives).
2. Make a Venn diagram by drawing two large overlapping circles. On one side write SLUG; on the other side write TOAD; where they overlap, write SAME. Students make suggestions as you write them under the proper heading.

PUBLISHING

Students fold 16" X 11" heavy stock paper in half. On another sheet of paper, they draw and cut out the letter S. They cut out a large letter S and staple it to the front back page.

Inside they write a story using as many S words as possible. Display under the heading WE ARE SOME SMUG STUDENTS ABOUT S SOUNDS!

SING A SONG OF CIRCUS

Harcourt Brace

Ward Schumaker

PHONICS CONCEPTS:

- NG Consonant Sound: NG Nasal, Regular Digraph as in *siNG;*
- *Generalization:*
    REGULAR DIGRAPHS INCLUDES TWO-LETTER COMBINATIONS THAT REPRESENT A SOUND NOT ORDINARILY ASSOCIATED WITH EITHER CONSONANT.
- C Consonant Sound: S Sound, sometimes called the soft C as in *Circus;*
- *Generalization:*
    WHEN C IS FOLLOWED BY E, I, OR Y THE SOUND OF S IS LIKELY TO BE HEARD.
- C Consonant Sound: K Sound, sometimes called the hard C as in *cirCus;*
- S Consonant Sound as in *Sing, Song, circuS;*
- IR Vowel Sound: R Sound as in *cIRcus;*
- *Generalization:*
    WHEN A VOWEL IS FOLLOWED BY R, THE R INFLUENCES THE VOWEL SOUND. THESE SOUNDS ARE CALLED R-CONTROLLED VOWEL SOUNDS.

LANGUAGE ARTS CONCEPT:

- Personification

Artifacts: Orange and yellow balloons
Summary: An orange and a yellow balloon escape from their bunch to join the circus. There they work doing all sorts of things: help the clowns, save the man on the flying trapeze, give the dogs something to jump over, and so forth. While carrying a sign that announces an act, they deflate. The balloon man picks them up and gives them air. The illustrations are delightfully done in the manner of children's books in the 1940s.

READING/WRITING CONNECTION

1. Make five 24" balloons out of yellow, orange, red, blue, and green paper. Arrange

these on the front board or wall. Use ribbon or cord for their strings. These are BALLOON WORD BANKS!

- On the yellow balloon, print a 12" NG as in si*NG*.
- On the orange balloon, print a 12" C followed by *soft sound* in 6" letters as in *Circus*.
- On the red balloon, print a 12" IR as in c*IR*cus.
- On the blue balloon, print a 12" C followed by *hard sound* in 6" letters as in cir*Cus*.
- On the green balloon, print a 12" S as in *Song*.

2. Gather the students around the balloons, point to the letters on each balloon, and say their sound. Students echo. When they pronounce the NG ask them to put their thumb and index finger over their noses to feel the vibration the sound makes.

3. Tell students they will meet balloons in *Sing a Song of Circus*. These balloons make sounds because they talk, think, and act like people. Show their little faces in the book. Tell students that this is called personification. Write the word on board or chart. Show students the smaller word *person* in the word *personification* to remind them that the word is used when things or animals that usually do not speak talk like persons.

4. Encourage students to point out the sounds they just learned from the balloons in the book's title–two NGs, three Ss, one C (soft), one IR, and one C (hard).

5. Ask students if they have been to a circus or have ever seen one on television.

6. Allow plenty of time for students to talk about their experiences related to the circus.

7. Read the book, stopping to allow students to follow and talk about the antics of the twin balloons.

8. Distribute two balloons and two strips of light weight paper to each student. On one strip, students write each sound the way it is written on the four balloons. On the other strip, students write the book's title and underline the sounds they find in the four balloons. Encourage students to repeat quietly to themselves each sound and word as they write it.

9. Students put one strip inside one balloon and the other strip inside the other balloon. They blow them up, tie them off, and bounce them back and forth to each other.

10. As they tap a balloon back to a friend, tell them to make one of the sounds or to say one of the words with which they have been working. This is a fun way to practice the sounds.

EXTENSIONS

1. Reread the book. Invite students to identify any word that contains the sounds found in their five paper balloons. Write their words on the appropriate balloon, e.g *kangaroo, could* (hard), *soft, announce* (soft), *circus*, and so forth. This serves as both a comprehension check and provides words for later reference.

2. This book invites song. Students in small groups write a song about the circus.
   - Start them off by helping them choose a simple melody they know well such as "Happy Birthday."
   - Invite them to play around with circus words to fit the tune. For example, the following came from a group of second-graders. Sing to the tune of "Twinkle, Twinkle."

Circus, circus so much fun
When you're here we all run
Tents and food, clowns and acts
We love everything, that's a fact.

3. Brainstorm the animals usually associated with a circus: elephants, lions, tigers, monkeys, horses, dogs, bears, and so forth. Students write a crazy recipe for that animal's food. Model first, then the students:

    • choose an animal: (elephant);
    • title their recipe: ("Elephant Stew");
    • list the ingredients: 4 cups of peanuts, 1 cup of peanut butter, 2 cups peanut oil, 6 cups of peanut flour, and 3 cups of water;
    • give directions: Take shells off peanuts and mix into peanut butter. Add oil and flour. Stir. Mix in the water. Cook for 4 hours. Serve cold to the nearest elephant.

RELATED BOOKS

Sing, Sophie! by Dayle Ann Dodds tells the story of a how Sophie's singing soothes her baby brother during thunderstorms.

1. Students can join in on the refrain of Sophie's songs.
2. Review the S consonant sound. See if students can find it in the title. Say the sound. Students echo. Follow the same procedure with the NG nasal sound.
3. They can practice the nasal NG because the words *song, sing, singing, sang* as well as other -ing forms are used often in the book. Aside from the title, the NG sound is used approximately thirty-six times and one *fixin'*. When the students hear that NG sound, tell them to put their thumb and index finger over their noses to feel the vibrations. This will also indicate their level of understanding when hearing the sound.
4. Upon second reading, make a slash mark on the board every time the NG sound is heard. Have fun counting these sounds after reading the book.

Fish and Flamingo by Nancy White Carlstrom tells the story of two unlikely friends who tell each other stories about their lives.

1. Ask students if they can find the NG sound somewhere in the title. Since it is in the medial position and not at the end of the word as it so often is, students will have to look and listen closely.
2. Read the book through and then return to each page so students can find any of the five sounds. Add these words to the words on the five paper balloons.
3. Make a T-Chart. On one side, write FISH. On the other side, write FLAMINGO. Ask the students to tell you things about each. Write their offerings under the proper column.

PUBLISHING

To celebrate sounds have a sing-along. Students write invitations to their parents and friends. Photocopy some familiar tunes known to the students such as "Three Little Fishes," and "Down by the Bay." Students sing. Encourage guests to join in. Decorate the room with a banner that reads WE SING SONGS ABOUT SOUNDS!

LITTLE CLOUD

Philomel

Eric Carle

PHONICS CONCEPTS:

- CL Consonant Sound: CL Blend as in *CLoud;*
- OU Vowel Sound: OU Diphthong as in *clOUd;*
- T Consonant Sound: TT Plosive as in *liTTle;*
- *Generalization:*
    WHEN TWO OF THE SAME CONSONANTS ARE SIDE BY SIDE, ONLY ONE USUALLY IS HEARD.
- *Generalization:*
    IF THE FIRST VOWEL SOUND IN A WORD IS FOLLOWED BY TWO CONSONANTS, THE FIRST SYL-LABLE USUALLY ENDS WITH THE FIRST OF THE TWO CONSONANTS.
- *Generalization:*
    IF THE LAST SYLLABLE OF A WORD ENDS IN LE, THE CONSONANT PRECEDING THE LE USU-ALLY BEGINS THE LAST SYLLABLE.

LANGUAGE ARTS CONCEPT:

- Syllabication

Artifacts: Cotton balls
Summary: A little cloud turns into several things–airplane, shark, trees, clown–before joining other clouds and raining.

READING/WRITING CONNECTION

1. Before beginning this lesson, make a 2' cloud out of white paper. Write *Little Cloud* on it. Take some cotton balls, pull them apart, and glue them around the edge of the cloud to give a wispy appearance. This becomes the CLOUD WORD BANK. Display near students.
2. Distribute a cotton ball to each student. Ask students to look at the cotton balls and tell things that are like cotton.
3. Model for the students: "If I gently pull my cotton ball apart a bit, it reminds me of cotton candy because I can pull it apart the same way I can pull the cotton candy apart." Write cotton candy on the CLOUD WORD BANK.
4. Follow the same procedure as the students share. Be sure to encourage them to share

the reasons for their associations. (If a student does not offer the word cloud, at some point intervene by sharing that word.)

5. As a way of introducing the book, tell students that just as cotton balls remind us of different things, sometimes when people look at clouds they are reminded of different things.

6. Read the book.

7. Before the second reading, underline CL in the title on the COTTON WORD BANK. Pronounce the sound. Students echo. Tell students that including the title they will hear that sound thirty times in words in the book (the word *cloud* is used twenty-eight times in addition to the words *close* and *clown*). Tell students you want their help saying it. Give a signal, perhaps by lifting your cotton ball, to invite their help.

8. Underline OU in cloud. Pronounce its sound. Students echo.

9. Underline TT in *little*. Pronounce its sound. Students echo.

10. Introduce the concept of syllables. Tell students that sometimes a word is divided or broken up into smaller parts that we call syllables. Pronounce the word *cloud*. Pronounce the word *little*. Clap once for cloud; clap twice for little. Give students other words from the book to clap out the syllables: *sky, sight, shark, rabbit, huddle*. Depending upon the level of students, you may share one or more of the generalizations about syllabication.

EXTENSION

1. Students do finger-painting with white and light blue paints (show the end pages as an example).

2. When they are finished with their finger-painting and as the sheets are drying, call students back to the CLOUD WORD BANK. Read through all their offerings. Then show them how Eric Carle cut out his finger-painting (end pages) into the different shapes used throughout the book (hat, trees, and so forth).

3. Brainstorm other objects or animals not used in the book such as: *cat, car, ball, chicken*, and so forth. Each student chooses an object to draw on and cut out of his or her finger-painting. This can be an opportunity for thinking and oral language experiences. Again, encourage students to talk about their connections.

4. Students return to their places to draw and cut out their objects.

5. Distribute darker blue paper. Students glue their cloud objects or animals onto the paper.

6. Give them a sentence starter: Little Cloud changed into....

RELATED BOOKS

The Cloud Book by Tomie dePaola introduces the ten most common categories of clouds, myths about clouds, and how people can tell about the weather by studying the clouds.

1. Read the book and make a list of the ten types of clouds. To make this easy, demonstrate how to use the "Cloud Index" in the back of the book. Students choose one type of cloud and do research to find something other than what de Paola wrote. Two examples: Cumulus clouds are usually associated with fair weather. Cirrus clouds are made of ice crystals.

2. Students go outside with their notebooks to look at the clouds. They write down as

many shapes as they see.

3. Working in small groups, students write a myth about the clouds–how they came to be or what they could see or tell by them. This could be connected with the study of myths.

Cloudy with a Chance of Meatballs by Judi Barrett is a silly book about clouds, rain, and how the residents of Chewandswallow respond to their unique weather. It discusses what happens when their "weather" goes out of control.

1. Since this is such a silly book, model writing on chart paper a silly book called "Cloudy with a Chance of _____." Students suggest the last word of the title, for example: soda pop, black-eyed peas, chicken soup. Then they help write the story.

2. After writing a story together, students write their own version of "Cloudy with a Chance of _____" story.

Cloud Nine by Norman Silver plays on the idiom "to be on Cloud Nine" because Armstrong, a young boy who finds his house too noisy, builds a ladder up to the clouds where he enjoys the quiet.

1. After reading the book, provide a list of sayings about clouds and together infer the meanings:
   - every cloud has a silver lining;
   - to cast a cloud over something;
   - to be under a cloud;
   - to be on Cloud Nine;
   - to have a cloud lifted from over someone;
   - wait till the clouds roll by.

2. Students, working in pairs, create their own sayings about the clouds. One first-grade student wrote, "When you do numbers, sometimes clouds get in your head."

For an ancillary non-fiction book, Claire Llewellyn's *Why Do We Have Wind and Rain?* contains two chapters on clouds and many references to clouds.

1. Students conduct an experiment to see how water droplets in clouds become rain.
   - Fill an eye dropper with water.
   - Hold a coffee can lid with its bottom side up.
   - Squeeze several drops of water on the lid.
   - Turn the lid over and use a pencil point or some other pointed object to move the droplets together. Do this quickly.
   - As the droplets join other droplets and get bigger, they fall.

2. Talk about how the coffee can lid is like a cloud, collecting droplets until it gets so full the water falls to earth as rain. (For more of these kid-friendly experiments, see Janice Van Cleave's *Earth Science for Every Kid: 101 Easy Experiments that Really Work*.)

PUBLISHING

Cover the ceiling of the room (or one section of it) with blue tissue paper and white tissue paper to represent the sky and clouds. Make a mobile from a white coat hanger which says WE'RE LITTLE CLOUDS WHO KNOW OUR SOUNDS!

ONE ZILLION VALENTINES

Mulberry

Frank Modell

PHONICS CONCEPT:
• V Consonant Sound: Fricative as in *Valentine*

LANGUAGE ARTS CONCEPTS:
• Capital letters;
• Adjectives (describing words)

Artifacts: Valentine cards
Summary: Marvin and Milton make Valentines for everybody in the neighborhood, and they get a Valentine reward for their efforts.

READING/WRITING CONNECTION

1. On white chart paper, make a large curved V with a red marker. Pronounce the name of the letter and make its sound. Remind students that since they create some friction in the mouth when they say this letter, it is called a fricative because something gets in the way of the breath coming out of the lungs. Show students how the lower lip touches the upper teeth to make the V sound. Students make the sound.

2. With the red marker make a heart out of the red V. Write the words *Valentine, even, love* inside the heart. This becomes the VALENTINE WORD BANK.

3. Ask students to find the V sound. Talk about how one V sound is at the beginning of the word, one is in the medial position, and the V in love is considered in the final position because the E is silent.

4. Read the title of the book. Point again to the word *Valentine*. Ask them why the V in this word is larger than the other letters in the word. Students find the other capital letters in the title.

5. Ask students how many make a zillion. Help them know we use this word when we mean too many to count. Looking at the picture on the cover, ask students to predict the story. Ask if Marvin and Milton really have a zillion Valentines in their boxes and wagons.

6. With this prereading completed, read the book.

7. Upon rereading, highlight the word *Valentine* with highlighter tape. Count the number of times it is used. (20 times) Marvin's name is used repeatedly, and there are other words such as *everybody, never, ever, even*, and *favorite* which contain the V consonant sound and could be highlighted. Write these words on the VALENTINE WORD BANK so students can listen for them. Pronounce them and invite students to echo.

8. Distribute large pieces of white paper. Ask the students to describe the Valentines in the book, for example: skinny, polka dot, and so forth. Write their descriptions

on the VALENTINE WORD BANK. With their red or pink crayons, students draw the hearts they described all over the paper. They make each heart by beginning with the letter V. Also, use this as a way to teach descriptive words (adjectives).
- big hearts;
- little hearts;
- skinny hearts;
- fat hearts;
- polka-dot hearts;
- striped hearts;

9. When they are finished, they fold the paper so the hearts are on the outside. Students write a Valentine's Day message inside. Talk about appropriate messages, but remind students they must use the word *Valentine*.
10. Students share their Valentine's Day cards in the Author's Chair before sending or giving them to someone. One kindergarten student wrote:

   2 Momi   MI litle hart Ur big hart

EXTENSIONS

Since Marvin and Milton sold their cards, this book lends itself to a mathematics activity.

1. Divide the students into groups of three. Distribute five three-inch hearts: one red, two purple, and two pink. Students count the hearts and identify the colors.
2. Read the following word problem: "Maria bet Jesse he couldn't build a pole of hearts using five hearts and five clues. Jesse did. Can you? Here are the clues:
   - No hearts of the same color are next to each other.
   - The top heart is not pink.
   - The heart in the center is not red.
   - One pink heart is just below a red one.
   - The bottom heart is not pink."
3. Distribute additional hearts and white paper. Students make up another design and glue their designs on the paper. They write their clues on the paper.

RELATED BOOKS

One Very Best Valentine's Day by Joan W. Blos is a delightfully warm story about how Barbara turns the disappointment of her broken bracelet into Valentines for her entire family.

1. Students identify the colors of the hearts on the end pages; they also count the hearts.
2. This is a good book for predicting. Ask the students what they think Barbara will do after her bracelet breaks. Ask them to predict her secret.
3. Students make Valentine bracelets by gluing the candy hearts in a circle on pink paper.
4. When they come to share, students tell to whom they would give each of the hearts.

Love Bugs by David A. Carter is a delightful Valentine pop-up book.
1. Give each student an artificial rose and two small plastic eyes.
2. Students glue the eyes on the rose petals and make a nose and smile with marker

using the roses in the book as a model.

3. They write a message on a pink index card and attach it to the stem of the rose.

The Valentine Star by Patricia Reilly Giff tells about the kids in Ms. Rooney's room making cards for the Valentine box. This is one of "The Kids of the Polk Street School" series. Couple this with *Nate the Great and the Mushy Valentine* by Marjorie Weinman Sharmat for two excellent books to recommend for the independent reader.

In *Roses Are Pink, Your Feet Really Stink* by Diane de Groat, Gilbert learns a valuable lesson about writing nice and nasty poems in Valentine's Day cards for his classmates.

1. Students practice writing nice poems to their classmates for Valentine's Day.
2. Get cookies that are shaped like hearts and say "Happy Valentine's Day!" Give one to each student after he or she identifies the V, makes the V consonant sound, and reads the message.

Cranberry Valentine by Wende and Harry Devlin tells how the sewing circle at Cranberryport made Mr. Whiskers happy by sending secret Valentine's Day cards.

1. This is a good story to practice predicting skills. When reading, stop often to ask students to predict who is sending Mr. Whiskers Valentine's Day cards.
2. Provide students with ribbon, lace, and plenty of pink, red, and white paper so they can make fancy cards. When they complete the card, put a dot of perfume on each card.

Eve Bunting's *The Valentine Bears* is a sweet story about how Mrs. Bear plans a Valentine's Day surprise celebration for Mr. Bear. Students learn about hibernation; find out what bears eat; make up other "treats" besides chocolate-covered ants and sweet termites.

Arthur's Valentine by Marc Brown, a favorite of young readers, follows the secret admirer theme.

1. Students, like those in Arthur's class, each make a Valentine box.
2. On Valentine's Day, give each student a kiss—the kind Arthur gave Francine—chocolate.

Arthur's Great Big Valentine by Lillian Hoban is a level 2 "I Can Read Book" in which Arthur and his friend Norman have a falling out but make up with special Valentines.

1. Divide students into small groups. Distribute candy hearts to each group.
2. Students use the hearts as math counters, using them to do calculations.

PUBLISHING

Create a display of all the students work on Valentines. Make a red banner with white letters and lots of hearts that proclaims V is for VICTORY and VALENTINE'S DAY.

RAISING DRAGONS

Harcourt Brace

Jerdine Nolen

PHONICS CONCEPTS:
- DR Consonant Sound: DR Blend as in *DRagon;*
- A Vowel Sound: Short A as in *drAgon;*
- G Consonant Sound: Guttural Sound as in *draGon;*
- O Vowel Sound: Short O as in *dragOn;*
- N Consonant Sound as in *dragoN*

LANGUAGE ARTS CONCEPTS:
- Prediction;
- Elements of a narrative: characters, setting, plot, problem, and solution

Phonics Friendly Books
103

Artifacts: Neon dragons in assorted colors (available from U. S. Toy)
Summary: This is a story about a young farmer's daughter who raises a dragon from the time it cracks out of its egg. This wonderful adventure is punctuated with love, loyalty, and the joys of the unexpected.

READING/WRITING CONNECTION

1. Show the book's cover. Ask students to identify the creature they see. Ask them to describe it. Talk about dragons, stories they have heard or read about them. Help students realize dragons come to us from mythology and usually represent everything from fear to good fortune. (Point of information: *dragon* comes from the Greek word *drakon* meaning "to see" or "to watch" which is probably why dragons so often watch or guard over castles and royalty.)
2. Write the title on board or chart.
3. Underline the DR blend. Pronounce it. Students echo.
4. Point to each letter in the word *dragon*. Identify each letter. Pronounce each sound. Students echo.
5. Put all the sounds together and help students see how this sounding out of letters helps them read whole words. Use the comparison of a big rubberband that stretches and then comes together tight and taut.

6. Next, check comprehension. Be sure that the students know what the words *raising* and *dragon* mean. Ask, "If a baby dragon appeared in a story, would the people in the story be afraid?" Talk about that.
7. Show the end pages. Ask students to describe what they see. Students make predictions about the dragon on the cover. Ask students why there are volcanoes on the title page.
8. Read the story, showing each page and giving students ample time to study the pictures and to talk about what they see.
9. Use this story as an opportunity to talk about taking care of pets; talk about responsibility; talk about losing a pet or something or someone you love.
10. Distribute the artifacts and a large index card. Students write the word *dragon* at the top of the card. Under *dragon*, they write as many words as they can find or think of that begin with the DR blend.

EXTENSIONS

1. On chart paper, begin the story. Read the first two sentences in several books to help the students think of a good opener.
   • Nudge them into characters, setting, action or plot, problem, and solution.
   • After the collective story is written, divide students into four groups.
2. Students create a story mural.
   • Give students old newsprint to spread out in their working area.
   • Give them plenty of tissue paper and watercolor paint.
   • Model how to carefully paint the tissue paper using a variety of colors.
   • Students paint the tissue paper.
   • Attach a long piece of beige or tan butcher paper horizontally along a wall. Explain that this will serve as the background for a mural they are about to make.
   • Begin this project by asking students to write a story with you about a dragon.
   • One group draws the characters and cuts them out of their painted tissue paper.
   • One group designs the setting(s) and makes sets out of their painted tissue paper.
   • One group figures a way to show the problem (which will probably be the dragon) by cutting their painted tissue paper.
   • One group creates the solution by cutting it from their painted tissue paper.
   • Students adhere their cut-outs to the mural, under teacher supervision, so that the art matches the story.

RELATED BOOKS

Eric Carle's Dragons Dragons & Other Creatures that Never Were compiled by Laura Whipple contains poetry on mythical animals from "The Manticore" to "Centaurs."
1. Students in small groups create a make-believe animal. They may draw it or use other materials such as Styrofoam™, odds and ends of fabrics, string, and so forth.
2. They name their imaginary animal.
3. They write a poem about their mythical animal.

The Secret in the Matchbox by Val Willis matches the imaginary secret with an imaginary dragon who grows with the tale.
1. Distribute empty matchboxes.
2. Students decorate the matchboxes.
3. Brainstorm secrets that could be placed in the matchboxes.
4. Students choose one from the list and write about it.

Komodo! by Peter Sis includes actual factual information about the Komodo dragon in this fanciful tale of a young boy who loves dragons. He goes with his parents to the Indonesian island of Komodo in hopes of seeing a real dragon.
1. Students find the island of Komodo in Indonesia on a map or globe in the classroom using the map in the book.
2. Use this book to help students distinguish between fiction and non-fiction.

Max's Dragon Shirt by Rosemary Wells (complete with a free iron-on decal), describes a shopping expedition undertaken by Ruby, Max's sister, in order to buy him pants. From the outset Max wants a dragon shirt and he ultimately gets one.
1. Use the double-page spread of the store to encourage students to talk about what they see, if they can find Max and Ruby, and what it's like when they go shopping.
2. Students design a dragon shirt.

Elvira by Margaret Shannon is the story of a young female dragon who wants to dress like a princess. Since the word *dragon* is used repeatedly throughout the book, it reinforces this sound.

The trio of books about Elmer Elevator and the flying baby dragon, *Elmer and the Dragon, My Father's Dragon,* and *The Dragons of Blueland* by Ruth Stiles Gannett, make wonderful books for the independent reader interested in dragons.

PUBLISHING

Students invite parents, friends, other teachers, and administrators to the "premiere showing of their story mural." In a way designated by the teacher, students read their story and point to the accompanying art. Above the mural, place a banner: A DRAGON DRAMA!

SATURDAY NIGHT AT THE DINOSAUR STOMP

Candlewick

Carol Diggory Shields

PHONICS CONCEPT:
• AU Vowel Sound: Broad O as in *dinosAUr*

LANGUAGE ARTS CONCEPTS:
• Predicting rhyming words;
• Common and proper nouns: dinosaur, Tyrannosaurus Rex;
• Lower case and capital letters

Artifacts: 6" Vinyl Bendable Dinosaur Assortment (available from Oriental Trading Co.)
Summary: It is rock-and-roll time in prehistoric times. All the dinosaurs gather to twist, twirl, tromp, and stomp. Written in rhyme, this book delightfully conveys the names of different dinosaurs, their characteristics, and the names of different prehistoric periods.

READING/WRITING CONNECTION

1. Before beginning this lesson, make a 3' DINOSAUR WORD BANK out of green paper. Write the word DINOSAUR on it and underline the AU. Display it in the front of the room.
2. Distribute percussion instruments to the students. Tell them they are going to softly beat out the rhythm of the book you are about to read. Model how they are to tap the instruments. (If there are no instruments available, students may clap their hands or tap their pencils on desks or tables.)
3. Open the book fully so students can see the entire scene. Ask them to describe what is going on. Read the title. Talk about the word *stomp*. Tell students that one of its meanings is to dance.
4. Read the book through in rhythm. (Practice beforehand to achieve the full effect of the book's rhyme and rhythm.)
5. Before the second reading, point out the AU vowel sound in the word dinosaur. Help students hear it as a broad O. Students repeat the sound.
6. Tell students every time they hear the AU sound, they are to raise their hands and you will write that word on the DINOSAUR WORD BANK. You want them to help you spell it each time.
7. Distinguish between the word *dinosaur* and the names of specific dinosaurs. Point out that the word *dinosaur* begins with a lower case letter whereas the special or specific names of dinosaurs begin with a capital letters. Draw parallels between their names and just being called a girl or boy. Draw parallels between the word teacher and your name. When the book is finished, together reread the names of the dinosaurs.

8. Students will count the word *dinosaur* twelve times (teachable time to use the word *dozen*). They will read the following specific names with the AU broad O sound: *Plesiosaurus, Maiasaur, Ultrasaurus, Ankylosaurus, Allosaurus, Stegosaur, Brontosaurus, Tyrannosaurus Rex,* and *Carnosaurs.*

9. Distribute the bendable dinosaurs and paper. Students bend their dinosaurs in different positions as if they were dancing.

10. Students write about what happens when their dinosaur goes to the Dinosaur Stomp! Encourage them to refer to the DINOSAUR WORD BANK for correct spellings.

EXTENSIONS

1. Show students the end pages. Challenge them to figure out what is pictured there. (dinosaur dance steps)

2. Use these steps as a motor skill development lesson. Students move their bodies, heads, arms, and legs to the rhythm of the reading. Play a variety of music which may include Beethoven's *Symphony Number Five* for its opening measures to approximate the coming of the dinosaurs, San Souci's *Carnival of the Animals* for its different tempos, some rock-and-roll favorite such as the *Twist* by Chubby Checker, and a Western stomp such as *Cotton-Eyed-Joe.*

3. Reread the book. When you come to a rhyming word, stop. Ask the students to supply a word that might fit.

RELATED BOOKS

The Dinosaurs Are Back and It's All Your Fault Edward! by Wendy Hartmann and Niki Daly is an unusual and funny book about the imagination of two brothers. Engrossed in a dinosaur book at bedtime, Edward becomes more and more nervous about dinosaurs lurking about because of his big brother's teasing.

1. Since this is a "what if..." story, begin by inviting oral speculation about "What if you found a dinosaur egg under your bed? What if it hatched?"

2. Students write a story about what would happen.

The *Dinosaur's Paw* by Patricia Reilly Giff is another great Polk Street School book for the independent reader. It is about dinosaur day, a ruler with dinosaur's initials, and how Richard deals with the missing ruler. These books are designed to entertain and enlighten young people and encourage the independent reader with high-interest text.

Four fine non-fiction books about dinosaurs:
• Patricia Lauber's *How Dinosaurs Came to Be* tells about important events that led up to the age of dinosaurs; this book contains an index.
• Donald Silver's *Extinction Is Forever* speculates why dinosaurs disappeared from the face of the Earth.
• Don Lessem's two books *Seismosaurus: The Longest Dinosaur* and *Utahraptor: The Deadliest Dinosaur* explore specific dinosaurs as well as the scientific and archaeological research that led to their findings.

Noelle Sterne's *Tyrannosaurus Wrecks: A Book of Dinosaur Riddles* is filled with language that plays on the characteristics of dinosaurs. This is a wonderful motivator for students to try their hand at writing riddles.

Bernard Most's *Where to Look for a Dinosaur* not only invites connections with social studies, as all the dinosaurs mentioned in the book are globally placed, but it also contains an extensive list of museums that count dinosaurs in their holdings.

PUBLISHING

Celebrate DINOSAUR DAY! Display a wide assortment of dinosaur books and the bendable dinosaurs dancing at the stomp. Play dinosaur music and let the students dance like dinosaurs and keep the rhythm with percussion instruments. At the conclusion of the celebration, students read their papers about what happens when their dinosaurs went to the Dinosaur Stomp!

TWELVE SNAILS TO ONE LIZARD: A TALE OF MISCHIEF AND MEASUREMENT

Simon & Schuster

Susan Hightower

PHONICS CONCEPTS:
- TW Consonant Sound: TW Blend as in *TWelve* (initial and medial positions)
- AI Vowel Sound: Long A as in *snAIl;*
- *Generalization:*
    THE FIRST VOWEL IS USUALLY LONG AND THE SECOND SILENT IN THE DIGRAPHS AI, EA, OA, UI.

LANGUAGE ARTS CONCEPTS:
- Measurements in words; reading measurements;
- Inference

Artifacts: 12" Plastic OUR EARTH ® WIGGLE RULERS (available from Oriental Trading Co.)
Summary: Milo the beaver wants to build a dam. He receives help from Bubba the bullfrog who explains the concepts of inches, feet, and yards.

READING/WRITING CONNECTION

1. After gathering the students around, hold up a yardstick and identify it. Ask students to look closely and tell what they see on the yardstick. When they say "numbers" have them count as you point to each number. Use the yardstick to draw a line down the middle of chart paper.
2. Write the words *two* and *twelve* on the board or chart. Say these numbers.
3. Ask students what they see in these words that is the same. Underline the TW. Tell students that TW makes a sound like a bird's twitter. Make the sound. Students echo. Write TW at the top of one column. Write the words *twitter* and *twelve* under it. Read the words. Students echo.
4. Ask students if they can think of any other TW words. They may suggest words such as: *twenty, twice, twig, twins, twilight, twelfth,* and so forth. Add to list.
5. Stand two students together; stand between them. Add the word between to the list. Show students the TW sound in this word is in the medial position. Add to list.
6. Show students the book. Ask if anyone can find the TW sound in the title. Ask if anyone can read the word. Add it to the list.
7. Tell students there is another sound you want them to listen for in the title. Tell them that sometimes the two vowels A and I sound like the letter A saying its own name.

8. Begin another list. Label it AI. Write words such as *ail, aim, aid, rain,* saying each word and exaggerating the AI sound. Ask students for onsets for these words. Add to list such words as: *train, tail, pain, sail, nail,* and so forth.
9. Read the book showing the measurements on the yardstick that Bubba talks about.
10. Distribute the rulers along with several different size sheets of paper to students. Students measure the paper and write the numbers on the paper. Advanced students may also write the measurement in words. Share.

EXTENSIONS

Measurement
1. Collect an assortment of boxes: cereal boxes, shoe boxes, crayon boxes, lunch boxes, and various other boxes that come from the grocery store.
2. Divide students into four groups. Give each group several different size boxes.
3. Using their rulers, students measure all the sides of the boxes. Advanced students may add up all the sides to arrive at the surface area. Share results.
4. Talk about how much easier it was for Milo the beaver to use the yardstick than to line up snails, iguanas, or a boa constrictor.
5. Use the measurement facts in the back of the book to reinforce concepts found in the book.
6. Take time to measure things such as the desk top, the board, the door using their hands or things. Then measure the same things using the yardstick. Reinforce the ease of using a standard measurement device.

Reading Skills: Inference
1. Use the four wordless double-page spreads with four pictures each to sow the seeds of inference skills.
2. Students examine each picture and orally recount what is happening.
3. Students connect what is happening in the wordless pictures to the context of the story.

RELATED BOOK

Twilight Comes Twice by Ralph Fletcher describes dusk and dawn in poetic prose. It also describes various activities that take place between those two times.
1. Show the cover of the book. Challenge students to find the TW sound in the title.
2. Ask if someone can read the title.
3. Write the word *dusk* on one end of the board. Tell students that is the name for *twilight* in the evening.
4. Write the word *dawn* on the other end of the board. Tell students that is the name for *twilight* in the morning.
5. Explain that this book is about those two times.
6. Students render landscapes of dusk and dawn using watercolors or pastels.

PUBLISHING

Under a banner which reads WE CAN TWITTER AND TWEET LIKE BIRDS ABOUT OUR TW AND AI SOUNDS!

LILLY'S PURPLE PLASTIC PURSE

Greenwillow

Kevin Henkes

PHONICS CONCEPTS:
- PL Consonant Sound: PL Blend as in *purPLe* and *PLastic;*
- L Consonant Sound: Liquid as in *LiLLy;*
- UR Vowel Sound: R Sound as in *pURple, pURse;*
- *Generalization:*
  WHEN A VOWEL IS FOLLOWED BY R, THE R INFLUENCES THE VOWEL SOUND.
- P Consonant Sound: Plosive as in *Purple, Purse;*
- A Vowel Sound: Short A as in *plAstic*

LANGUAGE ARTS CONCEPT:
- Main character in a book or story

Artifacts: Purple paper purses, wallets, backpacks

Summary: Lilly loves everything about school. After going shopping with Grammy, Lilly brings to school: a pair of movie star sunglasses, three shiny quarters, and a brand new purple plastic purse that plays a tune when opened. She wants to show these to her classmates immediately, but Mr. Slinger, the teacher, asks her to wait. She does not. Therein lies the lesson and the story.

READING/WRITING CONNECTION

1. Begin by encouraging students to talk about how they feel when they get something new. Ask if they get excited about some new things more than other new things. Talk about that. At some point, if students have not already brought up sharing in school, lead them to consider it. You might say, "Sometimes after I get something new and share it with my family and friends, I want to bring it to school and share it with my friends here and with you. Do you?"

2. If the students know other books by Henkes, review them. Talk about how they always have a strong main character. Remind them of his character Lilly. Encourage students to tell you what they remember about Lilly. If the students do not know other books by Henkes, tell them that the main character they are about to meet

lives in two other books by the same author (*Chester's Way* and *Julius, the Baby of the World*). And she may appear again.

3. Write the title on the board or chart.
   - Underline all the Ls in *Lilly*. Tell students this sound is called a liquid because it seems to flow on or around the tongue like water instead of being clicked like the TIC in *plastic* or popped or hissed like the P and S in *purse*.
   - Make the L sound. Show students how the tongue goes to the roof of the mouth behind the top teeth when making this sound. Students echo.
   - Teach the P sound. Tell students it is called a plosive because when you say it, it explodes. Say the sound. Students echo.
   - Put the P sound and L sound together: a tiny explosion followed by the tongue to the roof of the mouth behind the top teeth. Make the sound. Students echo.
   - Teach the UR sound. Make the sound. Students echo.
   - Teach the short A sound. Make the sound. Students echo.
   - Students put all the sounds together to read the title of the book.
4. After they read the title, talk about what the words mean.
5. Students study the pictures of Lilly and make predictions about the book.
6. If possible, get glittery glasses and Lilly's purse (available from MerryMakers or from children's book stores) to use as props when you read the story.
7. After reading the book, have available purple paper in a variety of hues, weights, and sizes. Also have the small brass-colored brads, buttons, lace, and odds and ends students may use to make their own purple plastic purses, wallets, or backpacks.
8. As students work, distribute plain white paper.
9. When students complete their task, they write to Lilly on the white paper. It may be a letter, story, essay, a persuasive writing that their purple purse, wallet, or backpack is the best, or they may write her directions on how to make a purse, wallet, or backpack.
10. Students place their writing inside and display their purses, wallets, or backpacks somewhere in the room.

EXTENSIONS

Main Character.
1. Bring in a Lilly doll (also available from MerryMaker, or from children's book stores). Show students the doll. Talk about the way Lilly is dressed. Put some small piece of writing in her purse, one you could invite a student to open during the lesson, perhaps a note that would generate more thought, more talk, "Do you like the color purple?" (If a Lilly doll is unavailable, do this with a purse, wallet, or backpack you have constructed out of paper.)
2. Tell students when a book or story revolves around one character or is mostly about one character, we say that is the main character of the book. Lilly is the main character in this book.
3. Ask students if they can think of main characters in other books they are reading. They may say the hungry caterpillar or the grouchy ladybug. Extend them to characters with first and/or last names such as Rosie Rabbit or Koala Lou.
4. Receive all student responses.

Music.
1. Since Lilly's purse plays "Twinkle, Twinkle, Little Star," write a verse on board or

chart. Students identify the L sound in the song's title. If they have studied the TW, they also identify the TW.

2. Students compose a "Twinkle Twinkle..." with the new sounds they have learned.
   For example: Twinkle twinkle little bell
                    You make the sound of liquid L
                    In other words you sound so swell
                    Knowing you makes us yell!

RELATED BOOKS

1. One way to instill the notion of a corpus of work by an author is by sharing many books by that author. In this case, each of Henkes's books reinforces the concept of main character:
   • *Sheila Rae the Brave* tells how Sheila Rae, who boasts of her fearlessness, learns a lesson from her sister Louise.
   • *Grandpa & Bo* recounts the closeness between a grandfather and his grandson.
   • *Owen* captures the stubbornness of a child who doesn't want to give up his blanket.
   • *Chrysanthemum* loves her name until her classmates make fun of it.
   • *A Weekend with Wendell* chronicles Wendell's stay with Sophie which starts off one way and ends up another way.
   • *Bailey Goes Camping* is about Bailey who is not yet a Bunny Scout but gets to eat hot dogs and do all the camping things because his parents understand.
   • *Jessica* is Ruthie's pretend playmate until she goes to kindergarten and meets a real Jessica.
   • *Chester's Way* is about how Chester and Wilson share the same way of doing things until Lilly moves into the neighborhood and teaches them some new tricks.
   • *Julius, the Baby of the World* describes how Lilly treats her new baby brother.
2. In each of these books there is a strong, easily identified main character. Students will be able to see how the story centers on that character. If students are ready, the concept of minor characters may also be introduced.
3. A C.A.S.P.A.R. Chart may be used after reading one or each of these books.
   • Divide a long sheet of butcher paper into six sections. Label each section with each of the letters that spells out C.A.S.P.A.R.
   • Under C, students tell you the characters: main characters; minor characters.
   • Under A, record adjectives, words that describe the characters.
   • Under S, write down the setting, where the story takes place.
   • Under P, put the problem.
   • Skip A at this point.
   • Under R, tell how the story ends, the resolution or solution to the problem.
   • Go back to A, record the actions that bring about the solution.

PUBLISHING

On "Lilly's Purple Purse Day" everyone goes shopping. Each student chooses someone else's creation, takes it back to their place, reads what is inside, responds, and returns the purse, wallet, or backpack to its original owner. Eventually, all the creations are displayed again under the title: WE LOVE THE SOUND OF PURPLE!

WATERMELON DAY

Henry Holt

Kathi Appelt

PHONICS CONCEPTS:

- W Consonant Sound as in *Watermelon;*
- AY Vowel Sound, Vowel Digraph: Long A Sound or Long Vowel Digraph as in *dAY;*
- *Generalization:*
    IN AY, THE Y IS SILENT AND GIVES A ITS LONG SOUND.

LANGUAGE ARTS CONCEPT:

- Similes

Artifacts: Fresh pieces of watermelon and watermelon stationery or watermelon stickers

Summary: Jesse waits all summer for her watermelon to ripen. When it does, Pappy cuts it from its vine and sets it in the cold lake water. Later, when the relatives arrive, everyone celebrates "A Watermelon Day!"

READING/WRITING CONNECTION

1. Make a 2' slice of watermelon out of pink butcher paper to make a WATERMELON WORD BANK. Add seeds with black marker and rind with green marker. Hang it near where you will gather the students.
2. Bring in a large watermelon. Place it where you intend to read to the students.
3. The sight of it will cause students to comment and conjecture, so this provides a great opportunity for oral language.
4. Encourage students to share how they feel about eating watermelon, when they usually eat it, how they eat it, or if they eat it. Encourage students to share stories that relate to watermelons: growing one, picking one out, buying one or more, picnics or parties where watermelon was served, and so forth. Write these responses on the WATERMELON WORD BANK.
5. Before reading the book, ask students to think what a "Watermelon Day" might be. Write "Watermelon Day" on the WATERMELON WORD BANK and on the real watermelon. Receive all responses.
6. Tell students Kathi Appelt is an author who wrote about a watermelon day. Show them the book and read the title. Write the title on the paper watermelon. Underline the W and the AY. Pronounce the W sound. Students echo. Pronounce the AY sound. Students echo. Tell students it makes the same sound as A saying its own name, long A and the Y is silent.

7. Ask a volunteer to write the title on the watermelon. Ask for volunteers to underline the W and the AY. Pronounce the W sound. Students echo. Pronounce the AY sound. Invite the students to listen for these sounds as you read the story.

8. Be sure to begin the reading with the title page. As is the case with most contemporary children's literature, the story often begins before the first page. In this book the title page is replete with inference. Talk about the double-page spread on the copyright and dedication pages.

9. After the story, cut the real watermelon and give each student a piece of watermelon and a watermelon shaped paper or regular paper with a watermelon sticker on it.

10. Students write about a watermelon day they have experienced or they may plan a watermelon day. Encourage them to refer to the WATERMELON WORD BANK. Share.

EXTENSIONS

Social Studies.
1. Since watermelon is native to Africa, find Africa on a map or globe.
2. Since watermelon grows in tropical, subtropical, and temperate regions. Show these regions on the map or globe and explain in simple terms the range of heat associated with those regions. Knowing that, ask students to examine the map or globe and speculate about where watermelons are not grown.

Mathematics.
1. Cut the watermelon. Use each cut to reinforce the concepts of whole, half, quarter, eighths.
2. Students keep the seeds from their pieces of watermelon and glue them on pink index cards. Each student counts his or her seeds and writes the number on the card.
3. Graph the seeds in the watermelon according to the cards.

Language Arts.
1. This book is filled with apt similes. Explain that sometimes authors compare one thing to another so readers will better understand or get better pictures (images) in their heads as they are reading. Tell the students that authors use the words *like* or *as* to signal a comparison. Depending on level, you may introduce the word *similes*.
2. Write "not as big as her fist" on the board or chart. Invite students to make a fist with their hands. Ask them which gives them a better, clearer picture of the size of the watermelon, the comparison, "It was not as big as her fist, but it was bigger than the other melons..." or just saying, "It was small."
3. Reenter the book. Write each simile on the WATERMELON WORD BANK. After each, talk about how much clearer the comparison makes the reading. Encourage students to try similes when they are writing so their readers will get a clear pictures in their minds.

Science.
1. Watermelons are part of the gourd family. Bring in other species for exhibit: pumpkin, summer squashes, winter squashes, cucumbers, gherkins, all melons.
2. After examining the gourds, encourage students to generalize about what makes an edible plant a gourd.

Art.

1. Students make papier-mâché watermelons of different sizes.
2. They write similes, comparing the size of their watermelons to something else. For example, students have written:

   Mine is as big as a dinosaur.

   My watermelon is as little as my foot.

   Our watermelon takes up as much space as the globe.

Music.

1. Jesse hears the sweet song of her watermelon. Later she sings a watermelon song. Divide the students into small groups to make up a watermelon song.
2. Each group sings its song.

   • One group made their song fit the tune "Deep in the Heart of Texas." While digging up watermelons is suspect, these students sang their watermelon song with gusto.

   The watermelons we dig are ripe and big

   Deep in the summer of Texas.

   Reminds us of other melons we love

   Deep in the summer of Texas.

RELATED BOOKs

The Enormous Watermelon, retold by Brenda Parks and Judith Smith, places Old Mother Hubbard in the garden planting a watermelon seed. When the watermelon is ready to be picked, it has grown so enormous that she calls other nursery-rhyme characters to help her pick it.

1. As you read the book, encourage students to examine the clues and predict the next nursery-rhyme character.
2. Reread the book many times so the students may join in on the repetitions and reinforce the sound/letter correspondences in the words.
3. Point out how the red print and the two marks (called quotation marks) mean that Old Mother Hubbard is talking. Tell them that the two marks are like two lips. They show when someone begins to talk and when someone finishes talking.
4. Read those parts in an Old Mother Hubbard voice.

Walk with a Wolf by Janni Howker takes the reader into the world of wolves to follow a lone female wolf as she hunts, howls to her pack, and greets her cubs and mate. This book is replete with the W consonant sound and will reinforce learning the sound.

PUBLISHING

Make a watermelon patch. Place the papier-mâché watermelons, books, pictures, students' writing, real watermelons in and around the vines, leaves, and tendrils. On one vine write: WE KNOW THE W AND AY SOUNDS. THEY HELP MAKE WATERMELON MUSIC. Celebrate WATERMELON DAY! Invite other classes, parents, administrators, and friends and family to visit the watermelon patch and share in its delights!

THE GHOST-EYE TREE

Henry Holt

Bill Martin, Jr. and John Archambault

PHONICS CONCEPTS:
• G Consonant Sound: Guttural as in *Ghost;*
• GH: Silent H as in *gHost;*
• *Generalization:*
  WHEN THE LETTERS GH BEGIN A WORD, THE H IS SILENT AND THE G TAKES THE HARD GUTTURAL SOUND.

LANGUAGE ARTS CONCEPT:
• Setting in a story

Artifacts: Thin branches and twigs with one or two leaves on them
Summary: Told in rhyme in the first person, the narrator and his sister Ellie run an errand for their Mama and encounter the Ghost-eye tree.

READING/WRITING CONNECTION

1. Show students the book's dust jacket as you read the title and authors. Ask students what the word ghost means (remind them of Casper).
2. Point to the GH in the title.
   • Tell students that an easy way to remember the sound GH makes at the beginning of a word is to think of ghost.
   • Tell students that the G sounds hard because the sound is made in the throat and sometimes sounds disagreeable like someone afraid of a ghost.
   • You can see the H but you can't hear it. The H in words that begin with GH is as silent as a ghost. All you hear is the G.
   • Pronounce the sound and say the word. Students echo.
3. Read the book. When you get to the Ghost-eye tree, lower your voice to a whisper and read with expression.
4. After completing the book, ask students if they would have gone back for the hat. Talk about why the narrator was so frightened. Ask students to talk about times when something frightened them.
5. Distribute the tiny branches and twigs. Turn the room lights off and the overhead

projector on.

6. In groups of two or three, students become the Ghost-eye tree and slowly wave their branches and twigs in front of the light to produce a scary effect. Introduce the word *shadow*. As tree shadows, they may even make the E, O, OW sounds the tree makes in the book.

7. Talk about the setting in the book and how setting helps tell the story. In this book the setting helps set a "scary" atmosphere. Ask the students what else in the setting, in the time and place of the story, makes it scary. (night, wind blowing, tree branches moving)

8. Talk about the setting in other books.

9. Give students dark grey paper on which they write about a time when they were frightened or about a time when someone else was frightened and they were not.

10. Share in the Author's Chair with the lights off and the author reading by flashlight.

EXTENSIONS

1. Take students deeper into setting. Invite students to speculate about three things: the time of year the story takes place, where it takes place, and the age of the narrator and his sister. When students answer, ask them to find some evidence in the book to support their answer. For example: the fall of the year—no snow yet on the ground, only a few leaves on the trees, the blowing wind, the children wearing coats and hats; the cat looks like a Halloween cat, the moon seems cold, and so forth.

2. Students construct a Ghost-eye tree in the room. By twining big pieces of black butcher paper, they make the trunk. Smaller pieces make the branches. The more spidery they make them, the scarier they look. They may cut out various sizes of leaves from black construction paper. They may put a moon behind the tree on the wall. Finally, they make two eyes out of yellow paper and affix them on the tree.

3. Students choose a branch upon which to hang their writing.

RELATED BOOKS

The Ghost of Sifty Sifty Sam by Angela Shelf Medearis puts a modern and culinary twist on the old folktale of a person agreeing to stay in a supposedly haunted house overnight for a reward.

1. Point out the hard G sound and the silent H in the title. Pronounce the word. Students echo. Read the title.

2. Read this book quickly, with expression, and in rhythm.

3. Use the first and last end pages for the reading skill of inference.

In *The Ghost of Greyfriar's Bobby*, Ruth Brown retells a true tale of a loyal dog in Edinburgh, Scotland.

1. Find Edinburgh, Scotland, on the map or globe.

2. Point out the hard G sound and the silent H in the title. Pronounce the words. Students echo.

3. Read the story and talk about the loyalty of dogs, their pets, and animals in general.

For advanced or older students, use Alice McLerran's *The Ghost Dance*, which is also based on fact. McLerran recounts the story of the Paiute Native Americans, who, in listening to their spiritual leaders, joined together in a sacred dance that was misinterpreted for a war-dance. This misinterpretation ultimately led to the massacre at Wounded Knee.

1. Point out the hard G sound and the silent H in the title.

2. After reading the story, ask students which pictures strike them most and why.

3. Let students reenact the ghost dance. Talk about how it could have been misinterpreted.

Also, older students will enjoy *Ghosts of the White House* by Cheryl Harness. George Washington's ghost pulls a girl out of her school's White House Tour and takes her on a personal tour of the building. He introduces her to the ghosts of previous presidents and to the history of the White House of the United States.

• Use this book to reteach the GH sound and the meaning of the word *ghost*.

• Connect this to social studies.

PUBLISHING

Give students mini magic slates (available from U. S. Toy). They write GH words (*ghost, ghetto, ghastly, ghostly, ghoul*) on their slates and then lift the sheet to remove the words. Talk about letters being there and then disappearing. Connect this to the ghostly H that remains silent. Suspend these gray slates from branches on the tree. Label the entire exhibit OUR GHOST-EYED TREE!

FREIGHT TRAIN

Greenwillow

Donald Crews

PHONICS CONCEPTS:

- GH: Silent Consonants as in *freiGHt;*
- *Generalization:*
    WHEN THE LETTERS GHT APPEAR TOGETHER IN A WORD, THE LETTERS GH ARE SILENT.
- FR Consonant Sound: FR Blend as in *FReight;*
- TR Consonant Sound: TR Blend as in *TRain;*
- T Consonant Sound: Plosive as in *freighT;*
- AI Vowel Sound: Long A as in *trAIn;*
- N Consonant Sound: Nasal as in *traiN*

LANGUAGE ARTS CONCEPT:

- Sequencing

Artifacts: Oversized train whistles (available from U. S. Toy) or Train Counters (available from Lakeshore Learning Materials or from teacher supply stores)

Summary: This simple book traces the route of a train through tunnels, by cities, moving until it is gone. The parts of the train are described by color and function from the black engine to the red caboose.

READING/WRITING CONNECTION

1. Before beginning, make a FREIGHT TRAIN WORD BANK. Display near the reading area.
2. To create a train, line students up in groups of eight, face-to-back.
    - Each student bends his or her arms as if carrying a tray.
    - Except for the first student in line, each student holds the elbows of the student directly in front of him or her.
    - Standing in place, students move their arms back and forth in the manner of train wheels and say in rhythm a slow "Chugga, chugga. Chugga, chugga." Next, students blow their train whistles if you chose that artifact, or they say "Whooo, whooooo!"

3. Use this experience to introduce the book. Open the book so students can see the entire train.

   • Read the title on both the front and back covers. Write it on the Freight Train Word Bank.

   • A volunteer underlines the GH.

   • Cover everything but the FR sound. Say the sound. Students echo.

   • Cover the FR so students see the word *eight*. Ask who can read that number.

   • Pronounce the two preceding sounds together. Students echo.

   • Say the word *freight* with exaggeration. Ask students to listen carefully for its sounds. (They will hear a long A sound and a T plosive.)

   • Ask them what letters they do not hear. (GH)

   • Ask, "When we can't hear letters, what do we call them?" (Silent)

   • Give students the generalization.

   • Write other words with the silent GH on the Freight Train Word Bank for students to read: *night, sight, right, might, slight, straight, weight, freight, flight, blight, bright, fright, height, knight.*

   • Cover AIN and ask students to say the TR blend.

   • Cover the TR and ask students to say the AI long A sound and the N nasal.

   • Students put all the sounds together as you point to each letter reading the title.

4. Point out the Caldecott Medal on the book's cover as an award for illustrations. Give students time to look at the illustrations. Ask for volunteers to identify the colors

5. Ask if students know what each car is called. Some students may know the caboose, tank, engine. Tell students they will learn the names of the other parts of the train in this book.

6. Read the book. Afterwards, challenge students to identify both the color and the name of each car in sequence. Talk about sequence, how things sometimes go in order. Review the order of the train, how things are ordered in class, and so forth. Write these on the Freight Train Word Bank.

7. Return to the title you have written on board or chart. After asking a student to read it again, ask the following questions and write them under the title.

   • What is a freight train? What does it do? What is its purpose?

   • Who has seen a freight train?

   • Who has seen the television show called "Thomas the Train"?

   • What other kinds of trains are there? What do they do? (passenger, Amtrak, express, wagon, train of a dress, to train as in to teach, chain and so forth)

8. Put out seven colors of paper (both the tender and engine are black) so students may choose one of the colors.

9. They draw and cut out the part of the train that corresponds to their paper color.

10. Students write about train. Depending upon level, they write the sounds, the words, what trains do, an experience they had riding a train, a toy train they have, or about train whistles. They arrange these in proper sequence around the room.

EXTENSIONS

1. Obtain foam sheets (available in craft stores) in the seven colors of the cars of the freight train. Cut them into twelve-inch ovals. Cut out a smaller oval to fit the head of each student. These will serve as conductor caps for each student. Older students can make their own caps.

• To create a train, line students up in groups of eight matching their conductor's caps to the order of colors of the freight train's cars.

• Repeat the "Chugga, chugga. Chugga, chugga. Whooo, whooooo!" prereading experience, adding the name of the car, its color, and where it goes. Encourage students to make up destinations. For example:

"Chugga, chugga. Chugga, chugga. Whooo, whooooo!" says the red caboose of the freight train as it goes through tunnels.

"Chugga, chugga. Chugga, chugga. Whooo, whooooo!" says the orange tank car of the freight train as it goes over mountains.

• Use desks, chairs, and other students to pretend to be mountains, tunnels, towns, and so forth. Be sure every student gets to be part of the train.

2. Working in small groups, students construct a freight train out of various size cereal boxes.

3. Students do a writing roulette train story with their group members. After brainstorming possible stories, and reviewing the sequence of stories, make the point that stories, like freight trains, have a sequence

• each student takes out a sheet of paper and writes his or her name in the top right-hand corner;

• each student begins a freight train story that will be passed on to another student;

• students write quickly for several minutes until you call time;

• at that signal, each student passes his or her paper to the right;

• the student receiving the paper reads what is written and continues the story;

• continue writing and passing until time is called;

• all students conclude the story they have before them;

• share stories aloud.

RELATED BOOKS

Ten, Nine, Eight by Molly Bang is a lullaby counting book and winner of the Caldecott Medal. It was also designated an ALA Notable Book.

1. Write the book's title on the board or chart. A volunteer underlines the GH. Read the title together. Ask each to read the title. Remind them of the GHT generalization.

2. Read the book. Students count the objects for each page.

Amelia's Fantastic Flight by Rose Bursik tells about Amelia's trip to six continents and fourteen countries.

1. Write the book's title on the board or chart. A volunteer underlines the GH. Read the title together. Ask individuals to read the title. Remind students of the GHT generalization

2. Show students each of the inset maps as the students follow Amelia's trip.

3. When the book is completed, students retrace the adventure on the two full-spread maps located in the back.

PUBLISHING

Display students' work, trains, books on trains, and pictures of trains in an exhibit called WE'RE ON A FREIGHT TRAIN OF LETTERS!

FLUTE'S JOURNEY: THE LIFE OF A WOOD THRUSH

Harcourt Brace

Lynne Cherry

PHONICS CONCEPTS:
- U Vowel Sound: 2-Dot U as in *flUte;*
- FL Consonant Sound: FL Blend as in *FLute;*
- THR Consonant Sound: THR 3-Letter Blend as in *THRush;*
- U Vowel Sound: Short U as in *thrUsh*

LANGUAGE ARTS CONCEPT:
- Letter writing

Artifacts: Plastic 3" bird whistles (available from U. S. Toy)
Summary: This book traces the migration of a wood thrush named Flute from his nesting ground in a forest preserve in Maryland to his winter home in Costa Rica and back again. The book's end pages provide maps of his trip as well as pictures of other migratory song birds.

READING/WRITING CONNECTION

1. Begin by constructing a 2' bird out of blue butcher paper as a BIRD WORD BANK. Display near the reading area.
2. Display a large map of North and Central America. Get map flags. Also get pitcher of water. Have all this prepared before beginning the book.
3. Distribute the bird whistles. Fill each student's bird whistle with water so that when they blow the whistle it will make a warbling sound. Explain to students that you are about to read a book about a songbird. Sometimes when birds sing, we call it a warble. Write this new vocabulary word on the BIRD WORD BANK.
4. Transition to the sound of words. Tell students just as people can tell what kind of bird it is by its sound, people can tell a word by its letters and sound.
5. Write the word *flute* on the BIRD WORD BANK. Underline the U. Make its sound. Students echo. Write other words with the 2-dot U vowel sound: *June, July, tuna, tuba, duty, prune, junior, rule, ruby,* and so forth. Pronounce the U sound in each word. Students echo. Pronounce the word. Students echo.
6. Compare this U vowel sound to the short U sound in *thrush*. Pronounce the sound

and the word. Students echo. Add other words with the short U sound: *up, us, umbrella, but, cut* so students can hear the differences, sometimes subtle, the way people who study birds can tell their different songs. (At this point let students warble with their whistles one more time before you begin reading.)

7. Show students *Flute's Journey*. Write the title on the BIRD WORD BANK. Underline the FL blend, pronounce and invite students to echo. Do the same with the three-letter THR blend. Explain that Flute is a wood thrush and that they will follow him on his migration. Add migration to the BIRD WORD BANK.

8. As you read the introductory page, invite students to warble with their whistles to approximate "the calls of hundreds of migratory songbirds." Show the dedication page and elicit responses about the forest. It is important to show the pictures since this book is chocked full of information. As you read through the book, add other vocabulary words related to birds on the BIRD WORD BANK.

9. Beginning with the turquoise eggs in the Maryland nest, flag that area on the map. Then, as you read through the book, continue to flag Flute's journey. This book is a best divided into several days to approximate the different segments of the migration.

10. When the book is completed, review Flute's journey by looking at the flags and talking about what the students remember. Students write a letter persuading Flute to be careful on his journey.

EXTENSIONS

1. Students write for more information about how to make the world safer for songbirds. Depending upon the level of students, these letters may be individual or one letter may be generated by the entire class. The address is

    Save the Land You Love
    The Center for Children's Environmental Literature
    P.O. Box 5995
    Washington, D. C. 20016

2. Since so much of Flute's journey revolves around his search for food, students can help the feeding process by making an all-purpose feeder out of an empty egg carton.

    • Cut off the top;
    • Loop wire or string around the two ends of the carton;
    • Attach the wires to the bottom of a wire hanger;
    • Fill the egg carton compartments with different bird seeds;
    • Hang outside the classroom window or in a nearby tree.

RELATED BOOKS

While any books related to birds or more specifically songbirds would connect to the theme, the related books below have been chosen to reinforce the 2-dot U vowel sound.

Junior Kroll by Betty Paraskevas is a quirky poetry book about the events of a young boy's life. The title provides another look at the U vowel 2-dot sound.

1. Junior and Junior Kroll are mentioned several times in each poem. Write these on the

board or chart. When you come to one or the other, point to the word and the students read it with you.

2. Each poem is replete with allusions such as: Benny Goodman, W. C. Fields, Mickey Mouse, Good & Plenty, King Kong, double-breasted suit, Key Lime Pie, and so forth, which invites rich discussion, vocabulary development, and expansion of knowledge.

June 29, 1999 by David Wiesner tells the tale of Holly Evans's science experiment. Holly launched seedlings into the sky to study the effects of extraterrestrial conditions upon their growth.

1. Reinforce the 2-dot U vowel sound in the title.
2. Encourage speculation about what is on the cover, the page preceding the copyright page, and the title page.
3. Ask students to make predictions about what is about to happen. Continue this process of prediction throughout the book.

PUBLISHING

Students celebrate Flute's return by gathering in a U with their warblers and their persuasive letters to Flute. Each reads in turn. When a student finishes, other students show their appreciation by warbling their whistles. Call this CELEBRATING FLUTE'S SOUND!

Dr. JAC 44

LIBRARY LIL

Dial Books for Young Readers

Suzanne Williams

PHONICS CONCEPTS:

• BR Consonant Sound: BR Blend as in *liBRary;*
• AR Vowel Sound: AIR Sound as in *librARy;*
• L Consonant Sound as in *Library LiL*

LANGUAGE ARTS CONCEPTS:

• Library research
• Alliteration

Artifacts: Colorful library pockets (available from Top Notch)
Summary: Library Lil is an up-town, up-to-date librarian who not only turns resistant residents into readers, but also turns a visiting, tough motorcycle gang into lovers of books. In a real sense Library Lil proves that knowledge is power.

READING/WRITING CONNECTION

1. Give every student a brightly-colored library pocket and three brightly-colored cards that fit into the pocket. Each student writes his or her name on the outside of each pocket. Explain that these are going to be collection cards of sounds. Compare to other types of card collections: bubble gum, sports, dinosaurs, and so forth.

2. Say the BR sound, write it on the board or chart, say the sound again, and invite students to echo. After saying the sound, students print BR in large letters on the first card and put it in the pocket.

3. Say the AR (AIR) sound, write it on the board or chart, say the sound again, and invite students to echo. After saying the sound, students print AR in large letters on the second card and put it in the pocket.

4. Say the L sound, write it on the board or chart, say the sound again, and invite students to echo. After saying the sound, students print L as a large letter on the third card and put it in the pocket.

5. Tell students that these sounds occur again and again in the title and throughout the book you are about to share. Show the book and invite students to read the title.

6. Open to the title page. Ask students what Library Lil is holding. As you point to each volume, students say the letter of the alphabet and its sound. Help students see the deeper level of the picture, that Library Lil is strong because she can read, because she holds knowledge.

7. Ask what students see in the background. Invite speculation about what motorcycles might have to do with Library Lil.
8. Because Steven Kellogg's detailed illustrations greatly enhance the meaning of the words, be sure to stop and ask the students what they see and how that relates to the story.
9. After the reading, talk about why the gang acted so tough, why Bust-'em-up Bill kept his word with Lil after she moved the motorcycles, why all the guys fought over the book *The Mouse and the Motorcycle*.
10. Students talk and then write about the kinds of books they like to read.

EXTENSIONS

1. Students take out their three cards. They write *library* on each of the first two cards, underlining BR on one and AR on the other. They write *Lil* on the third card and underline the two Ls. Review the sounds with the students echoing.
   - Divide students into small groups of three or four.
   - Take the students to the library. Seat each group at a library table.
   - Explain that they are going to do library research. They are to get a library book and use it to find other words that contain the BR, AR, and L sounds. Be sure to distinguish the AR as AIR sound as in *February* from the AR sound as in *are*, *March*, or *farm*.
   - Give the students guidelines:
     - No more than four books at a time at a table;
     - They say the sounds with their three-inch voices; when they think they have a match, they test the sound and word on their group;
     - They are to neatly write the words they find on the appropriate cards.
   - Returning to the classroom, groups share their words.
2. Upon rereading the focal book, students could use their cards and slash marks to keep count of the number of times *library*, *librarian(s)*, and *Lil* were used (over fifty references).
3. After collecting all the cards, point out the repetition of the letter *L*. Talk about alliteration.

RELATED BOOKS

Carmen Agra Deedy's *The Library Dragon* tells the story of how Miss Lotta Scales, the library dragon, changes into Miss Lotty, librarian and storyteller.
1. Students make scaly bookmarks;
2. They record all the references and idioms related to dragons.

Aunt Chip and the Great Triple Creek Dam Affair by Patricia Polacco parallels the story of Library Lil. In Polacco's version, Aunt Chip saves the town of Triple Creek, where everyone has forgotten how to read because of television, by reminding them of the joy of reading.
1. Students role play what it would be like to teach someone how to read.
2. In groups, students come up with a list of favorite books to put into the new school's library.

For the BR sound in the initial position, use *Bottomley the Brave* by Peter Harris and Doffy Weir. Bottomley exaggerates his capture of burglars.

•Students make the BR sound in the word *brave* and compare it to the sound in the word *library*.

• Returning to the story, students compare what the words say to what the pictures say. Draw some conclusions about the importance of examining the pictures, of inferring meaning, and of reading both words and pictures for meaning.

PUBLISHING

Display the students library pockets on the bulletin board. Call the display: WE BROUGHT OUR LIBRARY POCKETS FILLED WITH SOUNDS!

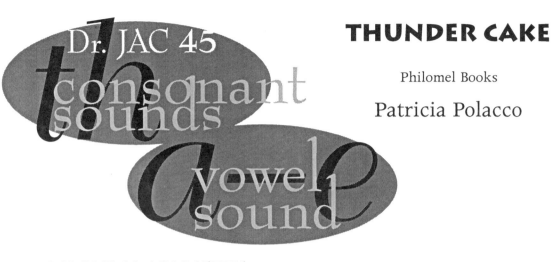

THUNDER CAKE

Philomel Books

Patricia Polacco

PHONICS CONCEPTS:
- TH Consonant Sound: TH Digraph Voiceless as in *THunder;*
- TH Consonant Sound: TH Digraph Voiced as in *THe, THem;*
- A–E Vowel Sound: Long A–Final E Silent as in *cAkE;*
- *Generalization I:*
    When there are two vowels in a one-syllable word, one of which is final E, separated from the first vowel by one consonant, the first vowel is usually long and the E is usually silent.
  - *Generalization II:*
    When words end with silent E, the preceding A or I is usually long.

LANGUAGE ARTS CONCEPT:
- The mythology of thunder

Artifact: A piece of Thunder Cake (most any cake will do if you do not make the actual recipe "My Grandma's Thunder Cake," which can be found at the conclusion of the book).

Summary: Grandma (Babushka) has found a wise and wonderful way to distract her grandchild and help her overcome her fear of thunderstorms.

READING/WRITING CONNECTION

1. Make a 3' cloud out of grey butcher paper. This will be the THUNDER CAKE WORD BANK.
2. Call students around you and talk about weather, storms, rain, what happens during a thunderstorm, and so forth. Encourage students to tell about times when they were in a storm, or when the lights went out. Talk about how people know when a storm is coming, what they do during a storm, and how they feel during the storm. If they have pets, ask the students if they notice their pets acting differently before or during a thunderstorm.
3. Show the book and write the title on the THUNDER CAKE WORD BANK. Examine the dust jacket, ask the students to describe what they notice. Go to the title page. Call students' attention to the sky. Compare it to the dedication and the introductory page. Look at the animals. What is the person in the picture doing? Ask them to

infer the weather and give their reasons.

4. Point to the word *thunder*. Underline the TH. Tell students this sound is called a "dental sound" because the tongue goes between the teeth.
   • Say the word *the*. Students echo and listen to the TH sound. (voiced)
   • Say the word *thigh*. Students echo and listen to the TH sound. (unvoiced)
   • Ask students in which of those two words do they hear the TH sound (*the*).
   • Return to the TH in the word *thunder*. Determine if students can tell if its voiced or unvoiced. Compare it to distant thunder, just the hint of a storm. Since this is a difficult concept for young students, have students construct TH words using their magnetic or tactile letters.

5. Move to the word cake. Share the two generalizations applicable to this word. Say the word. Students echo. Point out how *cake* says the letter A (long) but keeps its E silent. Ask students if they can think of other words that rhyme with cake. Write these on the THUNDER CAKE WORD BANK.

6. Create several other lists of word families conveying these generalizations: *–ace; –ade; –age; –ale; –ame; –ane; –ape*, and so forth. Students offer words belonging to these families.

7. Read the book, stopping often to look at the weather pictured in the sky, and to add words to the THUNDER CAKE WORD BANK. (At some point you may want to dim the lights or even play thunder sound effects as background.)

8. When the book is completed, take off the dust jacket and show students the picture of the thunder cake in the window. Give each student a piece of Thunder Cake.

9. While they are eating, write on the overhead about a storm you remember or some baked good you remember, one perhaps associated with a holiday or time of year, one you especially liked. Do this as a model for the upcoming writing you will invite from the students.

10. Give students two choices of paper: grey if they want to write about a storm they remember; brown if they want to write about a cake or something baked they remember.

EXTENSIONS

Language Arts.

Tell students that in Norse mythology there is a god of thunder called Thor. He carried a thunderbolt. People believed he lived in the clouds and from there he would hurl his thunderbolt when he was angry. From his name comes the word *Thursday*. Help students realize that the TH sound is the same in *Thor, Thursday,* and in *Thunder*. Write these on the THUNDER CAKE WORD BANK.

Arts.

Students make a Thunder Cake out of Styrofoam™ which they paint. Crumbled paper painted red with green stems makes effective strawberries.

Mathematics.

Use the recipe in the book to teach measurement. Bring in measuring cups and spoons. Students fill them with colored sand and colored water to approximate the ingredients in "My Grandma's Thunder Cake."

RELATED BOOKS

Nick Ward's Don't Worry Grandpa parallels Polacco's book except that Charlie, the grandson, distracts his worried Grandpa with a story of giants playing until the storm passes.

1. Use this book in conjunction with *Thunder Cake* for comparison and contrast.
2. Tape two grey butcher paper clouds together to make a Venn diagram. Make sure they overlap. On one cloud print THUNDER CAKE on the other print DON'T WORRY; where they overlap, print SAME.
3. Review both books by asking the students to tell you something about one story, then compare or contrast it with the other. For example.

THUNDER CAKE	SAME	DON'T WORRY
Grandma	a grandparent is a character	Grandpa
girl grandchild	a grandchild is a character	boy grandchild
made a cake	both have a distraction	told a story

Molly Wigand's *Stormy Weather* is part of the Rugrats' series of Nickelodeon® and the "Ready-to-Read Simon Spotlight." In this book a group of babies comfort each other during a storm.

Storms by Seymour Simon is an excellent non-fiction book. It contains descriptions of atmospheric conditions which create thunderstorms, lightning, and other violent weather.

1. Use this book in conjunction with science.
2. Show the pictures to help students understand the nature of thunderstorms.
3. Review the TH sound.

PUBLISHING

Suspend students' writing from coat-hangers that have been covered with tissue paper painted with grey paint to look like thunder clouds. Call the display WE ARE THUNDERHEADS OVER SOUNDS!

IN THE SMALL, SMALL POND

Henry Holt

Denise Fleming

PHONICS CONCEPTS:

- AL Vowel Sound: Broad O as in *smALl;*
- FR Consonant Sound: FR Blend as in *FRog;*
- LL Double Consonant of the Same Letter as in *smaLL;*
- *Generalization:*
  WHEN TWO OF THE SAME CONSONANTS ARE SIDE BY SIDE ONLY ONE IS HEARD.
- SM Consonant Sound: SM Blend as in *SMall*

LANGUAGE ARTS CONCEPT:

- Commas between two words that are the same

Artifact: Mini-frog Erasers in three assorted styles (available from U. S. Toy)
Summary: Through colorful, simple illustrations and rhyming text, this book describes the activities of animals living in or near a pond as spring moves into autumn.

READING/WRITING CONNECTION

1. Before beginning this book, make a POND WORD BANK out of light blue butcher paper. Color or paint some reeds, grasses, and a bit of sand around it. Make three frogs out of green construction paper or felt that can be affixed in the pond. Have these ready to attach later in the lesson. Hang the POND WORD BANK near the reading circle.

2. After students have settled down, show the book and its cover and point out the title and author.

3. Call students' attention to the repeated word *small, small* by pointing to each word. Note the comma between the words. Ask if someone can make the SM sound. Ask for volunteers to read some or all of the title.

4. On the POND WORD BANK, write the word *small.* Say the word. Students echo. Underline the AL. Say the sound. Students echo. Tell students that sound is like a broad O. Repeat several times with students echoing.

5. Say the word again. This time ask students how many L sounds do they hear. After they respond correctly with "one," share the generalization. Elicit other words in the ALL family and ask students to listen for one sound. Add to POND WORD BANK.

Try other words with double like consonants such as: *guess, add, bell, sheriff, mitt*.

6. Ask students to describe what they see on the cover. Talk about the child's expression. Explain what this book does (refer to summary). Read through the book once.

7. Before the second reading, challenge students to look for something that appears on every double-page spread. (the frog)

8. Call upon individual students to read each double-page spread. As each finishes, give that student a frog eraser. (Be sure every student reads and receives a frog eraser.)

9. Conclude by asking what appears on each page. When students say "frog," write the word on the board or chart and point out the FR consonant blend. Attach the paper or felt frogs onto the paper pond.

10. Distribute green paper. Students write about frogs, their frog eraser, or a story about frogs. Very young students just coming to this word, may practice writing the FR blend and the word *frog*.

EXTENSIONS

1. Ask students what a pond is. Brainstorm other bodies of water. As they offer some of the following, depending upon their age, abilities, and experience, write them on the POND WORD BANK. Feel free to add one or two others in order to expand their vocabulary: sea, ocean, lake, creek, stream, lagoon, pool, tarn, reservoir, river, brook, bayou, tank, waterfall, rapids, fountain, geyser, spa.

2. Talk about the size of these bodies of water. Look each up in the dictionary with the young students but encourage older students to use their dictionary skills to look each up. Circle in red all the big bodies of water. Circle in green all the small bodies of water.

3. Talk about each body of water listed on the POND WORD BANK.

4. Locate oceans and lakes on maps and globes.

5. Make a miniature pond in the classroom. Use an inexpensive plastic child's wading pool.

RELATED BOOKS

Linnea's Almanac by Christina Bjork is a rich book with many extensions because it basically chronicles Linnea's entries into her almanac. There she keeps track of her indoor and outdoor activities all year long. This book also includes an index called "Planning of the Year."

1. Point to Linnea's name. Ask students what generalization they have just learned that fits her name. Ask students to say her name.

2. Point to the word almanac. Say the word. Point out the AL at the beginning of the word. Ask students the sound of those letters. If they have problems, remind them of the word *small*. Say the word. Students echo. Together say the entire title. Show students a copy of an almanac, perhaps *The Farmer's Almanac*. Explain its function.

3. Read the introduction to Linnea's Almanac. Talk about Linnea's expression "I'm an asphalt flower," and how she plays with the idiom "green thumb" when she calls Mr. Bloom's thumb "blue."

4. Turn to the section about the pond in the "August" section. Connect to the book *In the Small, Small Pond*. Talk about the allusion to *Thumbelina* and why the author

Christina Bjork and illustrator Lena Anderson might use that allusion rather than some other fairy tale. (Bjork and Anderson come from Sweden and share by heritage and inclination the folklore of that part of the world.)

5. Note that "Victoria" is a giant water lily that originated in the Amazon River. Connect to work on bodies of water.
6. Students begin writing their own almanac.

Frogs in Three Dimensions by Jill Bailey shows in an interesting format the habitats, feeding, movement, reproduction, and defense of frogs.

1. Use this book to reinforce the FR consonant sound.
2. Connect to science and the study of amphibians.

PUBLISHING

Fill the plastic child's wading pool with students' work. Call the display: BIG, BIG WORK ON SOUNDS IN A SMALL, SMALL POND!

THIS OLD MAN

Child's Play

Pam Adams
(illustrator)

PHONICS CONCEPTS:
- M Consonant Sound as in *Man*;
- A Vowel Sound: Short A as in *mAn*;
- N Consonant Sound: Nasal as in *maN*;
- TH Consonant Sound: TH Digraph Voiced as in *THis*

LANGUAGE ARTS CONCEPT:
- Predicting

Artifacts: Wooden Number Beads (available at 300 pieces per unit from Oriental Trading Co.)
Summary: This version of the favorite old song couples rhythm and rhyme with words, numbers, numerals, and simple addition.

READING/WRITING CONNECTION

1. Before beginning this book, cut two sheets of paper (about 3' square). On one, cut a 2' peep hole. Staple or tape together with the peep-hole sheet on top. On the top sheet, directly under the peep hole, write the words THIS OLD MAN. Display near where the students will gather. This becomes their PEEP-HOLE AND NUMBER BANK. Using the peep hole not only focuses the students but looks like the pages in the book. The peep-hole acts as a visual mnemonic device.
2. Ask volunteers to underline the TH sound in *this*, the M consonant sound in *man*, the short A in *man*, and the N consonant sound in *man*. Say the sounds; students echo. Very young students may be introduced to the above phonics concepts one skill at a time.
3. Under each underline, ask students to think of other words that have that sound. Write correct responses under the appropriate sound. Share.
4. Show the title page. Point to the peep-hole in the book and identify the character as "This old man." Repeat the sounds or ask students to repeat the sounds as you point to them.
5. Read the book. As you say the number, for example, "He plays one," ask a student to point to the numeral near the peep-hole and count the number of flowers in that numeral. Ask students if they can find the numeral anywhere on the old man (on his pocket). As you say the object, for example drum, ask students if they can find

the object. Ask students if they can find one of anything else on that page, for example one boy, one bunny. Follow this procedure throughout the book.

6. Distribute the plastic number beads so that each student receives beads that number zero through nine and an extra one. Distribute paper.

7. Reread the book. As you read the number, students find it among their beads.

8. They write the number symbols and the spelled-out numbers on their papers as you write them in the Peep-Hole and Number Bank. (Leave enough room for ten.)

9. When the second reading is completed, point to each number symbol as students read it. Point to each word number as students read it.

10. Point to the underlined letters as students sound them out to read the title.

EXTENSIONS

Mathematics.

Return to the book for mathematics concepts. For this, every student needs extra number one and two beads.

• Reenter the book. Students lay out their beads to match the addition in the book.

For example:

• bead with the numeral 1 on it + 1 bead with the numeral 1 on it = 1 bead with the numeral 2 on it.

• Proceed through the book in this manner.

Building Words.

Use the rhyming words to make words.

• Working with a pocket chart, begin with the letter A.

• Have the other letters of the alphabet available.

• Place the A in the pocket. Remind students that every word contains a vowel.

• Talk about the word A.

• Place an N after the A. Talk about the word *an*.

• Ask students what letter might they put in front of *an*.

• Working with their suggestions, build words and eliminate non-words.

• Students take out their mini-folders, magnetic or tactile letters. Beginning with the letter A, they build words at their desks.

• Be sure students get the chance to share their words and the processes by which they built their words.

RELATED BOOK

This Old Man, illustrated by Carol Jones, also contains peep-holes. These provide a perfect way for students to predict the next object by looking through the peep hole and rhyming it with the number. For example, the peep-hole for the number four shows a section of a door.

• This version of the book contains a page of music, so it invites song. Sing the line, stop so students can study the picture, think about the number, and predict, then go on to sing the next line. Everyone sings the chorus. As the students become familiar with the song, they can sing it again and again.

• Go back through the book. Show students the picture. Write the name of the object on the board or chart. Underline its initial letter. Students find other objects in the picture that begin with or contain that letter. For example: *drum, D*. Students' name: *dog, doll, duck, grandfather, drape, desk, dollhouse*, and so forth.

 • Students make a double page with a peep-hole. On the top page they write

   This old man he played...

      peep-hole

   Here they write the number

   He played nick nack on my...

On the second page they draw an object whose name rhymes with the number so that it shows through the peep-hole. On the back of the second page they identify the object's name and write the chorus.

PUBLISHING

Conduct a SING-A-LONG OF SOUNDS! Students sing their pages of "This Old Man." Invite parents, other students, administrators, and friends for this songfest.

THE BLUE BALLOON

Little, Brown

Mick Inkpen

PHONICS CONCEPT:
- BL Consonant Sound: BL Blend as in *BLue, BLew*

LANGUAGE ARTS CONCEPT:
- Homophones especially *Blue* and *Blew*

Artifact: A light blue balloon
Summary: Through pages that open in various ways, the reader sees a little boy blow up a wonderful balloon that never bursts, despite being stretched, squeezed, squashed, whacked, run over, and let fly.

READING/WRITING CONNECTION

1. Before beginning this book, make a BALLOON WORD BANK in the shape of a balloon out of light blue paper. Tie a real string or ribbon around its tail to make it look realistic. Display near students.
2. After the students are settled, take out a blue balloon. Ask students to
    - identify what it is;
    - tell its color;
    - describe what it's made of;
    - share things to do with a balloon;
    - tell places where someone might get a balloon or might be able to bring a balloon;
    - explain how balloons are used for celebrations
3. Write responses on BALLOON WORD BANK.
4. Ask a volunteer to underline the BL blend in the word blue and anywhere else the blend may appear on the BALLOON WORD BANK. For example, the students are likely to say they "blow up a balloon" or they "blew one up." (If they do not suggest the word *blew*, make that suggestion.)
5. Pronounce the BL blend. Students echo. Have students place their hands near their mouth so they can feel the air. Use this to introduce the homophones *blue* and *blew*. Make the connection between blowing up and the blue balloon.
6. Write both words with magnetic letters
    - Cover the words so that only the BL shows. Students read the blend.
    - Uncover the UE so that the entire word blue shows. Pronounce the word. Show the color. Ask students to find the color blue in the room. Talk about the different shades of blue:

    eggshell blue, navy blue, royal blue, light blue, dark blue, dusty blue, powder blue, marine blue, peacock blue, robin's egg blue, sea blue, turquoise blue, reddish blue, slate blue, cobalt blue, midnight blue, periwinkle blue, wisteria blue, and so on. Write these under the word *blue*.

• Uncover the EW so that the entire word *blew* shows. Pronounce the word. Blow gently. Ask students to blow gently; then ask them to wave their arms. Talk about what makes air move: wind, fans, people. Talk about what happens when something blows: it moves.

• Tell students they can remember which *blew* means moving air by looking at the last letter in the word blew W. This letter begins the word wind. Wind is moving air; it blows. If the W is not at the end, the word is a color.

7. Read the book. Point out the homophones as you meet them. Ask the students to tell you which *blue/blew* the author means by finding the W and by how the word is used in the story. Also, help students examine the pictures for clues. This helps young students realize the value of using pictorial context as a reading strategy.

8. After the book, distribute the blue balloons. Permit students to have some fun blowing up their balloons and playing with them as the boy did in the story.

9. At your signal, playing stops. Distribute blue index cards to each student. Write on the board or chart the following question: If blowing causes air to move, how does it make your blue balloon get bigger?

10. Students think about your question and write their answers on the cards. Share responses.

EXTENSIONS

1. Air power: Show how to lift a book without touching it. Put a balloon on a table so its opening hangs over the table's edge. Place a book on top of the balloon. Raise the book by blowing up the balloon. Talk about how air under pressure can move heavy objects.

2. Static electricity: Show how to stick a balloon on a wall. Take a blown-up balloon and rub it against something woolen or against hair. Put the balloon against a wall and let it stick. Talk about how the balloon became charged.

3. Teach students the definition of homophones. Ask students to think of other words that sound the same but have different meanings: *too, two, to; so, sew, sow; tale, tail; tow, toe; red, read; pear, pare, pair*, and so forth. List these on the BALLOON WORD BANK.

RELATED BOOKS

A great book to use with this lesson is *The Wind Blew* by Pat Hutchins because in a playful rhyming way it describes the antics of a capricious wind that takes everything with it including a blue balloon.

1. Ask students to highlight the BL blend in the title with highlighter tape. Ask them what kind of blue/blew is this book going to be about.

2. Ask them to find the blue balloon on the cover. Ask them what kind of blue/blew it is. Ask them to find other blue things on the cover.

3. This book also uses wonderful verbs: *took, snatched, swept, whipped, grabbed, tossed, plucked, lifted, whirled, stole, pulled, sent, mixed, and threw*. After reading the book, ask individual students to role-play the wind. Each in turn pantomimes the wind's actions.

The Well-Mannered Balloon by Nancy Willard is another book about a blue balloon. This balloon belongs to James. It is well-mannered until late at night when it asks to eat everything in the house. This book helps students understand personification since the balloon speaks.

1. Students may do as James did and paint faces on their balloons.
2. In groups, they make a list of other things a balloon may ask to eat.

Why Is the Sky Blue? by Sally Grindley is a book about friends, sharing, and, most importantly, it is about learning. Because of the repetition of the question, the BL sound is repeated approximately ten times, making it a perfect book to reinforce the BL consonant blend sound.

1. Write the title on the board or chart. Ask for volunteers to read it.
2. Tell students that when you come to that question, you will point to it so that everyone can read it together.
3. Ask students which blue/blew this story is about.

PUBLISHING

Create a display of blue balloons and books that have *blue/blew* in their titles. Call the display WE BLEW THE BL SOUND OUT OF THE BLUE!

THE BOAT OF MANY ROOMS: THE STORY OF NOAH

Atheneum

J. Patrick Lewis

PHONICS CONCEPTS:
- OA Vowel Sound: Long O Digraph as in b*OA*t;
- *Generalization:*
  THE FIRST VOWEL IS USUALLY LONG AND THE SECOND SILENT IN THE OA DIGRAPH.
- *Exception to the generalization:*
  WHEN THE O AND A ARE NOT PRONOUNCED AS A DIGRAPH AS IN THE TWO-SYLLABLE NAME NOAH, THE GENERALIZATION DOES NOT HOLD.
- M Consonant Sound in the Initial and Medial position as in *M*any and roo*M*s

LANGUAGE ARTS CONCEPT:
- Synonyms

Artifacts: Religious erasers (available in an assortment of three—ark, dove, cross—from U. S. Toy)

Summary: A poetic retelling of the story of Noah's ark, which saves two of every kind of animal while the rains cause a flood and destroy everything on the earth.

READING/WRITING CONNECTION

1. Show the cover. Ask the students to name what they see there. Read the title. Ask the students if they know another name for a boat with many rooms. If they do not, add hints such as, "A man named Noah made it." "It held two of each animal." "Noah built it when it began to rain and rain." If they do not know the word ark, provide it.
2. Write the words *boat* and *ark* on the board or chart. Tell students that when words mean almost the same thing, they are called synonyms.
3. Explain that while both boats and arks travel in water, an ark is usually associated with a vessel that provides protection or safety.
4. Write the title of the book on board or chart. Read the title. Ask for a volunteer to underline OA in both the title and in Noah's name.
5. Pronounce the sound in the word *boat*; students echo. Say the word.
6. Pronounce the sound in Noah's name. Say his name. Ask if students hear the difference. Share the generalization and the exception.
7. Ask a volunteer to underline the M consonant sounds in the title. Make the sound.

Students echo.

8. Read the book, stopping to show the pictures and discuss the events.
9. Attach a 6' sheet of butcher paper horizontally to the wall for a Noah's Ark mural. Explain to students that just as the ark was divided into rooms, you are dividing the mural into parts so they can retell the story. Divide the paper into six 1' segments. Divide students into six groups.
   • Group One designs and writes the first part where God instructs Noah.
   • Group Two designs and writes the part where Noah builds the ark.
   • Group Three designs and writes about the animals coming aboard.
   • Group Four designs and writes about the rain and how the animals reacted.
   • Group Five designs and writes about the rain stopping and the dove leaving.
   • Group Six designs and writes about the ending.
10. When the mural is completed, give each student an eraser artifact that matches their part of the story.

EXTENSIONS

1. Create a Noah's Ark Shadow Box.
   • Using egg cartons, students fill the "rooms" with drawings, miniature plastic animals, pictures of animals two by two.
   • On the flat inside lid, students write their version of the story. This may be done on paper and glued inside.
   • They decorate the outside lid after putting their name and title on it.
2. Read and talk about floods, what causes them, when they occur, and where they occur.

RELATED BOOKS

Noah's Ark by Lucy Cousins is a sturdy board book that provides a simple retelling of the story. This book was chosen as a Parents Magazine Best Book of the Year.
   • Very young children can name the different animals pictured on each page.
   • Write forty and 40. Ask a volunteer to read each. Students see that amounts can be expressed through two different symbolizing systems: words and numbers.

Noah's Ark by Sophie Windham uniquely retells the story of how Noah and the animals survived the flood through text and peek-through-window illustrations. This is an excellent book to use for predictions.

Sister Yessa's Story by Karen Greenfield is a tale within a tale. The book juxtaposes the story of Sister Yessa collecting animals two by two as rain clouds gather with the story she tells of Great Turtle carrying animals on his back and depositing them in various places on earth. Both tales end as she arrives at her brother Noah's. He is building an ark as the rain begins.
   • Use this book to consider different versions that deal with Noah.
   • Make a T-Chart and list this version on one side of the T and one of the other versions on the other side of the T.
   • Students revisit the two stories as they fill in the chart.

Aardvarks, Disembark! by Ann Jonas is a great book to use to culminate the study. It begins with the rainbow. Noah has landed. He calls out of the ark a variety of little-known animals, many of which are now endangered. The last page of the book tells about each animal and whether it is designated as extinct or endangered.

• Since this book is an alphabet book that begins with Z and ends with A, it may be used to review the alphabet in reverse.

• Many advanced students enjoy researching some of the odd animals such as: meerkats, hartbeests, boomslangs, aardwolves, and others.

PUBLISHING

Invite a priest, minister, or rabbi to class. Students share their mural version of Noah's Ark and discuss parts of the story with the guest. Call the day NOAH'S STORY IS FULL OF SOUNDS WE KNOW!

THE MUSICIANS OF BREMEN

Simon & Schuster

Jane Yolen

PHONICS CONCEPT:

- U Vowel Sound: Long U as in *mUsicians*

LANGUAGE ARTS CONCEPT:

Synecdoche

Artifacts: Gold coins (available from U. S. Toy)

Summary: Four animals who have been driven off by their masters decide to become musicians. On the way to the town of Bremen, they see a light, think it is a house, and go there intending to sing for their supper. What they encounter is a robbers' den. The animals use their wits and talents to scare off the thieves and reap the benefits. There is an interesting "Note" in the back of the book worth sharing with students.

This version of the story comes from the German, *Kletke* where it was called "The Street Musicians." The original story may be found in *The Grey Fairy Book*, edited by Andrew Lang and first published in 1900 by Longmans, Green, and Co. A paperback edition of this original is now available from Dover Publications in New York.

READING/WRITING CONNECTION

1. Begin the lesson by playing music. As students settle into their places for reading, ask them about what they heard, what it is called. Write the word music on the board or chart.

2. Invite a volunteer to underline the long U sound in the word. Remind students that long vowels say their own name. Say the sound. Students echo. Pronounce the word. Students echo.

3. Ask students if they know what people are called who make music. Write *musicians* on the board or chart. Follow the same procedure as above to emphasize the long U vowel sound.

4. Explain to students that the story you are about to read has animals as musicians. Tell them there is also something special about the way Donkey addresses each animal. Ask them to listen carefully and see if they can tell you that special way. When Donkey calls the dog "Growler," the cat "Whiskers," and the rooster "Red-Comb," he is using synecdoche, a poetic device that singles out some part of a thing, person, animal as important enough to stand for the whole. Walt Disney used it for the Seven Dwarfs, "Sleepy," "Dopey," and children use this technique quite easily when they make up nick names for each other based upon some prominent characteristic, such as "Stilts" as a moniker for a long-legged friend.

5. Read the book and point out the wonderful illustrations. When you get to the discovery of the robbers, ask students to predict what the four animals will do.

6. Discuss how the animals used their minds and how they used their talents. Be sure to clarify exactly what the robbers thought when they heard them and when Jock went back to check it out.

7. Stop after "and were never heard from again."

8. Distribute paper to students. Explain that you stopped the story after the robbers ran away, but there is more to the story. Ask them to write what they think happens to the animals.

9. As they share their endings, distribute the gold coins. This artifact should remind them how the animals were rewarded for using their wits and talents. Encourage them to talk about that.

10. Conclude by reading the end of the book. Compare and contrast it with those written by students.

EXTENSIONS

1. Making Musical Instruments. Students make drums and guitars.

   • Students bring in empty extra large coffee cans (2 lbs. 2.5 oz.) with the plastic tops. They may cover them with paper, paint them, or leave them as is, depending upon the class. These serve as drums. Students may tap these with their hands, sticks, or pieces of wood covered on one end with material or leather and tied with string or leather strips.

   • Large cereal boxes make great guitars. Simply cut out a portion of one side and wrap rubber bands around the box to serve as strings. Students may strum their guitars with their fingers or they may use mathematics chips or counters.

2. Making Music. Students become musicians. They sing and play the following adaptation to Stephen Foster's "Camptown Races."

   Bremen Musicians sing this song
      Long U, long U
   Bremen Musicians got the gold
      Oh, the long U day

   Make music all night
   Make music all day
   And use the long U every way
      Oh, the long U day!

RELATED BOOKS

Musicians of the Sun is Gerald McDermott's retelling of the Aztec myth of how the Lord of Night frees the four musicians that Sun holds as prisoners so they can bring joy to the world.

   • Since there are four musicians in this book and in the focal book, both books, lend themselves to the mathematical concept of four: counting to four, adding and subtracting to read four.

   • The four musicians are in the colors blue, yellow, red, and green. Students identify these colors, work with these colors, find these colors in the crayon box, and so forth.

The Unicorn Alphabet by Marianna Mayer repeats the word *unicorn* on almost every page, thereby reinforcing the long U sound in the initial position. Additionally, this book pictures a flower bordering every page. At the conclusion of the book, each flower is identified along with a brief description of its derivation, use, and symbolism.

• Ask individual students to choose a letter. Read that page. Every time you read the word *unicorn*, ask students to chorus its sound.

• Use the flowers to introduce a study of flowers.

Utahraptor: The Deadliest Dinosaur by Don Lessem provides information on one of the most recent dinosaur discoveries—a huge, vicious hunter called the Utahraptor.

• After pronouncing *Utahraptor* with the students echoing, tell students that this dinosaur was discovered in 1993 by a Dr. Kirkland who also named the dinosaur.

• Show students a map of the United States. If students do not already know the concept of "states," explain them in a general way. Challenge students to study the map to find a state that has a name like the dinosaur. After they discover Utah, ask them to figure out why the dinosaur was so named.

PUBLISHING

Create a 3' U out of heavy stock paper or a box. Cover with colorful paper. With a marker, write WE USE THE LONG U, make music notes all over the U, and intersperse the students writing among the notes. Suspend the U in the room.

MOON ROPE: A PERUVIAN FOLKTALE

Harcourt Brace Jovanovich

Lois Ehlert
(translated into Spanish by Amy Prince)

PHONICS CONCEPTS:
- O–E Vowel Sound: Long O as in *rOpe;*
- *Generalization:*
    WHEN THERE ARE TWO VOWELS IN A ONE-SYLLABLE WORD, ONE OF WHICH IS THE FINAL E, SEPARATED FROM THE FIRST VOWEL BY ONE CONSONANT, THE FIRST VOWEL IS USUALLY LONG AND THE E IS USUALLY SILENT.
- OO Vowel Sound: 2-Dot U or Long OO as in *mOOn;*
- M Consonant Sound: Nasal as in *Moon;*
- N Consonant Sound: Nasal as in *mooN*

LANGUAGE ARTS CONCEPT:
- Stories written in two languages

Artifacts: Lengths of hemp rope, about 2' for each student (available in craft and hobby stores)

Summary: Fox convinces Mole to climb to the moon with him on a rope of woven grass. Mole slips on the way, lands on a bird, and makes it safely to earth. When he lands the other creatures laugh at him so he digs a deep tunnel and only comes out at night. Fox perhaps made it to the moon because on clear nights the birds say they can see him looking down on earth.

READING/WRITING CONNECTION

1. Make a 2' moon out of silver paper. Use it for the MOON WORD BANK.
2. Write the title of the book on the MOON WORD BANK. Ask for a volunteer to underline the O in rope. Tell students that the long O says its name. Give students the generalization. Say the word *rope*. Students echo. If you have taught Dr. JAC 45, remind them of the word *cake*, long A and silent E and repeat the generalization.
3. Ask for volunteers to underline the M and the N. Make the sounds. Students echo. Point out how the nasal sounds M and N tickle the nose.
4. Ask for a volunteer to underline the OO sound. Pronounce the long OO sound.

Students echo. Say the word *moon*. (If teaching number 3 & 4 overload learners with too many phonics concepts at one time, introduce on a different day.)

5. Explain to students that knowing all those sounds help them read the title of the book you are going to share. Show the book. Ask for volunteers to put the sounds together and read the title. Ask students to speculate about the meaning of the title and predict what the book will be about.

6. Show students some of the pictures in the book. Tell them the pictures are based upon Peruvian art and that in Peru people speak Spanish.

7. Show how the words in the book are in both English and Spanish.

8. Dim the lights, read the book by using a flashlight. Shine the flashlight on the silvery sections of the book. When you get to the last page, shimmer the book so that the face in the moon shows.

9. Distribute the lengths of rope and grey or silver paper. Students write about one or more of the following:
   • how they would use their ropes to get to the moon;
   • what they would do on the moon;
   • who, if anyone, they would take to the moon;
   • how they would use their ropes to return from the moon.

10. Students share in Author's Chair.

EXTENSIONS

Writing, Art, and Social Studies:
   • Brainstorm animals other than those used in the book.
   • Using those animals as a basis, students create their own Peruvian designs.
   • For materials, give students access to silver, gold, and other Japanese origami paper (available at craft or hobby stores), large sheets of heavier stock paper, and rope.
   • After they create their designs, they model the book by writing a story that explains their design.
   • The teacher models the lesson by making a stylized face of a llama and another of an alpaca. Glue onto the paper. Glue a smaller moon between them in the distance with a piece of rope from the moon to one and the other animal. Show the picture to the students. After they have seen the picture, begin writing the story on the overhead. Talk/write so the students see and hear the process.
   • Begin by talking about Peru, its animals and topography. Mention that the Andes Mountains form the second largest mountain chain in the world. Suggest to yourself that you might want your story to be about Peruvian animals.
   • Start your story something like this: Two animals grazed up to the snow line of the Andes Mountains. Suddenly, they both looked up and saw the moon. "We must visit the moon," said the llama. "I am afraid," said the alpaca. "But if we go together," said the llama, "you'll be safe." Students may pick up the story from there, or they write their own version by using the same or different animals.

RELATED BOOKS

Rabbit and the Moon by Douglas Wood captures the Cree legend of the rabbit who longs to reach the moon and Crane who helps him. In the true spirit of legend, this tale explains how the Whooping Crane got his red headdress and his long legs.

- Students may write for information on the Whooping Crane to the
    International Crane Foundation
    P.O. Box 447
    Baraboo, WI 53913
- Collect other legends, especially about the rabbit.
- Bring a rabbit to class. Students observe the rabbit and keep a journal of their observations.
- Make a Venn diagram. Together with students compare this legend with the focal book.

Knots on a Counting Rope by Bill Martin, Jr. and John Archambault tells the story of a young Native American boy and his grandfather, how they reminisce about the boy's birth, first pony, first race, and how the grandfather teaches the boy to remember his love.
- Students keep their ropes, tying a knot each time they share their writing aloud.
- At the end of a marking period, all students count their knots to remind everyone who shared the most.

Anthony Reynoso: Born to Rope by Martha Cooper and Ginger Gordon is a non-fiction book about a young Mexican-American boy who learns how to do trick roping.
- Talk about the meaning of *rope* in the sentence, "As soon as I could stand, my dad gave me a rope."
- Then talk about the meaning of *rope* in the sentence, "It's a good thing I started when I was little, because it takes years to learn to rope."

PUBLISHING

Cover a wall or bulletin board with light brown paper. Affix heavy rope around as a border. Also with heavy rope, write out the title WE CAN ROPE OUR SOUNDS! Display the students' work within the borders.

CLIFFORD THE BIG RED DOG

Scholastic

Norman Bridwell

PHONICS CONCEPT:
• O Vowel Sound: Broad O as in *dOg*

LANGUAGE ARTS CONCEPTS:
• Common and proper nouns
• Prepositions

Artifacts: Red crayons
Summary: In this beloved classic, Emily Elizabeth tells about her big red dog Clifford.

READING/WRITING CONNECTION

1. Before beginning this lesson, make a 2' dog out of red paper. This is the CLIFFORD WORD BANK.

2. Use a stuffed Clifford dog to introduce the book. Ask students what kind of animal he is and what his name might be. Write the word *dog* on the CLIFFORD WORD BANK. Underline the O. Pronounce the sound. Students echo. Tell students this is called the broad O vowel sound.

3. Write the name *Clifford* on the CLIFFORD WORD BANK. Point to the capital letter in the word *Clifford* and the lower case letter in the word *dog*. Ask students the difference between dog and Clifford, between boy and James, between girl and Mary, between teacher and your name. Talk about dog as any dog. It is common, but Clifford is the proper name for a specific dog. Draw parallels with their names and yours.

4. Distribute red crayons from which you have removed the wrapping. Each student names its color. For example: bright red, dark red, light red, orange red, ruby red, cardinal, brownish red, pink, rose, cherry, and some may even think of Clifford red. Write these on the CLIFFORD WORD BANK.

5. Divide students into groups of two or three. On large pieces of white cardboard, each group draws their version of Clifford.

6. Each group places their Clifford somewhere in the room as if he were hiding. Together the other groups say, "We can find Clifford the big red dog no matter where he hides. He is hiding behind, under, near ..., the author's chair, the bookcase, the math center...," and they guess his hiding place.

7. Tell students that words such as *behind, near, by, under, over* are called prepositions. Show students the word *positions* in the word. Tell them these little words usually tell the position of someone or something and are usually followed by a place name.

8. Go back over Clifford's hiding places: behind the door, under the table, and so forth to make the function of prepositions clear.

9. After this oral language experience, students in groups list all the places where

Clifford the big red dog could hide on their version of Clifford. Have students use this experience and list in sentences about their Clifford.

10. Share.

EXTENSIONS

1. Make Fuzzy Clifford Cards.
   - Students cut out their versions of Clifford from furry red fabric (faux fur).
   - They use buttons for his eyes and nose.
   - Black strips of leather may be added for his collar.
   - Fold heavy stock to make the card.
   - On the outside they write *Clifford the Big Red Dog* with a black marker.
   - Brainstorm people to whom the card may be sent.
   - On the inside of the card, students write a message to a chosen person.
2. Ask students to bring to class their favorite dog book, dog picture, or stuffed dog. Set up a "Dog Show and Tell."

RELATED BOOKS

While there are any number of fine children's books about dogs, those described below are a small sampling of some old and new favorites.

Desmond the Dog by Nick Denchfield is a simple interactive book for primary students. By pulling Desmond's tail, students can make him splash, bark, and run.
- Students identify the D sound by finding the letter in the title and saying its sound. This also shows the D in the initial as well as the final position.
- Students take turns reading the pages. As a volunteer reads, that student gets to pull Desmond's tail. This simple reward encourages even reluctant students to risk the reading.

Tog the Dog by Colin and Jacqui Hawkins is a flip-the-page rhyming book about the antics of Tog. The following activity may be done before or after reading the book. In either case, ask individual students to read the word in bold print.
- Divide students into groups of four. Give each group a long strip of cashier tape.
- At the top they write the word family OG.
- Each group writes words in that family: *bog, clog, dog, flog, fog, grog, hog, jog, log, bullfrog, bulldog, groundhog*, and so forth.

Dogteam by Gary Paulsen recreates taking a dogteam out for a night run.
- This book lends itself to making a mural to capture the length of the team as pictured in the book.
- Locate Alaska on a map or globe.
- Talk about the Iditarod.

Open Me...I'm a Dog! by Art Spiegelman is a quirky little book that tries to convince the reader that it is a dog, not a book. For example, one page pops out so it looks like a dog's tail wagging. It even comes with a collar and leash attached to it.
- Use as a model for persuasive writing.

- After reading it, students go back through the book and list the proofs.
- Students notice the opener and the conclusion.
- Students add elaboration for each page. For example: What more could be added to the "Bow-wow" page to convince the reader it is a dog not a book.

Big Dog and Little Dog and *Big Dog and Little Dog Going for a Walk* by Dav Pilkey are two wonderful board books for the very young student. Both texts are predictable stories that lead the reader to read jointly and independently. The pictures and words so simple, the books so durable, students may pick them up and read them again and again.

Dog Breath: The Horrible Trouble with Hally Tosis by Dav Pilkey is the story of Hally Tosis and her terrible breath. Not only does this book introduce the word *halitosis*, but it tells how Hally used it for a good purpose.
- Students have fun finding out what Hally Tosis's bad breath causes to happen: wallpaper to roll up, fish to go belly up, and so forth.
- Design a poster about breath. Use those in the book as models.

I Really Want a Dog by Susan Breslow and Sally Blakemore is about a boy's longing for a dog.
- Use this book to introduce adjectives: *shaggy, curly, fearless*, and so forth.
- Use this book to reinforce questions and the question mark and answers.

The First Dog by Jan Brett tells the tale of Kip and the Palewolf. Because Palewolf proves his worth, Kip befriends him and christens him "dog."
- Students name the creatures pictured on the end pages and throughout the book.
- Talk about naming. In the book, Brett has Kip say, "And I will call you 'Dog,' which means 'One who wags his tail.'" Students share names of their pets or names they would give their pets and why they chose those names.

PUBLISHING

Make a display of the dog books, pictures, and stuffed dogs. Add students' writing and cards to the display and call it WE ARE BIG DOGS ABOUT OUR SOUNDS! Invite parents, friends, administrators, and other classes to see the display. Students sing, "How Much Is That Doggie in the Window?"

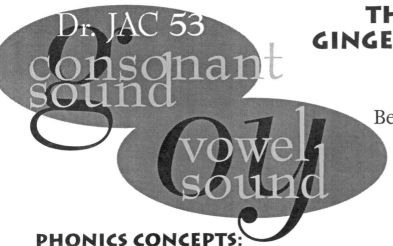

consonant sound

g

vowel sound

oy

THE CAJUN GINGERBREAD BOY

Hyperion

Berthe Amoss

PHONICS CONCEPTS:

- G Consonant Sound: J Sound as in *GinGerbread*
- *Generalization:*
    WHEN THE CONSONANT G IS FOLLOWED BY E, I, OR Y, THE G OFTEN HAS A SOUND SIMILAR TO THAT OF J IN JUMP. THIS SOUND IS CALLED THE SOFT G SOUND.
- OY Vowel Sound: OI Diphthong as in bOY

LANGUAGE ARTS CONCEPTS:

- How languages are assimilated;
- Capitalization

Artifacts: Cajun Gingerbread Boy Cookies (recipe in back of book, any gingerbread recipe, or store-bought gingerbread cookies)
Summary: This Cajun twist on the classic tale has a removeable gingerbread boy on the cover who travels through the book by being inserted into slits in the pages. The story, sprinkled with French and Cajun words, is set on Bayou Lafourche. The little old lady is a Cajun mawmaw, and the fox has been transformed into M'sieur Cocodrie, an alligator.

Note: This repetitive, cumulative tale comes to us from Scandinavia where it is called "The Pancake." Versions of this tale can be found in many countries, but it has been modernized as The Gingerbread Boy.

READING/WRITING CONNECTION

1. Before beginning this lesson, make a 3' GINGERBREAD BOY WORD BANK out of brown butcher paper to look like the removeable gingerbread boy in the book. Display near the reading area.
2. Call the students to the reading area and show them several versions of the classic story. If they know the story, invite retellings. If they do not know the story, read or tell one of the classic versions. (See "Related Books.")
3. Tell students that they will be working with two important sounds in gingerbread boy's name: the G consonant that sounds like the letter J and the OY vowel sound.
4. Say the word *gingerbread*. Students echo. Ask one volunteer to underline the two Gs in the word. Students repeat the sound after the underlining.

5. Say the word boy. Students echo. Ask one volunteer to underline the OY in the word. Students repeat the sound after the underlining. Make certain students hear the two sounds in this diphthong—the O and the I sound.

6. Show students the book and how the gingerbread boy can be removed from the alligator head. Read the title. Write the word Cajun on the word bank. Talk about why it is capitalized.

    •Tell students that Cajuns are descendants of people who immigrated to the state of Louisiana from a place once called Acadia but now called Nova Scotia.

    • People in Acadia spoke French.

    • Show students Nova Scotia on a map or globe. Show them France. Show them Louisiana. Speculate about how these people traveled.

    • Talk about how these people brought their language with them, but when they came to Louisiana, they learned English words. Talk about why that would happen. Talk about how they kept some French, mixed it with English, and created some unique words that were a combination of both.

7. Knowing that, invite students to predict how this version of the story might be different from the original. Ask them to "put on their listening ears" so that they can hear differences between the two stories. As you read, talk about the words that seem unusual: *Bayou Lafourche, mawmaw, piquant, merci, gumbo,* and so forth. Return to these words after you have read the story once. Talk about their meanings.

8. Ask a different student to place the gingerbread boy in each slit as you read through the pages of the book. When you come to the couplet, "Oh, my! Bon appetit!/ You smell good enough to eat!" ask the students to say it with you. When you come to the "Run, run, fast as you can!" refrain, invite the other students to make the soft G sound somewhat like a train chugging.

9. At the conclusion of the book, distribute the gingerbread cookies.

10. Divide students into groups of four. Each group draws a large gingerbread boy with a line down its middle. On one side of the gingerbread boy, students write characteristics of one story. On the other side, students write the characteristics of the Cajun story. Younger students draw their own gingerbread boys to use to write a story or practice writing their letters.

EXTENSIONS

1. Students make paper gingerbread boy books. Inside they write their version of the story. For example, they may write: The Texas Gingerbread Boy, The Gingerbread Girl, The Gingerbread Football Player, or in the manner of "The Pancake," students might create, "The Hamburger Boy," "The Pizza Boy," and so forth.

2. Connect this story to social studies by studying the state of Louisiana. The note on the back of book tells the route of the Gingerbread Boy, which students could trace on a map of Louisiana.

3. Students think about the French words and how they are used in the context. They try to figure out what each word means: *merci (thanks), bon appétit (good eating, may you enjoy the food), jamais (never), cher (dear), mes amis (my friends), m'sieur (monsieur, sir), bonjour (good day, hello), mais oui (but yes), merci beaucoup (thank you very much).* Students can also try decoding the Cajun words *fais-dodo* and *zydeco* by their context.

4. In science, students learn about swamps and bayous.

5. Students role play the story. In turn, students become the gingerbread boy. They run away, and other students try to catch him until he comes to the teacher!

RELATED BOOKS

The Gingerbread Boy by Paul Galdone tells the classic gingerbread boy story.
• The fun of this book is to challenge the students to remember each of the persons and animals the gingerbread boy has run away from.
• Read the refrain and pause for the students to insert the correct names.

The Gingerbread Man retold by Eric A. Kimmel gives a positive ending to this old favorite. This version ends with a poem that suggests the gingerbread man will return the next time someone bakes gingerbread.
• Talk about ginger. Bring in a ginger root (available at most supermarkets). Let the students hold it and look at it.
• Cut off tiny pieces for the students to smell and taste.
• Tell students that ginger is used as a food, spice, tea, and oil. The Chinese used it at least 2500 years ago as a medicine. People in Greece, India, Tibet, and Japan also use it.

In *The Stinky Cheese Man and other Fairly Stupid Tales* by Jon Scieszka and Lane Smith, the old lady decides to make a man not out of gingerbread but rather out of stinky cheese. The Stinky Cheese Man is so stinky no one wants to chase him, but he meets his fate because of a fox anyway.
• Students could construct "men" out of different food products such as: bread, marshmallows, fruit, vegetables.
• They write their version of the story based upon the ingredients of their "gingerbread man." For example, a "marshmallow man" may fall into a campfire or a "bread man" might get plucked from the ground by a crow.

PUBLISHING

Celebrate GINGERBREAD BOY DAY! Students prepare a display of books, stories, and art. Invite parents to bring gingerbread boy cookies. Students present a reenactment of the story. Small groups of students read the different versions of the story. Students read their own versions. Festoon a banner across the room which reads, GINGERBREAD BOYS TEACH US THEIR SOUNDS!

ARTHUR'S APRIL FOOL

Little, Brown

Marc Brown

PHONICS CONCEPTS:
- AR Vowel Sound: AR Sound as in *ARthur;*
- UR Vowel Sound: R Sound as in *ArthUR;*
- *Generalization:*
    WHEN A VOWEL IS FOLLOWED BY R, THE R INFLUENCES THE VOWEL SOUND.
- PR Consonant Sound: PR Blend as in *APRil;*
- TH Consonant Sound: TH Digraph Voiceless as in *ArTHur;*
- S Consonant Sound: Z Sound as in *Arthur'S;*
- A Vowel Sound: Long A as in *April;*
- I Vowel Sound: Short I as in *AprIl;*
- L Consonant Sound as in *ApriL, fooL;*
- F Consonant Sound as in *Fool;*
- OO Vowel Sound: 2-Dot U or Long OO as in *fOOl*

LANGUAGE ARTS CONCEPT:
- Apostrophes

Artifacts: Cardboard-tube telescopes
Summary: Binky threatens to ruin Arthur's tricks at the April Fool's Day assembly in school, but Arthur outsmarts him.

READING/WRITING CONNECTION

1. Make a three-dimensional top hat out of black construction paper before beginning this lesson. Inside the hat, place the two sets of letters you are about to introduce. Write AR on one large index card; write PR on another. Write the other sounds on additional index cards, but hold these out until you have taught these two vowel sounds first.
2. Gather the students around the hat. Invite one student to reach into the hat to pick one sound the class will learn today.
3. When the student produces the AR or PR sound, pronounce it. Students echo. Affix the index card on a nearby board or chart so students can see it. Follow this procedure for the next sound.
4. Drop the other index cards of sounds into the hat. Invite individual students, one at a time, to draw a card from the hat. Pronounce each sound. Students echo. Affix

the index card on board or chart.

5. Help students understand that knowing all those sounds will help them read the title of this book. Ask for reading volunteers.

6. Talk about April Fool's Day. Point out the apostrophe and explain why it is used. Talk about the meaning of the word fool. Elicit from students the kinds of tricks and pranks people play on this day. Explain that this is an old custom dating back to when April 1 marked the end of an eight-day New Year celebration. People who kept the custom of celebrating April 1 as the New Year even after the calendar was changed and January 1 marked the New Year were called the fools of April with April first becoming April Fool's Day.

7. Refocus students on the book's cover. Discuss what Arthur might be doing. Ask students to identify the clues that led them to their answers.

8. Talk about each of Arthur's friends pictured at the book's beginning. For oral language experience, ask students to tell what is funny about each picture.

9. Read the book. Point out the apostrophe in *Arthur's*. This book lends itself to frequent discussion of sequence and predictions.

10. Give students two cardboard tubes, one shorter than the other. Students insert one into the other to resemble a telescope. They tape clear food wrap or contact paper over the ends. They paint and decorate their telescopes. Then they write descriptions of what they see or imagine they see through their telescopes. Share.

EXTENSIONS

1. Make a class April Fool's Animal Alphabet Book. Create the first page together with students so they can use it as a model. Because Arthur is an aardvark, begin with Aardvark. Use this word to reinforce the AR sound.

2. Students create other pages individually or in small groups. They may do all or some of the following on their page:
   • They write the name of the animal.
   • Use words starting with the same letter to describe the animal, for instance, *angry aardvark*. Younger students may use any appropriate adjectives.
   • Write facts about the animal.
   • Draw the animal.
   • Write about the animal.
   • Give the animal a name, such as Arthur.
   • To play an April Fool's trick, students might hide something extra on their page.

RELATED BOOKS

Arthur Writes a Story by Marc Brown is another Arthur Adventure. Besides reinforcing the AR sound, this book reinforces the power of writing and what makes a good story.

1. Use Arthur's story to teach the elements of a story and appropriate elaboration.
2. Students write a story.

My Apron by Eric Carle tells how the narrator got an apron like his Uncle Adam's. It reinforces the power of modeling as well as the PR sound.

1. Students make aprons out of butcher paper. They decorate their aprons with the letters and sounds they have learned.

2. They write about a time when they received something from a relative.

PUBLISHING

Hold a "Find What's Hidden Huddle." Students form a group huddle with their telescopes, exchange animal alphabet pages, and search for the hidden extras. Bind and display the finished alphabet book. Call the display WE DON'T HIDE THE SOUNDS WE KNOW!

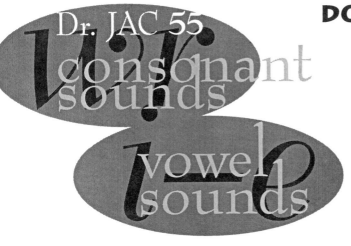

DON'T FORGET TO WRITE

Ideals Children's Books

Martina Selway

PHONICS CONCEPTS:
- WR Consonant Sound: R Sound as in *WRite;*
- *Generalization:*
    WHEN A WORD OR SYLLABLE STARTS WITH WR, THE W IS USUALLY SILENT.
- I–E Vowel Sound: Long I–Final E Silent as in *wrItE;*
- *Generalization:*
    WHEN THERE ARE TWO VOWELS IN A ONE-SYLLABLE WORD, ONE OF WHICH IS THE FINAL E, SEPARATED FROM THE FIRST VOWEL BY ONE CONSONANT, THE FIRST VOWEL IS USUALLY LONG AND THE E IS USUALLY SILENT.

LANGUAGE ARTS CONCEPT:
- Parts of a friendly letter

Artifacts: Sheets of stationery and envelopes
Summary: Rosie reluctantly leaves to visit Grandad's farm. Her mom's parting words are, "Don't forget to write." Rosie's letters turn into a daily journal which reflects her changing attitude toward this visit.

READING/WRITING CONNECTION

1. Before the lesson, prepare an enlarged sheet of stationery out of butcher paper to make a STATIONERY WORD BANK. Decorate it to look somewhat like the first page of stationery in the book. Write the title of the book on it.
2. Gather students around the stationery. Read the title. Ask students what sound they hear in the word *write*. When they say R, tell them they already know part of the day's lesson. Give them the generalization. Invite a student to underline the WR in the title.
3. Brainstorm other words that have the WR sound: *writing, written, wrong, wrap, wrestle, wrist, wren, wrinkle, typewriter, rewrite, handwriting,* and so forth. Write these on the STATIONERY WORD BANK.
4. Remind students of the second generalization in words such as *cake* and *rope*. Ask students if they can find another example of that generalization in the title.

Underline the word *write*. Point out how the I says its own name in the word but the E says nothing; it is silent.

5. Look back at the book's cover. Ask students to predict what might happen in the book.

6. Tell students to listen carefully to how the letter progresses and how the main character changes how she feels as she writes each page.

7. When reading, stop to show the students each progression of the letter, read the letter, and immediately discuss how Rosie is feeling.

8. This book invites rich oral language experiences: Ask students how they feel about making visits, if they have ever gone to visit someone and stayed over night or longer, how they feel about leaving home, why they might feel that way, who they may want to visit, where they would like to visit, who they would write to, and so forth.

9. Model writing a letter with the students as if you are on a visit. Use chart paper and encourage ideas from students. When they have finished their letter, they may decorate it the way Rosie did. Point out how Rosie's decorations match what she has written. Share.

EXTENSIONS

1. **Letter Writing.** Teach the parts of a friendly letter. Return to the letter at the beginning of the book. Talk about the return address, the salutation, indenting, and whatever else is on that first page that would be appropriate for your students. Even the youngest students could be exposed to the terminology.
   • Run through the body of the letter. Point out its elaboration, its punctuation—especially the correct use of quotation marks, and its block paragraphing.
   • Look again at the last page. Point out the closing and the signature. Use the envelope as a model for addressing envelopes.

2. **Motivation.** This is a good book to use as motivation for reading and writing. Teach the following poem, most often ascribed to Nikki Giovanni:
      If I can think it, I can say it.
      If I can say it, I can write it.
      If I can write it, I can read it.
Students should say this poem often, especially when they seem reluctant to write or to read their own writing.

RELATED BOOKS

If You Were a Writer by Joan Lowery Nixon tells how Melia wants to be a writer like her mother, so her mother gives her many helpful suggestions about good writing and about the elements of a narrative. This book is filled with possibilities for mini-lessons on the following topics:
      • imagery;
      • show don't tell ;
      • getting ideas;
      • starting a story;
      • inventing characters;

- problem and solution;
- genre.

Amelia's Notebook and *Amelia Writes Again* by Marissa Moss provide hand-lettered entries of a nine-year-old girl's notebook. She records her thoughts and feelings about moving, starting school, and dealing with her older sister. In the second book, Amelia is ten years old and writes more about her daily life.

- Brainstorm the things Amelia includes in her notebook.
- Students begin a notebook and use Amelia's as a model.

Write Up a Storm with the Polk Street School by Patricia Reilly Giff is another in the Polk Street series. This book is interactive; it helps young writers write a story. Each chapter tells the reader the steps Giff goes through in writing a story. This is a fine book for the independent reader and the neophyte writer because it models the writing. Giff presents an element of a story in a context, revisits it, gives students a turn, and then goes on to the next element. At the conclusion of the book, there are directions for making a book and inserts for pages.

PUBLISHING

Proclaim WE WRITE EVERY DAY! Display students' writing and books everywhere in the room. Conduct a read-a-thon. Write invitations to interested people.

NIGHT NOISES

Harcourt Brace

Mem Fox

PHONICS CONCEPTS:

- OI Vowel Sound: OI Diphthong as in *nOIse;*
- N Consonant Sound: Nasal as in *Night, Noises;*
- GH: Silent Consonants as in *niGHt;*
- *Generalization:*
  WHEN THE LETTER I IS FOLLOWED BY THE LETTERS GH, THE I USUALLY STANDS FOR ITS LONG SOUND AND THE GH IS SILENT.
- *Generalization:*
  WHEN THE LETTERS GHT APPEAR TOGETHER IN A WORD, THE LETTERS GH ARE SILENT.

LANGUAGE ARTS CONCEPTS:

- Subplots;
- Onomatopoeia

Artifacts: Noisemakers (available from Oriental Trading Co.)

Summary: Old Lily Laceby dozes by the fire, but her faithful dog hears different night noises. The surprise ending explains all the noise. The small pictures inserted to the left of the main pictures give hints about where the noise comes from, while the small pictures inserted to the right of the main pictures provide images of Lily's dreams. Interestingly, her dreams start in the recent past and progress backwards to her childhood. This book is a Horn Book Fanfare Selection, a Notable Children's Book in the Language Arts, and a Redbook Children's Picturebook Award.

READING/WRITING CONNECTION

1. Before the lesson begins, make a 3' NOISY WORD BANK with a border of stick figures holding their hands to their ears. Display near students. Write the title of the book at the top. Write each of the noisy words from the book on the NOISY WORD BANK so that you can point to them when meeting that word in the text: *click, clack, crinch,*

crunch, murmur, mutter, shhhh, twist, test, rattle, knick, knack, knock, yell, clatter, bang, creak, crack, snick, snack.

2. Begin the lesson by making noise with one of the noisemakers. Ask the students to describe what they hear. When one offers "noise," show them that word in the title.
3. Point out how the OI in the word noise sounds like the OY in boy. Make the sound; students echo.
4. Ask a volunteer to underline the N sound. Pronounce the nasal N. Students echo. Ask a volunteer to underline the GH. Say the word *night*. Ask students if they hear the GH. When they say they do not, ask what those letters are called. (silent) Invite a volunteer, based on these sounds, to read the title.
5. Tell the students that you will need help with the noises as you read this book. As you read and say the noise words, point to the word on the word bank so students can see the word as they repeat it. Since most of the words can be figured by onsets and rimes, this also helps students in that reading skill.
6. Upon second reading, show students the pictures on the left and right of the main pictures. Teach these as subplots. Talk about *sub* as something beneath or under something such as *submarine* or *subway*. Tell students that these other actions or subplots are also taking place while the main story takes place.
7. Take students outside or to some place in the school where they will not disturb others. Distribute the noisemakers. Let them make plenty of noise.
8. When they return, divide them into groups of three or four. Give each group paper. Tell them to write the words NOISY WORDS at the top of the paper. Ask them to underline the OI diphthong.
9. Explain that they just made noise with their noisemakers that everyone could hear, but when they write they must use noisy words so that readers can hear the sounds in their heads. Remind students of the noisy words in the book. Point to those and repeat them.
10. Students write these and other noisy words on their papers. Share.

EXTENSIONS

1. Students look through the books they are reading to find other noisy words to add to their lists. Ask students if OI is a sound or a noise. Talk about the difference.
2. Teach onomatopoeia. Explain to students that when we use a word that makes a sound like what it means, we call it onomatopoeia. If your students are ready, tell them that *onomatopoeia* means *name making* in Greek. It is as if nature makes its own name creating its sounds associated with it: *rumble, boom, crash*, and so forth. Ask students to give onomatopoeic words for the following sounds: (You may think of others.)
    • drop a penny in water
    • run your nail down the board
    • wad up a sheet of paper
    • use one of their noisemakers
    • push a book off a desk
    • ring a bell

RELATED BOOKS

Noisy Poems collected by Jill Bennett presents a dozen poems filled with noisy words. They range from David McCord's "Song of the Train" to Jack Prelutsky's "Spaghetti! Spaghetti!" The end pages are crammed with noisy words which the students may to add to their lists.

• Read the poems and ask the students to say the onomatopoeic words with you.

• Students write noisy poems. Challenge them to use the word *noise* or *noisy* in the poem and words from their noisy words lists.

Noisy Nora by Rosemary Wells tells how Nora, who feels neglected, makes more and more noise to attract her parents' attention.

• This is a good book to use for cause and effect. Talk about what causes different noises.

• Divide a portion of the board or chart in half. On one side, list the things Nora did to make noise. On the other side list the effect of that noise.

• Add things students do that make noise and their effect.

Too Much Noise by Ann McGovern is a classic cumulative tale that adds sounds as the book progresses.

• Students make the noises and repeat the onomatopoeic words in the story.

• Talk about why Peter felt the house was quiet at the end of the book when he thought those same sounds were noisy at the beginning of the book.

PUBLISHING

Proclaim NOISY DAY! Display students noisy writing, play noisy music, make noises, play with noisemakers.

EVEN IF I DID SOMETHING AWFUL

Aladdin

Barbara Shook Hazen

PHONICS CONCEPTS:
- AW Vowel Sound: Broad O as in *AWful, sAW;*
- Initial, medial, final positions

LANGUAGE ARTS CONCEPTS:
- Questions and question marks;
- Answers and periods

Artifacts: Orange crayons

Summary: Before revealing the awful thing she did, the main character, who is a little girl, tries to get her mother's assurance of unconditional love. This book is the winner of the Christopher Award, an award given by the Christopher Society to recognize books that reflect high moral standards.

READING/WRITING CONNECTION

1. In the middle of a 2' sheet of orange butcher paper write the letters AW about 12" high. This will be the AW WORD BANK. Display near the reading area.
2. Say the sound. Students echo. Ask students to think of times when they have heard somebody say that sound like a word. (Usually people say "aw" as an expression of incredulity, disgust, or sympathy.) Ask students if they might say the sound if they made a mistake, dropped something, or broke something. Model a situation (dropping the book, for example) that might be followed by saying, "Aw!"
3. Students role-play situations that are followed by saying, "Aw!" (missing a turn at a game, slipping, falling).
4. Show the cover of the book. Ask a volunteer to find the AW sound in the title and point it out. Repeat the sound. Students echo. Add *awful* to the word bank.
5. Show the first pages where the little girl plays with a football and subsequently breaks her mother's vase. Talk about what is happening and invite predictions.
6. Read the book through. Point out the mark that follows each question and the mark that follows each answer. Tell students the former is called a question mark and the latter is called a period. Explain that these marks tell us the thought is over, that the sentence is finished. They also tell us if it asks a questions or if it makes a statement.

7. Distribute orange crayons and paper.
8. Students write a question they would ask if they did something awful. Remind them to use the question mark.
9. Then they write an answer. Remind them to use the period.
10. Share in the Author's Chair.

EXTENSIONS

1. Refocus students' attention on the AW written on the butcher paper. Using magnetic letters on the board which allow for manipulation and interaction, show the AW in the initial position, so that the students see a large AW followed by other letters that make it a word. Say each word. Students echo. For example:

$$\begin{array}{l} \text{ful} \\ \textbf{AW}\text{e} \\ \text{fully} \end{array}$$

2. Using AW in the medial position, work with the words so that the students see a large AW preceded and followed by other letter(s) that makes it a word. Say each word. Students echo. For example:

l		n
dr	**AW**	n
h		k
y		n
cr		l

3. Using AW in the final position, move the letters about to make words so that the students see a large AW preceded by other letter(s) that makes it a word. Say each word. Students echo. For example:

l	
j	
dr	
str	**AW**
th	
p	
cl	
c	

4. Students use the letters in their minifolders, tactile letters, or their magnetic letters and boards to follow these models, saying the words as they do. This is good practice and helps students see patterns.

RELATED BOOK

What Faust Saw by Dutton Matt Ottley contains the AW vowel sound in the final position. This book casts Faust as the dutiful watchdog who does his best to warn the family about the bizarre events he sees taking place one night.

• Together write a version about Faust using as many of the AW words as possible.

For example, instead of "One night Faust saw something very strange," students might suggest "One night Faust saw something awful." Instead of "Faust hid," students might suggest "Faust crawled away."

PUBLISHING

Hold AN AWFULLY NICE DAY! As a variation of "Show and Tell," students bring to class something awfully nice to share. Each, in turn, begins the sharing by saying, "I have something awfully nice to share."

THE GLERP

Silver

David McPhail

PHONICS CONCEPT:
• GL Consonant Sound: GL Blend as in *GLasses* or *GLerp*

LANGUAGE ARTS CONCEPT:
• Quotation marks as a signal for dialogue

Artifacts: Large paper bags, grey if possible
Summary: The odd Glerp eats everything that gets in its way. The book reads like a secular version of Jonah and the whale.

READING/WRITING CONNECTION

1. Construct a three-foot "Glerp" out of grey butcher paper so that it resembles the one on the book's cover. Display near students. This will be the GLERP WORD BANK but do not identify it as such at this point.

2. Before showing the book, cover its title with a 7" strip of removable correction & cover-up tape. You may point out the author and ask students if they know other books by this author.

3. Ask students to identify the animals they see pictured on the cover. When they get to the large gray glob and are stumped, invite students to suggest names. Give them the hint that its name begins with GL. Make the sound. Students echo the sound.

4. Write students' suggestions on the GLERP WORD BANK. Interestingly, and probably because students pick up on the grey color, they typically suggest: *Glob, Globby, Gloomy, Gloppy* although one student suggested *Glove* and another *Glede*, which is a word, although he probably meant Gleed. Often students preface the name with an adjective such as *Foggy Glass* or *Gray Glitter*. In any case, accept all suggestions.

5. Underline the GL consonant sound in each suggestion, asking students to pronounce the sound each time.

6. Uncover the title. Discuss the names they offered and the name David McPhail used.

7. Read the book. Use a different voice when reading GLERP's dialogue to distinguish it from its name—GLERP.

8. After the story, return to the first page. Point out the GLERP and what it says in the picture. Since it is in a conversation bubble, it is easy for students to understand. Then point to the words below. Distinguish between the name and the dialogue. Make a connection between how you knew to change your voice for the dialogue and because of the quotation marks.

9. Tell students that when the GLERP talks, we put its words between two "little lips." Tell students these marks are called quotation marks. Reread the book, pointing to

the words in quotation marks.

10. Distribute the large paper bags which students transform into GLERPS by drawing mouths and eyes. Encourage them to have their GLERPS eat small items in and around their areas. Set this up by grouping students in several areas of the room where you have placed small objects. Afterwards, students write on their GLERPS the names of the items eaten or a story about their GLERPS. Share.

EXTENSION

Divide students into six groups: the elephant group; the cow group; the dog group; the lion group; the ant group; and the mouse group. Each group:
   • creates a diorama out of a shoe box for their animal;
   • researches what things their animal eats by reading or interviewing people such as parents, the librarian, or faculty members;
   • draws or finds pictures of what things their animal eats to place in their diorama;
   • gives their animal a name;
   • writes a dialogue between their animal and another animal in a different diorama (team up three groups with three other groups).

RELATED BOOKS

Use the poem "Gray" from *A Song of Colors* by Judy Hindley. Read the poem and add the three GL words *gleam, glisten, glint* to the GLERP WORD BANK.
   •Talk about the meaning of these words.
   •Talk about the different shades of grey mentioned in the poem.
   •Talk about the different things named that are grey in color. Ask if they are all the same shade of grey. Find these things in the picture.
   •Read other color poems that match the animals pictured in THE GLERP.

Frosted Glass by Denys Cazet tells how Gregory uses his imagination to draw wonderful things but is hampered when asked to draw a circle in front of the class.
   • Students draw circles and other shapes.
   • Using magic slates, students practice drawing a "perfect" circle.

Glasses (who needs 'em?) by Lane Smith repeats the GL sound fourteen times including the title, this permits much practice with the GL consonant sound. The story is about a boy who does not want to wear glasses until his doctor convinces him he should by pointing out an imaginative list of well-adjusted people who wear eyeglass.
   • Use this book for teaching persuasive writing.
   • Students design their own pair of eyeglasses. Then they actually make them out of heavy stock paper by making two lower case g's and joining them at the bridge over the nose. Each circle of the G fits over one eye and the tail of the G curls around the ear.

Eyeglasses by Margaret J. Goldstein is a non-fiction book about the history and development of eyeglasses. It includes a brief explanation of how the eye works and the vision problems that glasses can correct.
   • Students make pipe cleaner glasses according to the directions in the book.

• Students sing "The Star Spangled Banner" which begins with the line "Oh, say can you see?" Talk about the different ways of seeing.

• Point out the the "Glossary" at the conclusion of the book begins with the GL sound.

PUBLISHING

Declare GL DAY! Invite an ophthalmologist, optician, or optometrist to class to dialogue about eye care and the wearing of glasses. Display all the books and work done by the students.

A YOU'RE ADORABLE

Candlewick

Buddy Kaye, Fred Wise, and Sidney Lippman

PHONICS CONCEPT:
• The sounds of each letter in the alphabet

LANGUAGE ARTS CONCEPTS:
• Alphabetic Order;
• Alliteration

Artifacts: Alphabet stickers
Summary: Children and animals frolic through the letters of the alphabet in this illustrated presentation of a familiar song from the 1940s. Music for the song is included.

READING/WRITING CONNECTION

1. Review the alphabet in order and each sound as you read through the book. Students say the letter and echo its sound. Talk about the meaning of the word that starts with each letter. For example, the A page:
    • Teacher reads, "A you're adorable" and says the letter A.
    • Students echo the sentence and the letter.
    • Teacher pronounces the A Vowel Sound, the schwa in Adorable
    • Students echo the sound.
    • Talk about what adorable means.
    • Go to the next page, the next letter.
    • Follow this procedure throughout the book.
2. After the book, teach students the music to the song.
3. Sing the song several times.
4. Assign different students different letters; they sing their page; the class joins in.
5. This song is simple and lends itself to many variations. For example, boys sing some pages, girls sing others; one group of students sing the letter while the class sings the chorus; and so forth.
6. Distribute alphabet stickers and colorful paper.
7. Each student places his or her sticker somewhere on the paper.
8. Depending upon level and ability, the students write using that letter as their focus. For example, if a student received the letter B, he or she might:
    • practice writing the lower and upper case Bs;
    • compose a poem about a Bee;
    • write a story about a Bear;
    • persuade that B is the best letter in the alphabet;
    • compare or contrast B with other letters of the alphabet;
    • describe some exciting event using alliteration, such as BIG BEARS BREAK

Bottles;
- list fruits, vegetables, or animals that begin with their letter;
- list first names that begin with their letter;
- make up a tongue twister.
9. Students share in the Author's Chair.
10. Conclude by singing the song again.

EXTENSIONS

1. Reinforce the letters of the alphabet by making and playing the game "AL-FA-MATT," created by Alana Morris, consultant for Absey & Co.
   Materials
   - A white shower curtain liner
   - Sticky-backed tactile alphabet letters
   - Small pictures that relate to letters
   - Words that identify the picture
   - Small two-inch bean bags covered in various colored fabrics (may be made or purchased)

   Making the Game
   - Place the sticky-backed tactile letters randomly and rather densely on curtain.
   - Laminate the small pictures and words near related letters using laminate sheets or clear contact paper. For example, a picture of a wolf might be laminated near the letter W.

   Playing the Game
   - Place the curtain flat on the floor in an area where students may gather around it.
   - Students take turns tossing the bean bag onto the AL-FA-MATT.
   - Since there are many variations possible for playing, teachers may use the suggestions below and/or create others:
   - Students
     - say the letter the bean bag lands on;
     - say the letter the bean bag lands on and make its sound;
     - identify the picture and say the letter the picture begins with. For example, if the bean bag lands on a picture of a bird, students say "bird, B."
     - identify the picture, read the word, and say the letter and its sound.
     - compose a sentence using the word, letter, or picture.

2. There are two additional suggestions for using *A You're Adorable* on the inside cover of the book.

RELATED BOOK

Teachers may tap the resources in the library for alphabet books that are appropriate for the level and abilities they are teaching. One suggestion is a unique detective ABC book that tells a suspenseful story, *The ABC Mystery* by Doug Cushman.
1. Show the first wordless picture and invite inference and prediction by asking, "What do you think is happening? What do you think will happen next?"
2. Show the second wordless picture and continue to invite inference and prediction.

3. Read the book.
4. Students, working in small groups, create their own ABC book. This book may be connected to other subjects across the curriculum.

PUBLISHING

Celebrate ALPHABET DAY! Invite parents, friends, faculty, and administrators. Students sing their "A You're Adorable" and ask the audience to participate. Students give hand-made letters of the alphabet to guests before, during, or after the song.

THE EXTRAORDINARY GIFT

Abbeville

Florence Langlois

PHONICS CONCEPTS:
- TH Consonant Sound: TH Digraph Voiced as in *THe;*
- X Consonant Sound: KS Sound as in *eXtraordinary;*
- TR Consonant Sound: TR Blend as in *exTRaordinary;*
- A Vowel Sound: Schwa as in *extrAordinary;*
- OR Vowel Sound: OR Sound as in *extraORdinary;*
- AR Vowel Sound: AIR sound as in *extraordinARy;*
- *Generalization:*
    WHEN A VOWEL IS FOLLOWED BY R, THE R INFLUENCES THE VOWEL SOUND.
- D Consonant Sound: Plosive as in *extraorDinary;*
- I Vowel Sound: Short I as in *extraordInary, gIft;*
- N Consonant Sound: Nasal as in *extraordiNary;*
- Y Vowel Sound: Long E sound as in *extraordinarY;*
- *Generalization:*
    WHEN Y OR EY IS SEEN IN THE LAST SYLLABLE THAT IS NOT ACCENTED, THE LONG SOUND OF E IS HEARD.
- G Consonant Sound: Guttural as in *Gift;*
- F Consonant Sound: Fricative as in *giFt;*
- T Consonant Sound: Plosive as in *gifT*

LANGUAGE ARTS CONCEPT:
- Imagery while reading

Artifacts: Miniature books (available from Kirchen Bros.)

Summary: Paul's mother asks him what kind of gift he would like. Paul requests an extraordinary gift. He wants real things, each of which then folds out on an oversized page to reveal something creative and imaginative. On the final page, his wise mother grants his wish. She gives him the most extraordinary gift of all—a book!

READING/WRITING CONNECTION

1. Point to the book's title. Ask volunteers to read it.
2. After the reading, reteach the sounds by pointing to the letters, pronouncing the

sound, and asking students to echo. In this way students understand the process of sounding out words.

3. Explain that reading is both sounding out the words and understanding what those words mean.
4. Talk about the meaning of *extraordinary* and *gift*.
5. Proceed through the book by calling on volunteers to read each page.
6. The reader gets to open the gateway fold to read the second part of the page.
7. Each reader then picks the next reader.
8. Distribute the miniature books and sheets of paper.
9. Students write about why books are important or why it is important to read.
10. Author's Chair Share.

EXTENSIONS

1. Give each student two sheets of the same brightly-colored paper (8 1/2" X 14").
2. They fold the sheets in half, short end to short end.
3. They glue or paste the second half of one sheet to the back of the first half of the other sheet so that it creates a gatefold like those in the book.
4. Explain to students that they will write their own wishbook using the gatefolds the way they are used in the book. (For very young students, it helps to compare this "wish list" writing to writing a letter to Santa Claus.)
5. Students draw themselves on the left leaf and write "I'd like a ... and they write the name of the object or animal.
6. On the outside of the gatefold, students draw the object or animal.
7. Inside the gatefold students draw the imaginative version of the real thing or animal they want.

RELATED BOOKS

I Hate to Read! by Rita Marshall tells about Victor, who hates to read, unwillingly looking at a book only to discover that the characters come alive. These characters pique his interest so much he really begins to care about them, so he turns the pages and begins to read. Then he hates to stop reading.

Santa's Book of Names by David McPhail tells how Edward wants to read but has trouble doing so. On Christmas Eve, he finds a book Santa dropped and remembers that book starts with the letter B. He makes that letter in the snow to signal Santa, who takes him for a ride in his sleigh. Before the ride is over, Edward discovers how to read.

Edward and the Pirates by David McPhail is the sequel to *Santa's Book of Names*. In this book, Edward reads avidly and well, using his imagination to make books come alive.

For any one or all three of these related books, it is important to help students understand that good readers use their imagination to make the characters in books come alive, and that good readers see the action and adventure in their minds much the way they see a movie or a television show. After reading each or any of the above books, it is important to engage students in discussion about:

1. The characters in their favorite books;
2. What it means to have characters "come alive;"
3. How they learn to read new words;
4. How they feel when they read and understand something.

PUBLISHING

Hold a READ-A-THON. Students bring their favorite books. Each student reads his/her book and receives a certificate of reading success.

Dr. JAC Glossary of Language Arts Concepts

adjectives—most often called describing words because they modify nouns or pronouns.
   • **degrees of adjectives**—the ending on an adjective that shows different quality or amount. The positive is simply the adjective; the comparative degree takes the *-er* ending; the superlative degree takes the *-est* ending. Irregular adjectives become a different word, e.g. *good, better, best* when changing degree or take on the words *more, most, less, least*.

alliteration—is as old as language. It is a figurative language device that repeats consonant sounds at the beginning of words or syllables.

alphabet—a name composed of the names of the first two letters *alpha* and *beta* in the Greek alphabet. Letters evolved from thing-pictures to idea-pictures to word-sound pictures to syllable-sound pictures and finally to letter-sound pictures as a more efficient way to write. A true alphabet uses only letter-sound pictures (symbols). Oscar Ogg in *The 26 Letters* chronicles the history of the alphabet:

> From the standard Greek alphabet the Romans took A, B, E, Z, H, I, K, M, N, O, T, X, and Y with hardly any change at all. The letter B, was merely a rounded form of the Greek character. Remodeling and finishing other Greek letters, the Romans produced C (and G), L, S, P, R, D and V. F and Q were taken from two old characters abandoned by the Greeks themselves. And that makes twenty-three.

> Meanwhile you may have been wondering why Z comes at the end of the alphabet, for with the Greeks it had been number six. At first the Romans dropped Z entirely, then found they could not get along without it. When they allowed Z to return to the alphabet, it had lost its place in the regular order and had to get to the end of the line. We have kept Z there ever since.

> The three missing letters, J, U and W, were not used by the Romans at all. U and W developed from V about a thousand years ago, and J developed from the letter I about five hundred years ago. (106)

alphabetic knowledge—to be able to identify, name, and write the letters of the alphabet.

alphabetic order—to arrange something according to the order of the letters in the alphabet.

answers and periods—a telling statement, usually declaring something, giving an order, or directing and its terminal mark, a dot that indicates its end.

apostrophe—a punctuation mark used to show letters are missing as in a contraction; to show that someone owns something, as in possession; or to indicate the plural of letter and figures.

assimilating language—appropriating parts of words, words, phrases of one language into another language so thoroughly that the appropriated language becomes integral to the other language.

capital *I*—using an upper case letter for the pronoun *I*. Sometimes called *uncial* or *majuscule*, all writing was done in these large letters until an increasing demand for the work of scribes gradually led to lower case letters or small letters, called *semiunicals* or *minuscules*. These were more simplified and easier to write than the uncials or capitals.

cause and effect—show how facts, events, or concepts (EFFECTS) happen or come into being because of other facts, events, or concepts (CAUSES).

color words—words that convey a certain color or create a certain image.

comma—a punctuation mark that is used to signal a brief pause.

common nouns—the general names of persons, places, things, or ideas.

connotation—a range of secondary or accompanying meanings for a word as well as what it commonly suggests or implies.

consonants—speech sounds characterized by constriction, closure, or interference of the breath. Because consonants set up audible turbulence, they give vitality and energy to speech. Oscar Ogg in *The 26 Letters* states, "The Phoenicians, we believe, supplied the Greeks with nineteen characters—all consonants, no vowels. They wrote entirely with consonants, and it was up to the reader to decide where a vowel sound was intended and which one was needed" (87).

couplets—two lines of poetry.

corpus of work by an author—the collection or body of work done by one particular writer.

denotation—the primary meaning of a word, such as the dictionary ordinarily specifies.

elements of a narrative—or text structure, generally comprised of characters, action or plot (episodes in longer pieces), setting, problem, and solution.

exclamation mark—a terminal mark at the end of an exclamatory sentence to indicate surprise, excitement, or strong emotion.

fiction—stories or events that are not true, or are feigned or invented.

folk tale—a short story of unknown authorship, which was originally transmitted orally before being secured in writing. The term is usually extended to include stories by known authors, which, after they were printed, were adopted and retold over and over again.

glossary—a little dictionary in the back of a book. It tells about special words used in the book.

homophones—words that sound alike but have different spellings and meanings.

idioms—groups of words that actually do not mean what they literally say.

imagery—mental pictures experienced by the reader. It includes auditory, tactile/kinesthetic, olfactory, gustatory, and visual qualities evoked through the words.

inference—reading between the lines, drawing conclusions or generalizations from facts or premises, deriving meaning from thinking.

intonation—alterations in the tone of pronouncing words to signal changes in meaning and relationship.

language play—enjoying language, using words in different or humorous combinations, making up words, assigning different meaning to words, rearranging the letters in words or making them different sizes.

letter—a symbol that represents a speech sound by using a character of the alphabet.

letter writing—a particular genre meant to communicate with someone in writing.
   • friendly letters—a communique written to friends or relatives.
   • business letters—a communique written for or with information to companies or organizations.

library research—using the library to find information you need or want.

literary allusions—an "it-reminds-me-of" pattern because it is an incomplete reference to some other literary work.

main character—the protagonist upon which the story revolves.

measurements—words that convey dimension, capacity, amount, or degree.

mythology of a word—tracing certain words to mythology in order to understand their meaning.

non-fiction— stories that are historically or factually true.

numeration—the art of reading in words numbers expressed by numerals.

onomatopoeia—a term applied to a word or a combination of words whose sound seems to resemble the sound it denotes.

paragraph—while linguists avoid defining paragraphs because some follow specific patterns and others do not, because some are functional and others topical, and because the effectiveness of a paragraph depends upon how well it serves the reader not on how closely it adheres to a model, the generally accepted definition of a paragraph is that it is a self-contained unit of thought.

patterning—strong rhythms and linguistic repetitions that help students read even before they make accurate sound-to-print matches.

personification—attributing life to lifeless things.

prediction—a reading skill that anticipates with some degree of accuracy what the author is going to say or do next based upon previous information, pictures, context, and personal experience.

prepositions—these are functional words that relate a noun, pronoun, or gerund to another part of the sentence.

proper nouns—the specific names of persons, places, things, or ideas. They always begin with a capital letter.

questions and question marks—an interrogative or asking expression that seeks or expects knowledge and its unique terminal mark (?) that indicates a question.

quotation marks—punctuation that serves as a visual guide to tell readers someone is speaking or material is from another source.

reading for meaning—the basic responsibility of readers is to make sense of the text, to construct meaning during the reading process. Readers who focus only on calling words rather than on what the words mean, usually do not find the text meaningful. The most effective way to teach students how to read for meaning is by modeling. When teachers read aloud frequently and tell students how they are processing the text, they help students realize that reading involves interacting with the ideas presented by the author.

sentence—one or more words, punctuated as an independent unit, that say something. Because of their variety, sentences are difficult to explain in a way that includes all possibilities. Most elementary textbooks define a sentence as a group of words that make sense. They talk about the "naming" (subject) and "telling" (predicate) parts of a sentence.

sequencing—reconstructing the events or parts of the text in the same order as the author.

setting in a story—the general locale and the historical time in which the action occurs.

simile—a natural operation of the mind used to compare something or someone to its likeness. The word *simile* comes from the Latin word for *like*. Typically we think of similes as using the words *like,* or *as.*

story sequel—a story that continues the course of the narrative that started in a previous story.

story versions—variants of the original that have been preserved, altered, or adapted by the devices of storytellers or authors and have lived from generation to generation through the human voice, memory, or writing.

subplot—a second story within a story that is complete and interesting in its own right but which broadens and enhances the main plot.

syllabication—the little lumps of sound that words can be broken into—the vowel is central with whatever consonants attach themselves to either side.

synecdoche—singles out a characteristic or part of a thing or person for special notice so that the part becomes labeled as the whole, e.g. the names of the seven dwarfs in *Snow White.*

synonyms—words that express the same or almost the same meaning.

vowels—speech sounds characterized by unimpeded flow of breath. They are like musical notes because they carry frequency of sound. Interestingly, when considering the development of children's writing and their use of consonants before vowels, it was the Greeks who introduced vowels into the previously consonantal system of letters even appropriating the Semitic letter *alpha,* used as a consonant in the original Hebrew, to signify the vowel sound <u>A</u>.

word— a speech sound or a series of speech sounds that conveys meaning. In English, every word contains a vowel. This perhaps can be traced to the Romans refining of the Greek alphabet and the importance they placed upon vowels. With few exceptions, for example, the endings of the Latin nouns, verbs, and adjectives all contain at least one vowel.

* This glossary has been designed to fit the needs of teachers and students as they use the focal books in *Phonics Friendly Books.* This is not nor is it meant to be exhaustive. If further information is desired or needed, teachers are advised to consult a credible, up-to-date handbook.

Adams, Pam (illustrator). *There Was an Old Lady Who Swallowed a Fly*. Singapore: Child's Play International, 1973.

Adams, Pam (illustrator). *This Old Man*. Singapore: Child's Play International, 1974.

Ahlberg, Janet and Allan. *Funnybones*. New York: Mulberry Books, 1980.

Ahlberg, Janet and Allan. *Funnybones: Picture Card Game*. Bicester, Oxon: A Michael Stanfield Product. Ref. 7076, 1980.

Allen, Jonathan. *Wake Up, Sleeping Beauty! An Interactive Book with Sounds*. New York: Dial Books for Young Readers, 1997.

Amoss, Berthe. *The Cajun Gingerbread Boy*. New York: Hyperion, 1994.

Appelt, Kathi. *Bat Jamboree*. New York: Morrow Junior Books, 1996.

Appelt, Kathi. *Elephants Aloft*. New York: Harcourt Brace, 1993.

Appelt, Kathi. *Watermelon Day*. New York: Henry Holt, 1996.

Aruego, Jose and Ariane Dewey (illustrators). *Five Little Ducks*. New York: Random House, 1989.

Asch, Frank. *Just Like Daddy*. New York: Aladdin Paperbacks, Simon & Schuster, 1981.

Aylesworth, Jim. *Old Black Fly*. New York: Henry Holt, 1992.

Bailey, Jill. *Frogs in Three Dimensions*. New York: Viking, 1992.

Bang, Molly. *Ten, Nine, Eight*. New York: Greenwillow, 1983.

Barrett, Judi. *Cloudy with a Chance of Meatballs*. New York: Aladdin, 1978.

Barrett, Judi. *Old MacDonald Had an Apartment House*. New York: Atheneum, 1998.

Bayer, Jane. *A My Name is Alice*. New York: Dial, 1984.

Bennett, Jill. *Noisy Poems*. New York: Oxford University Press, 1996 (reprint).

Bennett, Jill. *Teeny Tiny*. New York: G. P. Putnam, 1986.

Berman, Ruth. *Ants*. Minnesota: Lerner Publications, 1996.

Bjork, Christina. *Linnea's Almanac*. New York: Farrar, Straus and Giroux, 1989.

Blos, Joan W. *One Very Best Valentine's Day*. New York: Aladdin, 1998.

Bornstein, Ruth Lercher. *That's How It Is When We Draw*. New York: Clarion, 1997.

Borovsky, Paul. *The Strange Blue Creature*. New York: Hyperion Books for Children, 1993.

Breslow, Susan and Sally Blakemore. *I Really Want a Dog*. New York: Dutton, 1990.

Brett, Jan. *The First Dog*. New York: Harcourt Brace Jovanovich, 1988.

Bridwell, Norman. *Clifford the Big Red Dog*. New York: Scholastic, 1985.

Brown, Marc. *Arthur Writes a Story*. Boston, MA: Little, Brown, 1996.

Brown, Marc. *Arthur's April Fool*. Boston, MA: Little, Brown, 1983.

Brown, Marc. *Arthur's Valentine*. Boston, MA: Little, Brown, 1980.

Brown, Marc. *Finger Rhymes*. New York: E. P. Dutton, 1980.

Brown, Marc. *Play Rhymes*. New York: E. P. Dutton, 1987.

Brown, Margaret Wise. *Goodnight Moon*. New York: Harper & Row, 1947.

Brown, Ruth. *The Ghost of Greyfriar's Bobby*. New York: Dutton Children's Books, 1995.

Brown, Ruth. *Toad*. New York: Dutton Children's Books, 1996.

Bryan, Ashley. *Ashley Bryan's ABC of African American Poetry*. New York: Atheneum Books for Young Readers, 1997.

Bunting, Eve. *The Valentine Bears*. New York: Clarion, 1983.

Bursik, Rose. *Amelia's Fantastic Flight*. New York: Henry Holt, 1992.

Carle, Eric. *Dragons Dragons & Other Creatures That Never Were*. New York: Philomel Books, 1991.

Carle, Eric. *Little Cloud*. New York: Philomel Books, 1996.

Carle, Eric. *My Apron*. New York: Philomel Books, 1994.

Carlstrom, Nancy White. *Fish and Flamingo*. Boston: Little, Brown, 1993.

Carter, David A. *Love Bugs*. New York: Simon & Schuster, 1995.

Cazet, Denys. *Frosted Glass*. New York: Bradbury Press, 1987.

Cherry, Lynne. *Flute's Journey: The Life of a Wood Thrush*. New York: Harcourt Brace, 1997.

Cole, Joanna. *The Magic School Bus on the Ocean Floor*. New York: Scholastic, 1992.

Cooner, Donna D. *I Know an Old Texan Who Swallowed a Fly*. Dallas, TX: Hendrick-Long, 1996.

Cooper, Martha and Ginger Gordon. *Anthony Reynoso: Born to Rope*. New York: Clarion, 1996.

Cousins, Lucy. *Maisy's Colors*. Cambridge, MA: Candlewick Press, 1997.

Cousins, Lucy. *Noah's Ark*. Cambridge, MA: Candlewick Press, 1993.

Crews, Donald. *Freight Train*. New York: Mulberry, 1992.

Cushman, Doug. *The ABC Mystery*. New York: Harper Collins, 1993.

Cuyler, Margery. *That's Good! That's Bad!* New York: Henry Holt, 1991.

Dakos, Kalli. *Get Out of the Alphabet, Number 2!* New York: Simon & Schuster Books for Young Readers, 1997.

Davol, Marguerite W. *The Paper Dragon*. New York: Atheneum Books, 1997.

de Groat, Diane. *Rose Are Pink, Your Feet Really Stink*. New York: Mulberry, 1996.

de Paola, Tomie. *The Cloud Book*. New York: Holiday House, 1975.

de Paola, Tomie. *The Legend of the Bluebonnet*. New York: G. P. Putnam's Sons, 1983,

Deedy, Carmen Agra. *Agatha's Feather Bed: Not Just Another Wild Goose Story*. Atlanta, GA: Peachtree, 1991.

Deedy, Carmen Agra. *The Library Dragon*. Atlanta, GA: Peachtree, 1994.

Degen, Bruce. *Jamberry*. New York: Harper Collins, 1992.

Denchfield, Nick. *Desmond the Dog*. New York: Harcourt Brace & Co., 1997.

Denchfield, Nick and Ant Parker. *Charlie the Chicken*. New York: Harcourt Brace & Co., Red Wagon Books, 1997.

Devlin, Wende and Harry. *Cranberry Valentine*. New York: Four Winds Press, 1986.

DK Direct Limited, *What's Inside? Insects*. Dorling Kindersley, 1992.

Dodds, Dayle Ann. *Sing, Sophie!* Cambridge, MA: Candlewick, 1997.

Dugan, Barbara. *Loop the Loop*. New York: Puffin, 1993.

Edwards, Pamela Duncan. *Four Famished Foxes and Fosdyke*. New York: Harper Trophy, 1995.

Edwards, Pamela Duncan. *Some Smug Slug*. New York: Harper Collins, 1996.

Ehlert, Lois. *Feathers for Lunch*. New York: Harcourt Brace Jovanovich, 1990.

Ehlert, Lois. *Hands*. Harcourt Brace, 1997.

Ehlert, Lois. *Moon Rope*. New York: Harcourt Brace Jovanovich, 1992.

Emberley, Rebecca. *Three Cool Kids*. New York: Little, Brown, 1995.

Faulkner, Keith. *A 3-D Look at Oceans*. New York: Little Simon, 1996.

Fleming, Denise. *In the Small, Small Pond*. New York: Henry Holt, 1993.

Fletcher, Ralph. *Twilight Comes Twice*. New York: Clarion, 1997.

Fox, Mem. *Feathers and Fools*. New York: Harcourt Brace, 1989.

Fox, Mem. *Night Noises*. New York: Harcourt Brace, 1989.

Frasier, Debra. *Out of the Ocean*. New York: Harcourt Brace Children's Books, 1998.

Galdone, Paul. *The Gingerbread Boy*. New York: Houghton Mifflin, 1975.

Gannett, Ruth Stiles. *Elmer and the Dragon*. New York: Alfred A. Knopf, 1950.

Gannett, Ruth Stiles. *My Father's Dragon*. New York: Alfred A. Knopf, 1948.

Gannett, Ruth Stiles. *The Dragons of Blueland*. New York: Alfred A. Knopf, 1951.

Giff, Patricia Reilly. *In the Dinosaur's Paw*. New York: Dell, 1985.

Giff, Patricia Reilly. *The Valentine Star*. New York: Dell, 1985.

Giff, Patricia Reilly. *Write Up a Storm with the Polk Street School*. New York: Yearling, 1993.

Goldstein, Margaret J. *Eyeglasses*. Minneapolis, MN: Carolrhoda Books, 1997.

Gray, Libba Moore. *Miss Tizzy*. New York: Simon & Schuster Book for Young Readers, 1993.

Greenfield, Karen. *Sister Yessa's Story*. New York: Harper Collins, 1992.

Gregoire, Caroline. *Uglypuss*. New York: Henry Holt, 1993.

Grindley, Sally. *Why is the Sky Blue?* New York: Simon & Schuster, 1997.

Grover, Max. *So Many Kinds of Shoes!* New York: Red Wagon Books, 1998.

Harness, Cheryl. *Ghosts of the White House*. New York: Simon & Schuster, 1998.

Harris, Peter and Doffy Weir. *Bottomley the Brave*. New York: Barron's, 1996.

Hartmann, Wendy and Niki Daly. *The Dinosaurs Are Back And It's All Your Fault Edward!* New York: Simon and Schuster, 1996.

Hawkins, Colin and Jacqui. *Tog the Dog*. New York: G.P. Putnam's Sons, 1986.

Hayes, Sarah. *The Candlewick Book of Fairy Tales*. Cambridge, MA: Candlewick, 1997.

Hazen, Barbara Shook. *Even If I Did Something Awful*. New York: Aladdin, 1992.

Hellen, Nancy. *Old MacDonald Had a Farm*. New York: Orchard, 1990.

Henkes, Kevin. *A Weekend with Wendell*. New York: Puffin, 1986.

Henkes, Kevin. *Bailey Goes Camping*. New York: Puffin, 1985.

Henkes, Kevin. *Chester's Way*. New York: Puffin, 1988.

Henkes, Kevin. *Chrysanthemum*. New York: Greenwillow, 1991.

Henkes, Kevin. *Grandpa & Bo*. New York: Greenwillow, 1986.

Henkes, Kevin. *Jessica*. New York: Greenwillow, 1989.

Henkes, Kevin. *Julius, the Baby of the World*. New York: Greenwillow, 1990.

Henkes, Kevin. *Lilly's Purple Plastic Purse*. New York: Greenwillow, 1996.

Henkes, Kevin. *Owen*. New York: Greenwillow, 1993.

Henkes, Kevin. *Sheila Rae, the Brave*. New York: Puffin, 1987.

Hennessy, B. G. *Eeney, Meeney, Miney, Mo*. New York: Viking, 1990.

Hightower, Susan. *Twelve Snails to One Lizard: A Tale of Mischief and Measurement*. New York: Simon & Schuster, 1997.

Hindley, Judy. *A Song of Colors*. Cambridge, MA: Candlewick Press, 1998.

Hoban, Lillian. *Arthur's Great Big Valentine*. New York: Harper Trophy, 1989.

Hutchins, Pat. *Good-Night, Owl!* New York: Aladdin, Simon & Schuster, 1990.

Hutchins, Pat. *The Doorbell Rang*. Boston: Houghton Mifflin, 1989. (Big Book)

Hutchins, Pat. *The Wind Blew*. New York: Aladdin, 1974.

Inkpen, Mick. *The Blue Balloon*. Boston, MA: Little, Brown, 1989.

Jackson, Alison. *I Know an Old Lady Who Swallowed a Pie*. New York: Dutton Children's Books, 1997.

Jeunesse, Gallimard and Pascale de Bourgoing. *The Ladybug and Other Insects*. New York: Scholastic, 1989.

Johnston, Tony. *Pages of Music*. New York: G. P. Putnam, 1988.

Johnston, Tony. *The Quilt Story*. New York: G. P. Putnam, 1985.

Jonas, Ann. *Aardvarks, Disembark!* New York: Greenwillow, 1990.

Jonas, Ann. *The Quilt*. New York: William Morrow, 1984.

Jones, Carol (illustrator). *Old MacDonald Had a Farm*. Boston: Houghton Mifflin, 1989.

Jones, Carol (illustrator). *This Old Man*. Boston, MA: Houghton Mifflin, 1990.

Julivert, Maria Ángels. *The Fascinating World of Ants*. New York: Barron's Educational Series, 1991.

Julivert, Maria Angels. *The Fascinating World of Birds of Prey*. New York: Barron's Educational Series, 1996.

Kaye, Buddy, Fred Wise, and Sidney Lippman. *A You're Adorable*. Cambridge, MA: Candlewick, 1997.

Keats, Ezra Jack. *The Snowy Day*. New York: Puffin, 1976.

Kimmel, Eric A. *I Took My Frog to the Library*. New York: Puffin, 1990.

Kimmel, Eric A. *The Gingerbread Man*. New York: Holiday House, 1993.

Kroll, Steven. *Loose Tooth*. New York: Holiday House, 1984.

Lang, Andrew. *The Grey Fairy Tale Book*. New York: Dover Publications, 1967.

Langlois, Florence. *The Extraordinary Gift*. New York: Abbeville Publishing, 1996.

Lauber, Patricia. *How Dinosaurs Came to Be*. New York: Simon & Schuster Books for Young Readers, 1996.

Lear, Edward. *The Owl and the Pussycat*. New York: G.P. Putnam's Sons, 1991.

Lessem, Don. *Seismosaurus: The Longest Dinosaur*. Minneapolis, MN: Carolrhoda Books, 1996.

Lessem, Don. *Utahraptor: The Deadliest Dinosaur*. Minneapolis, MN: Carolrhoda Books, 1996.

Lester, Helen. *A Porcupine Named Fluffy*. Boston, MA: Houghton Mifflin, 1986.

Lewis, J. Patrick. *The Boat of Many Rooms: The Story of Noah*. New York: Atheneum, 1997.

Lionni, Leo. *Inch by Inch*. New York: Astor-Honor, 1960.

Lionni, Leo. *The Alphabet Tree*. New York: Alfred A. Knopf, 1968.

Llewellyn, Claire. *Why Do We Have Wind and Rain?* New York: Barron's, 1995.

MacDonald, Suse. *Sea Shapes*. New York: Voyager Books, 1998.

Marshall, James. *Fox on the Job*. New York: Dial Books for Young Readers, 1988.

Marshall, James. *The Cut-Ups*. Puffin Books, 1986.

Marshall, Rita. *I Hate to Read!* Mankato, MN: Creative Editions, 1992.

Martin, Bill Jr. and John Archambault. *Chicka Chicka Boom Boom*. New York: Simon and Schuster Books for Young Readers, 1989.

Martin, Bill Jr. and John Archambault. *Knots on a Counting Rope*. New York: Henry Holt, 1987.

Martin, Bill Jr. and John Archambault. *The Ghost-Eye Tree*. New York: Henry Holt, 1985.

Martin, Bill Jr. and John Archambault. *These Are My Hands*. New York: Henry Holt, 1985.

Mayer, Marianna. *The Unicorn Alphabet*. New York: Dial, 1989.

McDermott, Gerald. *Musicians of the Sun*. New York: Simon & Schuster, 1997.

McDermott, Gerald. *Zomo the Rabbit: A Trickster Tale from West Africa*. Orlando, FL: Harcourt Brace, 1992.

McGovern, Ann. *Too Much Noise*. Boston, MA: Houghton Mifflin, 1967.

McKee, David. *Elmer and Wilbur*. New York: Lothrop, Lee & Shepard, 1994.

McKee, David. *Elmer*. New York: Lothrop, Lee & Shepard, 1968.

McLeod, Emilie Warren. *The Bear's Bicycle*. Boston: Little Brown, 1975.

McLerran, Alice. *Kisses*. New York: Scholastic, 1993.

McLerran, Alice. *Roxaboxen*. New York: Lothrop, Lee & Shepard, 1991.

McLerran, Alice. *The Ghost Dance*. New York: Clarion, 1995.

McLerran, Alice. *The Legacy of Roxaboxen: A Collection of Voices*. Spring, TX: Absey & Co., 1998.

McNaughton, Colin. *Oops!* New York: Harcourt Brace, 1996.

McPhail, David. *Edward and the Pirates*. Boston, MA: Little, Brown & Co., 1997.

McPhail, David. *Fix-It*. New York: E. P. Dutton, 1984.

McPhail, David. *Santa's Book of Names*. Boston, MA: Little, Brown & Co., 1993.

McPhail, David. *Snow Lion*. New York: Parents Magazine, 1982.

McPhail, David. *The Glerp*. Parsippany, NJ: Silver Press, 1995.

Medearis, Angela Shelf. *The Ghost of Sifty Sifty Sam*. New York: Scholastic, 1997.

Merriam, Eve. *Twelve Ways to Get to Eleven*. New York: Simon & Schuster Books for Children, 1993.

Meyers, Odette. *The Enchanted Umbrella*. New York: Gulliver Books, Harcourt Brace Jovanovich, 1988.

Micklethwait, Lucy. *I Spy: An Alphabet in Art*. New York: Greenwillow, 1992.

Minters, Frances. *Sleepless Beauty*. New York: Viking, Penguin, 1996.

Modell, Frank. *One Zillion Valentines*. New York, Mulberry, 1981.

Moss, Marissa. *Amelia Writes Again*. Berkeley, CA: Tricycle Press, 1996.

Moss, Marissa. *Amelia's Notebook*. Berkeley, CA: Tricycle Press, 1995.

Most, Bernard. *Cock-A-Doodle-Moo!* New York: Harcourt Brace, 1996.

Most, Bernard. *There's an Ant in Anthony*. New York: Mulberry, 1980.

Most, Bernard. *Where to Look for a Dinosaur*. New York: Harcourt Brace, 1997.

Mozelle, Shirley. *Zack's Alligator*. New York: Harper Trophy, 1989.

Murphy, Mary. *I Like It When...*New York: Harcourt Brace, 1997.

Nichelason, Margery G. *Shoes*. Minneapolis, MN: Carolrhoda Books, 1997.

Nixon, Joan Lowery. *If You Were a Writer*. New York: Four Winds Press, 1988.

Nolen, Jerdine. *Raising Dragons*. New York: Harcourt Brace, 1998.

Norman, Howard. *The Owl Scatterer*. New York: Little, Brown and Company, 1986.

Numeroff, Laura Joffe. *If You Give a Mouse a Cookie*. New York: Harper & Row, 1985.

O'Connor, Jane. *Sir Small and the Dragonfly*. New York: Random House, 1988.

Ottley, Matt. *What Faust Saw*. New York: Dutton, 1995.

Paraskevas, Betty. *Junior Kroll*. New York: Harcourt Brace Jovanovich, 1993.

Parker, Nancy Winslow and Joan Richards Wright. *Bugs*. New York: Mulberry, 1987.

Parkes, Brenda and Judith Smith. *The Enormous Watermelon*. Crystal Lake, IL: Rigby, 1986. (Reprinted, 1989).

Parsons, Alexandra. *Amazing Birds*. New York: Alfred A. Knopf, 1990.

Paul, Ann Whitford. *Eight Hands Round: A Patchwork Alphabet*. New York: Harper Collins, 1991.

Paulsen, Gary. *Dogteam*. New York: Delacorte, 1993.

Philpot, Lorna and Graham. *Amazing Anthony Ant*. New York: Random House, 1994.

Pilkey, Dav. *Big Dog and Little Dog*. New York: Harcourt Brace, 1997.

Pilkey, Dav. *Big Dog and Little Dog Going for a Walk*. New York: Harcourt Brace, 1997.

Pilkey, Dav. *Dog Breath: The Horrible Trouble with Hally Tosis*. New York: Scholastic, 1994.

Pinczes, Elinor J. *One Hundred Hungry Ants*. Boston: Houghton Mifflin, 1993.

Pinkney, Andrea and Brian. *Shake Shake Shake*. New York: Harcourt Brace, 1997.

Polacco, Patricia. *Aunt Chip and the Great Triple Creek Dam Affair*. New York: Philomel, 1996.

Polacco, Patricia. *Thunder Cake*. New York: Philomel, 1990.

Powell, Richard. *I Spy in the Garden*. New York: Penguin Books, Puffin, 1993.

Powell, Richard. *I Spy on the Farm*. New York: Penguin Books, Puffin, 1993.

Prelutsky, Jack. *Tyrannosaurus Was a Beast*. New York: Greenwillow, 1988.

Raschka, Chris. *Yo! Yes?* New York: Orchard, 1993.

Rosenthal, Paul. *Yo, Aesop! Get a Load of These Fables*. New York: Simon & Schuster, 1998.

Ryden, Hope. *ABC of Crawlers and Flyers*. New York: Clarion, 1996.

Sabuda, Robert. *Cookie Count*. New York: Simon & Schuster, 1997.

Saltzberg, Barney. *Phoebe and the Spelling Bee*. New York: Hyperion, 1996.

Sathre, Vivian. *Three Kind Mice*. New York: Harcourt Brace, 1997.

Sauvain, Philip. *Oceans*. Minneapolis, MN: Carolrhoda Books, 1996.

Schroeder, Alan. *Lily and the Wooden Bowl*. New York: Doubleday, 1994.

Schumaker, Ward. *Sing a Song of Circus*. New York: Harcourt Brace, 1997.

Scieszka, Jon and Lane Smith. *The Stinky Cheese Man and Other Fairly Stupid Tales*. New York: Viking, 1992.

Selway, Martina. *Don't Forget to Write*. Nashville, TN: Ideals Children's Books, 1992.

Shannon, Margaret. *Elvira*. New York: Ticknor & Fields, 1993.

Sharmat, Marjorie Weinman. *Nate the Great and the Mushy Valentine*. New York: Bantam Doubleday Dell Books for Young Readers, 1994.

Shaw, Eve. *Grandmother's Alphabet*. Duluth, MN: Pfeifer-Hamilton, 1997.

Shaw, Nancy. *Sheep in a Jeep*. Boston, MA: Houghton Mifflin, 1986.

Shaw, Nancy. *Sheep in a Shop*. Boston, MA: Houghton Mifflin, 1991.

Shaw, Nancy. *Sheep on a Ship*. Boston, MA: Houghton Mifflin, 1989.

Shaw, Nancy. *Sheep out to Eat*. Boston, MA: Houghton Mifflin, 1992.

Shaw, Nancy. *Sheep Take a Hike*. Boston, MA: Houghton Mifflin, 1994.

Shield, Carol Diggory. *Saturday Night at the Dinosaur Stomp*. Cambridge, MA: Candlewick, 1997.

Silver, Donald. *Extinction is Forever*. Parsippany, NJ: Silver Burdett, 1995.

Silverman, Erica. *Don't Fidget a Feather!* New York: Macmillan, 1994.

Simon, Seymour. *Storms*. New York: Morrow Junior, 1989.

Sis, Peter. *Komodo!* New York: Greenwillow, 1993.

Siver, Norman. *Cloud Nine*. New York: Clarion, 1995.

Smith, Lane. *Glasses (Who Needs 'Em?)* New York: Viking, 1991.

Snow, Alan. *The Monster Book of ABC Sounds*. New York: Puffin Pied Piper, 1991.

Spaulding, Dean T. *Watching Our Feathered Friends*. Minneapolis, MN: Lerner, 1997.

Spiegelman, Art. *I'm a Dog!* New York: Harper Collins, 1997.

Stanley, Diane. *Captain Whiz-Bang*. New York: William Morrow, 1987.

Sterne, Noelle. *Tyrannosaurus Wrecks: A Book of Dinosaur Riddles*. New York: Harper & Row, 1979.

Stevens, Janet. *The Three Billy Goats Gruff*. New York: Harcourt Brace Jovanovich, 1987.

Stubbs, Lisa. *Sonny's Beloved Boots*. New York: Barron's, 1997.

Taback, Simms. *There Was an Old Lady Who Swallowed a Fly*. New York: Viking: 1997

Tresselt, Alvin. *White Snow, Bright Snow*. New York: Lothrop, Lee and Shepard, 1988.

Turner, Priscilla. *The War between the Vowels and the Consonants*. New York: Garrar Straus Giroux, 1996.

Voake, Charlotte. *Mrs. Goose's Baby*. Cambridge, MA: Candlewick, 1989.

Waber, Bernard. *Ira Sleeps Over*. Boston: Houghton Mifflin, 1972.

Waddell, Martin. *Owl Babies*. Cambridge, MA: Candlewick Press, 1992.

Wallace, Karen. *Think of an Eel*. Cambridge, MA: Candlewick, 1993.

Ward, Nick. *Don't Worry, Grandpa*. New York: Barron's Educational Series, 1995.

Wells, Rosemary. *Max's Dragon Shirt*. New York: Puffin Pied Piper, 1991.

Wells, Rosemary. *Noisy Nora*. New York: Dial Book, 1997.

Wells, Rosemary. *Old MacDonald*. New York: Scholastic, 1998.

Westcott, Nadine Bernard. *The Pop-Up, Pull-Tab, Playtime House That Jack Built*. Los Angeles, CA: Intervisual Communications, 1991.

Whipple, Laura (compiler). *Eric Carle's Dragon Dragons and Other Creatures that Never Were*. New York: Philomel, 1991.

Wiesner, David. *June 29, 1999*. New York: Clarion Books, 1992.

Wigand, Molly. *Stormy Weather*. New York: Little Simon/Nickelodeon, 1997.

Willard, Nancy. *The Well-Mannered Balloon*. New York: Harcourt Brace Jovanovich, 1976.

Williams, Sue. *I Went Walking*. New York: Harcourt Brace Jovanovich, 1989.

Williams, Suzanne. *Library Lil*. New York: Dial, 1997.

Willis, Val. *The Secret in the Matchbox*. New York: Farrar, Straus and Giroux, 1988.

Windham, Sophie. *Noah's Ark*. New York: G. P. Putnam's Sons, 1988.

Winthrop, Elizabeth. *Shoes*. New York: Harper Collins, 1986.

Wolff, Patricia Rae. *The Toll-Bridge Troll*. New York: Harcourt Brace, 1995.

Wood, Audrey. *Quick as a Cricket*. Singapore: Child's Play International, 1982.

Wood, Audrey. *Silly Sally*. New York: Harcourt Brace, 1992.

Wood, Douglas. *Rabbit and the Moon*. New York: Simon & Schuster, 1998.

Yolen, Jane. *The Musicians of Bremen: A Tale from Germany*. New York: Simon & Schuster, 1996.

Yo-Yo, Professor. *The Little Book of Yo-Yos*. New York: Scholastic, 1998.

Yorinks, Arthur. *Ugh*. New York: Farrar, Straus and Giroux, 1990.

Zemach, Harve. *The Judge*. New York: Farrar, Straus and Giroux, 1991.

Dr. JAG Books and Articles for Teachers

Abram, David. *The Spell of the Sensuous*. New York: Vintage Books, 1996.

Adams, M. *Beginning to Read: Thinking and Learning about Print, A Summary*. Champaign, IL: Center for the Study of Reading, 1990.

Balmuth, M. *The Roots of Phonics*. NY: Teachers College Press, 1982.

Blevins, Wiley. *Phonics from A to Z: A Practical Guide*. New York: Scholastic, 1998.

Clymer, Theodore. "The Utility of Phonic Generalizations in the Primary Grades." *The Reading Teacher* 50 (3):182-187, 1996.

Cunningham, Patricia M. and Dorothy P. Hall. *Month-By-Month Phonics for First Grade: Systematic, Multilevel Instruction*. Greensboro, NC: Carson-Dellosa, 1997.

Cunningham, Patricia M. *Phonics They Use: Words for Reading and Writing*. (2nd ed.) New York: Harper Collins, 1995.

Ericson, Lita and Moira Fraser Juliebö. *The Phonological Awareness Handbook for Kindergarten and Primary Teachers*. Newark, DE: International Reading Association, 1998.

Fry, Edward Bernard, Jacqueline E. Kress and Dona Lee Fountoukidis. *The Reading Teacher's Book of Lists 3rd Ed.*, West Nyack, NY: The Center for Applied Research Education (Prentice Hall), 1993.

Goodman, Ken. *Phonics Phacts*. Portsmouth, NH: Heinemann, 1993.

Goswami, U. and F. Mead. "Onset and Rime Awareness and Analogies in Reading." *Reading Research Quarterly* 27: 150-162, 1992.

Griffith, P. L. and M. W. Olson. "Phonemic Awareness Helps Beginning Readers Break the Code." *The Reading Teacher* 45 (7): 516-523, 1992.

Gunning, Thomas G. "Word Building: A Strategic Approach to the Teaching of Phonics." *The Reading Teacher* 48 (6) 484-488, 1995.

Moustafa, Margaret. *Beyond Traditional Phonics: Research Discoveries and Reading Instruction*. Portsmouth, NH: Heinemann, 1997.

Moustafa, Margaret. "Children's Productive Phonological Recoding." *Reading Research Quarterly* 30 (3): 464-476.

Ogg, Oscar. *The 26 Letters*. New York: Thomas Y. Crowell, 1959.

Richgels, Donald J., Karla J. Poremba, and Lea M. McGee. "Kindergartners Talk about Print: Phonemic Awareness in Meaningful Contexts." *The Reading Teacher* 49 (8): 632-642, 1996.

Smith, Frank. *Reading without Nonsense*. (3rd ed.) NY: Teachers College Press, 1997.

Strickland, Dorothy S. *Teaching Phonics Today: A Primer for Educators*. Newark, DE: International Reading Association, 1998.

Venezky, R. L. "English Orthography: Its Graphical Structure and Its Relation to Sound." *Reading Research Quarterly* II: 75-106, 1967.

Wilde, Sandra. *What's a Schwa Sound Anyway? A Holistic Guide to Phonetics, Phonics, and Spelling*. Portsmouth, NH: Heinemann, 1997.

Wilson, Robert M. and Mary Anne Hall. *Programmed Word Attack for Teachers*. (6th ed.) Saddle River, NJ: Prentice Hall, 1997.

Wylie, R. E. and D. D. Durrell. "Teaching Vowels through Phonograms." *Elementary English* 47: 787-791, 1970.

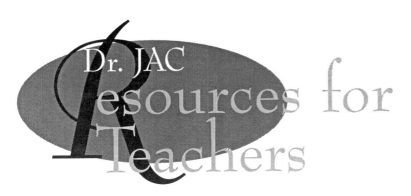

Balzac Earth Balloon Ball ™. Catco Inc., 529 West 42nd Street, New York, NY 10036.

Calloway House, Inc. 451 Richardson Drive, Lancaster, PA 17603. (800) 233-0290.

Carlson, Laurie. *Huzzah Means Hooray: Activities from the Days of Damsels, Jesters, and Blackbirds in a Pie*. Chicago, IL: Chicago Review Press, 1995.

Children's Book Express . (Contact Nancy Stone, former teacher, who is most helpful with finding and suggesting books.) 419 South Locust Street, Denton, TX. 76201-6019. (940) 380-1386; FAX (940) 380-0606.

Constructive Playthings. 1227 East 119th St., Grandview, MO 64030-1117. (This is a good source for instructional materials.)

Delta Education. P.O. Box 3000, Nashua, NH 03061-3000. (800) 442-5444.

Ekstrand, Florence. *Norwegian Trolls and Other Tales*. Mt. Vernon, WA: Welcome Press, 1990.

Evans, Ivor H. *Brewer's Dictionary of Phrase and Fable*. New York: Harper & Row, 1981.

Folkmanis, 1219 Park Avenue, Emeryville, CA 94608. (415) 658-7677. (These folks produce some of the most beautiful and enduring hand puppets.)

Gulland, Daphne M. and David Hinds-Howell. *English Idioms*. New York: Penguin, 1986.

Hajdusiewicz, Babs Bell. *Words and More Words: A Reference Book for Young Writers*. Glenview, IL: Good Year Books, 1997.

Hajdusiewicz, Babs Bell. *Words, Words, Words: A Reference Book for Beginning Writers*. Glenview, IL: Good Year Books, 1997.

Kirchen Bros. Box 1016, Skokie, IL 60076. (800) 378-5024.

Lakeshore Learning Materials. 2695 E. Dominguez St., Carson, CA 90749. (800) 421-5354. *jewels*

Lee Products Co. Dept. 5S, Minneapolis, MN 55420. (2" Highlighter tape–item # 13150.)

MerryMakers, Inc. San Francisco, CA 94104

National Week of the Ocean. P.O. Box 179, Fort Lauderdale, FL 33302

Oriental Trading Co., Inc. P.O. Box 3407, Omaha, NE 68103-0407. (800) 228-2269. (This is an inexpensive source of artifacts.)

Peter, Paul, and Mary. *Peter, Paul & Mommy, Too*. # 4-45216. New York: Warner Bros. Records Inc., 1993.

Resources for Reading ™ P.O. Box 9, La Honda, CA 94020-0009. (800) 278-7323.

Russon, Jacqueline. *Face Painting*. New York: Carolrhoda Books, Inc. Harper Collins, 1997.

Scholes, Robert, et al. *Elements of Literature* (5th edition). New York: Oxford University Press, 1982 (reference to *choragos*).

Sesame Street Platinum All-Time Favorites. Sesame Street, Inc. 1990. (800) 257-3880.

Top Notch Teacher Products. P.O. Box 849, Kerrville, Texas 78029. (210) 367-5311. (This is a good source for bright, colorful paper of different weights and library pockets. Ask about their discount.)

U. S. Toy Co. 1927 East Belt Line Rd., Carrollton, TX 75006. (972) 418-1860 or (800) 255-6124. (This is an inexpensive source of artifacts.)

Valenta, Barbara. *Pop-O-Mania: How to Create Your Own Pop-Ups*. New York: Dial Books for Young Readers, 1997. (This is an excellent and easy-to-follow book for making pop-ups.)

Van Cleave, Janice. *Earth Science for Every Kid: 101 Easy Experiments that Really Work*. New York: John Wiley & Sons, Inc., 1991.

Young, Sue. *The Scholastic Rhyming Dictionary*. New York: Scholastic Inc., 1994.

Dr. JAC Phonics Concepts Index

Dr. JAC Title and Author Index

H

I

J

K

L

M

W

Y

Z